SOFTWARE ENGINEERING
FOR INFORMATION SYSTEM_

INFORMATION SYSTEMS SERIES

Consulting Editors

D. E. AVISON
BA, MSc, FBCS
*Department of Computer Science and
Applied Mathematics, Aston University,
Birmingham, UK*

G. FITZGERALD
BA, MSc, MBCS
*Oxford Institute of Information Management
Templeton College, Oxford, UK*

This is a brand new series of student texts covering a wide variety of topics relating to information systems. It is designed to fulfil the needs of the growing number of courses on, and interest in, computing and information systems which do not focus purely on the technological aspects, but seek to relate these to business or organizational context.

INFORMATION SYSTEMS SERIES

SOFTWARE ENGINEERING FOR INFORMATION SYSTEMS

DONALD C. McDERMID,
BSc, MBA, MBCS, MBIM
Department of Computing Science,
Paisley College of Technology

OXFORD

BLACKWELL SCIENTIFIC PUBLICATIONS

LONDON EDINBURGH BOSTON

MELBOURNE PARIS BERLIN VIENNA

Blackwell Scientific Publications
Editorial offices:
Osney Mead, Oxford OX2 0EL
25 John Street, London WC1N 2BL
23 Ainslie Place, Edinburgh EH3 6AJ
238 Main Street, Cambridge
  Massachusetts 02142, USA
54 University Street, Carlton
  Victoria 3053, Australia

First published 1990
Reprinted 1993

Typeset by DP Photosetting,
Aylesbury, Bucks
Printed and bound in Great Britain by
Biddles Ltd, Guildford and King's Lynn

DISTRIBUTORS

Marston Book Services Ltd
PO Box 87
Oxford OX2 0DT
(Orders: Tel: 0865 791155
        Fax: 0865 791927
        Telex: 837515)

USA
  Blackwell Scientific Publications, Inc.
  238 Main Street
  Cambridge, MA 02142
  (Orders: Tel: 800 759-6102
          617 876-7000)

Canada
  Oxford University Press
  70 Wynford Drive
  Don Mills
  Ontario M3C 1J9
  (Orders: Tel: (416) 441-2941)

Australia
  Blackwell Scientific Publications Pty Ltd
  54 University Street
  Carlton, Victoria 3053
  (Orders: Tel: (03) 347-5552)

British Library
Cataloguing in Publication Data
McDermid, Donald C.
  Software engineering for information
  systems.
  1. Computer systems. Software. Design
  I. Title
  005.12

ISBN 0–632–02607–3

Library of Congress
Cataloging in Publication Data
McDermid, Donald C.
    Software engineering for information
    systems/Donald C. McDermid.
      p. cm.
    Includes bibliographical references.
    ISBN 0–632–02607–3
    1. Software engineering.
    2. System design.   I. Title
QA76.758.M35   1990   90–30108
                              CIP

Dedicated to my father

Contents

Foreword

The Blackwell Scientific Publications Series on Information Systems is a new series of student texts covering a wide variety of topics relating to information systems. It is designed to fulfil the needs of the growing number of courses on, and interest in, computing and information systems which do not focus purely on the technological aspects, but seek to relate these to business or organisational contexts.

Information systems have been defined as the effective design, delivery, use and impact of information technology in organisations and society. Utilising this fairly wide definition, it is clear that the subject area is somewhat interdisciplinary. Thus the series seeks to integrate technological disciplines with management and other disciplines, for example, psychology and philosophy. It is felt that currently these areas do not have a natural home, they are rarely represented by single departments in polytechnics and universities, and to put such books into a purely computer science or management series restricts potential readership and the benefits that such texts can provide. This series on information systems now provides such a home.

The books are mainly student texts, although certain topics may be dealt with at a deeper, more research orientated level.

The series is expected to include the following areas, although this is not an exhaustive list: information systems development methodologies, office information systems, management information systems, decision support systems, information modelling and databases, systems theory, human aspects and the human-computer interface, application systems, technology strategy, planning and control, and expert systems, knowledge acquisition and representation.

The latest addition to the Blackwell's Information Systems Series is *Software Engineering for Information Systems* by Donald McDermid. This book discusses and illustrates the principles of software engineering as they apply to information systems in the real world. The subject is not just addressed as a series of techniques but seeks to put them into an overall method and set the method in the wider context of information systems and related issues. This approach places Donald McDermid's book firmly within the philosophy of the Information Systems Series. We are very pleased to welcome this text to the Series and believe that it makes a significant contribution to the area.

David Avison and Guy Fitzgerald
Consulting Editors
Informations Systems Series

Preface

READERSHIP

This book is intended as an introductory textbook for those interested in developing information systems in a sound, professional manner. It assumes no prior knowledge except for some previous exposure to a programming language and some basic awareness of computer terminology. There are two main groups for whom this text is principally targeted. The first group are those students studying for a degree or diploma in a computer-related discipline (e.g. perhaps a qualification in computing science, computer studies, software engineering, information technology, information systems or whatever) and who, for the first time, are meeting the principles of software engineering as they are relevant to information systems. For example, at Paisley College of Technology, this book will be used on undergraduate degree programmes in Computing Science, Software Engineering and Business Information Technology as well as a postgraduate diploma course in Information Technology. For such readers, this may be the first text they have encountered in this area and therefore key texts have been identified as further reading so that a broad grounding can be obtained before specialisation takes place. Also, there are exercises at the end of most chapters, which are based on a case study. These exercises should help the reader acquire a level of skill in performing software engineering tasks.

The second group are those who are currently working in the computer industry. They could be in a variety of jobs – they might be programmers, sales people or support personnel. They may not have a formal qualification in computing. Indeed, the computing industry has moved so fast that even those with relatively recent qualifications may still derive much from this book. The common thread is that they will have an interest in or connection with 'information systems' and will be curious enough about 'software engineering' to wish to explore how it applies to information systems.

BOOK LAYOUT

The book is divided into three parts because it is felt that this is the best way to communicate the material. The aim is that, by the end of the book, the reader will have a well-rounded picture of what software engineering is as it applies to information systems and what some of the current major issues and challenges are. However, it is suggested that the best way to get there is in three stages. In the first stage (Part A) some level of skill in basic software engineering techniques is acquired. Only then do we move on to the second stage (Part B) in which a complete method is examined. In the third stage (Part C) a wider discussion of some important issues takes place to facilitate a broader appreciation.

Part A

Part A of the book describes important basic techniques and proposes that the reader acquire some skill in the execution of these before proceeding further. This is necessary because without at least some experience of using techniques it is all the harder for the reader to appreciate the rationale and arguments put forward in later parts of the book. Part A can therefore be considered a tutorial in the basic techniques of software engineering as applied to information systems. The techniques described include drawing dataflow diagrams, data modelling, drawing structure charts and normalisation. The appendix contains a case study which gives the reader practice in the techniques discussed.

Part B

There are many good ways of developing information systems. The method proposed in Part B is only one of those possible. It contains several widely used techniques, such as the ones mentioned in the previous paragraph; it contains others, such as the state dependency diagram, which are new at the time of writing. Part B demonstrates how such techniques can be integrated into a method in a practical way by discussing the rationale behind this particular method and why the techniques are used in the way they are. In doing so it is hoped that a general understanding of software engineering principles is imparted. The method in Part B is similar but not identical to SSADM and LSDM (though the method in this book also describes the system construction phase). All three share the common ethos that it is important to spend time analysing a problem as carefully and rigorously as possible. Each uses three different models or 'abstractions' of an information system. A model of the processes within an information system is described using dataflow diagrams, the data model specifies the data requirement and entity life histories provide a means of identifying the sequences of events which are critical to an information system. These models are regularly cross-referenced with each other in an attempt to identify inconsistencies and subsequently improve the quality of the specification. These methods are more mature than their predecessors in the sense that as well as incorporating the best models from earlier methods, they have also added significant new ones while preserving overall ease of use and power. It is submitted that methods like these contain the basic ideas which will be used by software engineers for many years to come. It is therefore essential for any student of software engineering to become thoroughly familiar with such concepts and Part B is designed to facilitate such an understanding.

Part C

But there is more to the practice of software engineering than understanding just one method and it is the purpose of Part C to explore the context and nature of the environment in which software engineering is performed so that a deeper, more realistic and critical view is formed. For example, the method in Part B is only part of a project in that there is no discussion of the planning and control of a project. Hence there is a chapter in Part C on project management which discusses what project management is and the relationship between a method and the project management tasks that surround it. To take another example, there is a chapter in Part C which critically examines the notion that any single method can or should be used in all circumstances. It proposes a view that on a situational basis, the analyst, designer and programmer should choose appropriate tools and techniques from a wide range available and that it is right that they should be able to exercise such discretion. So the purpose in Part C is to extend the discussion beyond the perspective of one software engineering method, and in doing so it is hoped that an appreciation of what constitutes mature software engineering is communicated.

Though it is intended that the book is approached serially from the beginning, it is possible to start to explore the method in part B more quickly. A road map for the book is shown below which indicates which chapters are prerequisites of others.

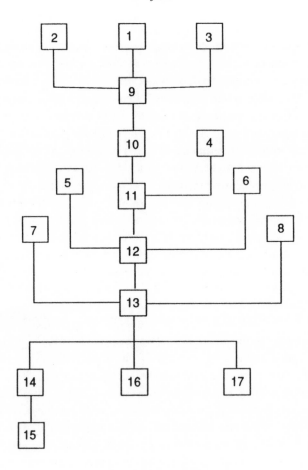

Road map for the book

ACKNOWLEDGEMENTS

Acknowledgements and thanks go to many people who in different ways have helped in the creation of this book. In particular to Paul Swatman, Boyd Johnstone, Richard Beeby, Malcolm Bronte-Stewart and Angus Quin for their help and suggestions. To Irene McKeown for her word-processing skills and patience and to Professor Malcolm Crowe for making her time and mine available. A special note of thanks goes to Glenn Michael of LBMS who reviewed early draughts and provided much useful insight into this business of ours. I should like to thank my wife Marion for her patience, understanding, support and sacrifice throughout this whole project. Lastly, I should like to say a big 'Hello, again' to my children, Suzanne, Carole and wee Donny, who now call me uncle.

Much of the text and diagrams relating to the State Dependency Diagram appear in an article by the author in the *Software Engineering Journal*. Copyright for this is vested in the IEE, from whom kind permission for reproduction here has been granted.

The discussion on Auto-Mate Plus, figures 15.2 to 15.10 and tables 15.1 to 15.6 are taken from the *Auto-Mate Plus Users Guide* which is the copyright of LBMS and from whom kind permission to reproduce here has been given.

The CCTA (UK) is the design authority for SSADM.

Figure 17.1 was kindly contributed by Mark McCracken, BA student in Business Information Technology at Paisley College of Technology, 1989.

Chapter 1
Introduction

1.1 WHAT IS SOFTWARE ENGINEERING?

The term 'software engineering' is sometimes confusing to the uninitiated. This is because the name software engineer is often used where someone is working at the hardware/software interface, i.e. in embedded systems where hardware and software are being developed in concert. Because of the close relationship with hardware, people assume that the 'engineering' component of the term comes from this source. In fact, software engineering as we will use it embraces all software development environments, not just those at the hardware/software interface. It also covers all phases of the software development process, i.e. analysis which decides what is required of the system, design which decides how the system will be implemented, construction which includes programming and documentation and lastly the subsequent maintenance of the implemented system.

Software engineering as a term was first coined in 1968 at a conference in West Germany held to discuss the software crisis. The software crisis is still with us today and refers to the fact that the computer industry is not meeting the demand for computing that the rest of industry has placed upon it. The 'engineering' component was incorporated to convey the sense of discipline and product orientation characteristic of most branches of engineering. In the 1960s, and to a large extent even today, software production was frequently undertaken in an ad-hoc, unprofessional manner. So the spirit of software engineering has much to offer today's software developers.

A second cause of confusion lies in the fact that there is no generally agreed definition of software engineering, although many are similar. For example, Boehm[1], states that 'software engineering is the application of science and mathematics by which the capabilities of computer equipment are made useful to man via computer programs, procedures and associated documentation.' Other definitions such as Fairley's[2] explicitly include the concerns of management in the software development process: 'Software engineering is the technological and managerial discipline concerned with systematic production and maintenance of software products that are developed and modified on time and within cost estimates.'

The size and to some extent the complexity of current software developments dictate that a group of engineers collectively develop a computer system. For a variety of reasons, including experience and flair, members of the team specialise in different aspects of the development, hence the terms systems analyst, designer, programmer and so on. Specialism enables individuals to aspire to high levels of competence in a specific field, but because of the interrelatedness of the software development process, the more members in a team there are, the more the need for communication between individuals within the team.

Given that large team environments are a fact of life, the challenge to software engineering is to minimise its adverse effects on software development. It does this through the provision of, for example, reviews which include both the originator and recipient of deliverables. Another example would be team environments where several members work on the same piece of code.

It was stated earlier that there are different phases or stages of development in a computer system. Taken together these stages are often called the systems (or software) life cycle, because every system follows a pattern very much like the life of a human, in which an idea for a system develops through stages into a fully mature system.

The waterfall model is a popular model of the system development process. It is given this name because the steps on a waterfall force water to move in

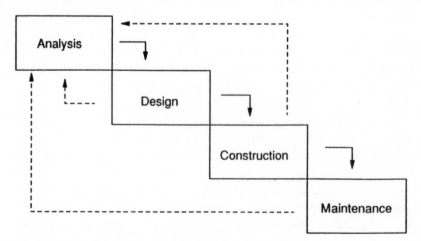

Fig. 1.1. Waterfall model of the systems life cycle.

a downward direction only from one step to the next. Similarly, the traditional view of systems development is that the stages of a life cycle inexorably move from one stage to the next. Moving back a stage is not permitted. See figure 1.1. The waterfall model is a useful model but there is a significant problem with it. It is that current practice indicates that information systems development is iterative. For example, if mistakes or omissions are found in one stage, it may be necessary to return to an earlier stage to correct them. This is inconsistent with the downward flow implied in the waterfall model.

The life cycle itself is only one aspect of the above definitions of software engineering. Software is engineered (or perhaps misengineered) in all sorts of environments. Sometimes it is done very poorly; sometimes very well. What is therefore important in studying software engineering is to identify those characteristics which help us to distinguish the good from the bad. These characteristics would include:

- use of method
- product ethos
- use of formal methods
- project management
- metrics
- quality assurance
- productivity ethos

1.1.1 Use of method

A method (or methodology as it is sometimes called) is a framework of integrated techniques which assist the software engineer in developing a system. For our purposes, a technique can be considered as a set of instructions or guidelines for completing a single task such as conducting an interview or coding a module. Ideally, one method should cover all aspects of the development. In practice this does not happen often. Methods tend to cover only part of the full life cycle and therefore have to be used in combination with one another in order to cover all of the total life cycle of the system.

Another problem is that there is no commonly agreed way of partitioning the life cycle. A very simple way of partitioning has, in fact, already been discussed and this is set out in table 1.1(a). This is basically the one we will use in this book as a means of partitioning the software development tasks,

(a)	analysis	(b)	terms of reference
	design		feasibility of study
	construction		system specification
	maintenance		outline design
			detailed design
			system development
			testing
			implementation
			review
			maintenance

Table 1.1. Two ways of partitioning the life cycle.

although because of the size of the analysis task it is further partitioned into three stages. A more comprehensive way of partitioning appears in table 1.1(b) and an explanation of these terms appears in table 1.2 for the purposes of comparison.

But why use a method at all? The use of a method brings a number of advantages. Firstly, it provides a pathway for the software engineer to follow. The software engineer knows that if the stages of a method are properly carried out, a good solution is likely. This is much less likely where there is no route to follow. So the risk factor is reduced if a method is used. This is especially significant in situations where some developers have little experience of systems development.

Secondly, inherent in the method is a model or models for solving the problem. So, for instance, a problem in concurrent programming would need a notation which could highlight simultaneous processes; a data processing problem might be documented using a dataflow diagram (discussed in chapter 2). Each method has underlying assumptions about the nature of the problem which are reflected in the models used within it. Most methods have evolved through experience with similar kinds of problem. Experience, in many cases of failure, has brought insight into the nature of the problem and so the proposed model or models underpinning the method aim to ensure that similar mistakes do not reoccur. Implicit, of course, is the assumption that the software engineer is able to select the most appropriate method.

Thirdly, good methods contain 'deliverables'. Although a clumsy word, the concept of a deliverable is important in a method. A deliverable is a tangible product generated by a task within a method. A task may produce one or more deliverables. A deliverable may be a compiled piece of code, or a diagram on a standard form, or a list of user problems. However, it must be tangible in the sense that someone else can confirm that the task has been

Terms of Reference

A definition of the scope of the system. Its purpose is to act as a guide to the systems analyst. This helps the systems analyst to delimit and put boundaries upon that which is to be considered for computerisation.

Feasibility Study

The purpose of the feasibility study is to confirm (or not) that the concept of the project is viable. Basically, what this means is that the systems analyst must perform some preliminary investigation into the system, to look at likely costs, benefits, timescales, problem areas (particularly logistical ones) and report back to management so that a decision to proceed or not may be taken.

System Specification

The next stage is to make high-level decisions about what will be implemented, i.e. which parts will be manual processes and which parts will be computerised. It might also specify to an extent how it will operate. For example, which parts would be on-line or batch, mainframe or micro-based.

The purpose of the system specification is to provide enough of a picture to management so that the proposed system can be easily visualised and therefore accepted. Then reasonably accurate estimates of costs can be calculated.

Outline Design

Design in this life cycle model is seen as a two-stage process, which separates "external" decisions from "internal" ones. For example, in outline design, the exact nature of the user interface i.e. screen formats, dialogue types, reports layouts would be specified, though how this is achieved is not specified.

Detailed Design

Detailed design has the task of defining all further items necessary to actually implement the system. So it must take account of the facilities and options available in the computer environment it will be implemented on. If a database is being used, knowledge of this and its facilities must be built into the design.

System Development

This includes all the programming activity i.e. the development of programming code, and compilation thereof as well as construction of program, user and operations documentation.

Testing

A phase often performed in parallel with system development is to test the programs or modules which have been written. A variety of approaches are available here.

Implementation

Implementation is the act of ensuring that the system runs on the computer. Files or databases must be set up or converted, security and back-up procedures implemented, users and operators trained.

Review

Once the system has been implemented for some time, say three months, a review is undertaken to determine if the original objectives of the system are being met.

Maintenance

At any time after its implementation, a system may require maintenance either due to errors in the original implementation or through business change which require changes or enhancements to the existing system. Maintenance is often viewed not as the end of life cycle, but the beginning of one since it may require system specification and so on.

Table 1.2. An alternative partitioning of the life cycle.

completed. The purpose of deliverables is to move away from statements like 'the code is 95% complete', which is misleading since there is no objective way of measuring such a statement. As long as tasks are relatively small, deliverables are a good way of measuring the progress of a software development. They also provide the basis for a checklist for the completion of a task within a method. Methods which do not explicitly define deliverables are not, in the author's view, true methods.

Lastly, good methods are designed in cognizance of the other characteristics of software engineering which are discussed here and seek to incorporate those characteristics within themselves. So, for example, a good method includes tasks to ensure the quality of deliverables is of an acceptable standard in line with the concept of quality assurance.

1.1.2 Product ethos

Software is manufactured in many ways and for a variety of purposes. Sometimes it is a single program written by a novice programmer which is, say, a problem in a Pascal textbook. This program will probably be discarded as soon as it is working properly. Sometimes, however, programs are written as part of a large complex system. People other than the developers, perhaps within the same organisation, perhaps not, will ultimately use such programs. Naturally, they will expect the program to be easy to use. If mistakes are made by the user in entering data, then the program should produce messages which are sensible to the user and the mistake should be easy to correct. All this implies that the program should be designed with these issues in mind and that documentation is provided which supports easy correction. It is no longer acceptable (as if it ever were) for code to be clumsy or undocumented. It is a software product which will become the property of someone else. Consequently, it must be easy to use and any error messages easy to understand.

Just like any other product, software must conform to minimum standards of quality, so comprehensive testing is mandatory. This is all the more important because typically such products are intended to be used for years to come and are likely to be modified significantly as changing requirements arise. Other staff may be asked to make the modifications because their predecessors have moved on. So the product needs to be designed for ease of maintenance and appropriate documentation must be generated so that it can be maintained by someone else.

A product ethos therefore implies a number of additional considerations in the way the software is engineered. Software engineers require a sound awareness of the need to view software as a product.

1.1.3 Use of formal methods

Software runs on machines which blindly follow the instructions fed into them. If the instructions are not quite what was intended, this makes no difference to the computer. Garbage in, garbage out! Programming languages are formal since they are developed from language theory, and hence there is no ambiguity in what is described in such an environment. Unfortunately, this is not so in the early stages of developing a system. In the analysis stage, the requirements of a system have to be gleaned from beings who communicate in English or other such imprecise languages. These languages are imperfect because they tolerate ambiguity and permit open interpretation in a way that computer languages do not. During the conversion from human to computer form, errors and oversights frequently creep in.

Formal methods in the analysis stage involve specifying the requirements as rigorously as possible. The obvious vehicle for this is to use the language of mathematics to describe what is required. Because the specification is precise, it is likely that conversion to computer interpretable form will be much less error-prone. Formal methods can also be used in the design and construction phase to demonstrate that each step of the conversion from requirements specification to final coded form is mathematically correct.

The use of formal methods in software engineering is not without its difficulties, not least of which are the level of mathematics required and the general inertia in some quarters to adopt more rigorous approaches. However, because of the opportunity it presents in reducing errors in software development, the role of formal methods in software engineering is an important one. The use of formal methods in the construction phase is demonstrated in this book.

1.1.4 Project management

The development of an information system is often referred to as a project. A project is a unique non-repetitive activity with associated constraints in terms of quality, time and budget. In other words, it is not enough that software is developed which meets requirements, it must also be tempered by a deadline and be within an agreed budget. The astute reader will recognise that these three factors are strongly interrelated. For example, raising quality impacts time and cost; a reduction in cost can be achieved by reducing quality, etc. It is now widely accepted in software engineering circles that the management aspects of software development are critical to overall success and therefore project management is not seen as something separate from software engineering but part of it.

1.1.5 Metrics

Metrics are concerned with measuring the characteristics of software. This really has two main uses. The first one is to use metrics to predict how long a task, such as writing a program, will take. The metric used in such a case might be the estimated lines of code in a program. The assumption here is that there is some kind of relationship between, in this case, estimated lines of code and the time it will take to actually develop the program. Secondly, once the software has been constructed it is possible to use metrics to measure the quality of the code.

1.1.6 Quality assurance

Quality assurance is concerned with establishing just how correct the software is. This is done by holding meetings specifically designed to assess particular aspects of the products being developed. These meetings may involve users if the issue is to do with aspects that they are able to comment on; equally meetings may be of a more technical nature where more detailed issues are being addressed and therefore may not be of direct interest to users.

1.1.7 Productivity ethos

Productivity is a difficult characteristic to define because so many factors affect it, but it certainly incorporates both efficiency and effectiveness considerations.

Clearly efficiency is important. If ways can be found to decrease the time spent on activities without reducing quality then this is obviously desirable. However, a trend in recent methods such as SSADM and LSDM has been to perform a more thorough and comprehensive analysis and design. This has meant that the overall length of the project has arguably increased, thereby increasing the pressure to reduce time spent in other ways. Computer Assisted Software Engineering (CASE) tools are playing a significant role in increasing the efficiency of software engineers. All systems need documenting, so word processors make a contribution to efficiency. This is not because the first version is necessarily produced quicker on a word processor than on a typewriter, but because revisions to the first attempt are so much faster, through being able to edit and move text. Revisions are inevitable and typically time-consuming when generating documentation. More interestingly, the same applies to the use of diagram editors. Once the first version of the diagram has been entered, typically many revisions ensue. As already explained, this is because the nature of analysis and design is an iterative one. So, here too, software can increase productivity.

Effectiveness is arguably more important than efficiency. Behind effectiveness lies the notion of quality. If an individual is effective then the quality of the products he produces is taken to be at least satisfactory. Certain types of software can improve the quality of the product. For example, validation programs can be run against diagrams or data definitions to determine if all necessary data has been supplied or to check the consistency of the data against pre-defined rules. In this way, omissions and errors are identified early and their consequent negative effect on the quality of the product avoided.

1.2 WHAT MAKES INFORMATION SYSTEMS DIFFERENT?

We are concerned with the software engineering of information systems, so it is worthwhile clarifying what makes the information systems context different before proceeding further. The critical point here is the domain of the problem being addressed. In other words, the nature of the problem dictates what kind of method, techniques, tools and quality criteria are appropriate. Perhaps the best way to illustrate this is to compare two different problem domains. Table 1.3 contains details of a small information system. Table 1.4

A company requires a Personnel system to provide information on the personal details of its employees. As staff join, leave or get transferred within the company, the system must aim to reflect this in the information produced. Reports on staff in each department and a variety of statistics on turnover are produced regularly and circulated within the organisation. Some staff are able to enquire on-line about individual staff details. As management have become more accustomed to the information they receive, several requests for additional reports have been received, for example, reports by age for manpower planning purposes and reports by grade for salary award negotiations. Requests have also been received for information which the Personnel system doesn't currently hold, such as qualifications and training details.

Table 1.3. The Personnel system.

A building has 11 floors and is to contain 3 lifts. A software system is required which will decide which lift is best suited to service a request at any one time.

Table 1.4. The lift problem.

contains a description of the lift problem, which is a classical embedded systems problem. For the sake of discussion, assume that each problem domain is typical of its class and that representative distinctions can be made, although in reality this is an over-simplification.

For one thing, the respective purposes of the systems are totally different. One is an information system, the other is an optimisation problem. In the lift problem, the parameters which influence the decision are well known and are identified through transducers and input to the system as variables to a linear programming algorithm. For the Personnel system, there is no single decision, as such, to be made. Indeed, the range of decisions which will be taken based on the information provided is not yet known. So it is not possible to know in advance exactly what information is required and how it should be packaged.

The nature of the maintenance problem is different too. With the lift problem, providing the system is working within agreed limits, no maintenance is required unless more floors or lifts are added. Personnel systems are prone to modification even if the software is performing to the specification. Modifications come from two sources. Firstly, new legislation or other rules change the information required to be shown. For example, new legislation on the amount of paid holiday leave each person in a company is entitled to would affect the calculation of an employee's paid leave in a computer program and therefore require the system to be modified. Here, the actual data field remains the same, it is simply that the calculation changes. Sometimes, however, as when VAT (a kind of sales tax) was introduced in the UK for the first time, new pieces of data are required.

Secondly, modifications arise through users of the information system understanding better what they require from the system. This may be in the form of requiring additional fields, or perhaps more or less detailed information. Through their experience of using the system, users decide what their real informational needs are. This is one reason why many systems analysts have difficulty in working with terms of reference and in performing a feasibility study. What is needed is a method which has an assumption model which, as far as possible, takes account of the fact that users do not always know 'up-front' what their detailed requirements are. Another problem is that as old users are replaced by others, it may be that their preferences for information change because they view the problem differently from their predecessors. Maintenance of information systems is almost always inevitable with user involvement mandatory, but with the lift problem, user involvement is not necessary to modify or indeed to specify the system.

Because the lift problem is dominated by physical factors such as the speed and acceleration of the lift, lift proximity and direction, the specification is naturally easier as it is quantifiable and lends itself to a more rigorous description. In terms of the parameters of the problem, the Personnel system is not so easily specified because users are not always clear about what they want, and in any case the rules might change. Different perceptions of what is required by different users do not help.

For the lift problem the specification lends itself to a mathematical description, i.e. in terms of formulae and time-based constraints. There is no direct equivalent for the Personnel system. The specification must clearly state what information is required, by whom, in what form and when – none of which, arguably, is naturally expressed in mathematical terms.

The data used in the lift problem is unlikely to be required for use elsewhere. This is not so with the Personnel system. In information systems, data is usually shared amongst many users. This is a fundamental and crucial difference in the problem that will be dealt with more fully in chapter 3. However, for the moment it is enough to recognise that the need to share the same data with other users may have consequences in how the problem is analysed and therefore in the models used to solve the problem.

1.3 SUMMARY

This chapter has attempted to map out the territory of software engineering. Software engineering is presented as a disciplined approach to information systems development which has come about because previous attempts at producing information systems were inadequate in several fundamental ways.

Software engineering is a relatively new field. Like the computer industry itself, it has not had time to mature to a state where definitions and terminology are universally accepted. An example of this phenomenon would include the variety of alternative waterfall models around. Even the boundary between analysis and design is still hotly debated in some quarters. That said, there is probably more agreement about what constitutes good software engineering practice. A list of software engineering 'characteristics' was presented which reflects this practice, and in the remainder of the book these characteristics reappear as underlying philosophies to the techniques and method discussed.

Lastly, it was felt important to introduce the 'information systems' dimension to the discussion. Information systems are different from other kinds of problem domain in fundamental respects, so much so that explicit techniques are required to address and manage these important differences.

1.4 FURTHER READING

1 Boehm, B. (1981) *Software Engineering Economics*, Prentice-Hall, Englewood Cliffs, New Jersey, provides a definition of software engineering which is used in this chapter.
2 Fairley, R. (1985) *Software Engineering Concepts*, McGraw-Hill, New York, provides another useful definition of software engineering. This is a good reference text for the practising software engineer and, in the author's opinion, aspiring software engineers can make good use of it once the ideas and techniques in this book have been mastered.

Part A
Basic Techniques

Chapter 2
Dataflow Diagrams and Data Dictionary Techniques

2.1 INTRODUCTION

A fundamental ability for any method is to be able to describe as succintly as possible what is going on inside the system itself. This is necessary when investigating how a system currently operates, as well as for describing how it will operate.

But what kind of data do we want to capture about an information system? Well, let's define what is meant by the term information system.

system	A set of components which are interrelated in some way. When these components are viewed together they are usually meaningful to the beholder.
information	This is data which has been presented in a way that is meaningful to the beholder.
information system	This is a type of system which generates, manipulates and communicates information.

If we think closely about the above definitions, it can be seen that to 'know what is going on inside' the information system the following are required:

(1) A technique which allows us to view the interrelationship of the components in the system. The technique we will use is called the dataflow diagram. It is a fundamental cornerstone of the software engineering method used in this book and is discussed in some depth shortly.

(2) A technique which allows us to define data or information. Such definitions are stored in a data dictionary which may or may not be computerised. As will be seen later in the chapter, data may be in an elementary form, but often it is in a more complicated form such as a document. So a way of defining its composition is required. Fortunately, a simple technique exists.

(3) A technique which allows us to describe what is going on inside a specific process. Look again at the definition of an information system. Clearly, processes are required to perform the generating, manipulating and communicating of information. So a way is needed to specify what is happening inside each process. Again, this is stored in a data dictionary.

Given that we have techniques for each of the above, then we should be in a position to describe an information system and hence capture the behaviour of it. The remainder of this chapter is given over to describing these basic techniques.

2.2 DATAFLOW DIAGRAMS

Perhaps the most widely-used aid for describing a system, the dataflow diagram (DFD) has been around in one form or another since the 1950s, largely because the alternatives of language and its written form, narrative, had been misinterpreted in many ways for all sorts of reasons. Intuitively, analysts seeking a more appropriate medium for describing business activities, deduced that a diagrammatic form which contained only those graphical objects which are actually needed, would be far more practical than using English in an unstructured or undisciplined manner.

The DFD contains four objects. These are the dataflow, process, datastore, and external entity. The dataflow represents packets of data moving to and from processes in the diagram; the processes themselves are simply transformations of incoming dataflows to outgoing dataflows. Datastores represent locations where data is stored, and external entities are used to show the source or destination of data when it is outside the area of analysis. The DFD is therefore a network of processes, datastores and external entities which are connected by dataflows.

Other attempts to use diagrammatic tools such as the flowchart suffered from placing too much emphasis on details of control, i.e. the rules for specifying under what conditions certain events had to occur. What was required was an approach which effectively forced the big picture to be painted first and which thereafter allowed other details to be completed. In other words, the solution to the problem was more than just using the right tool, i.e. the DFD, it lay also in the manner in which the DFD was to be used. Using DFDs in this way can therefore be considered a framework for capturing the important data early by focusing on dataflows and processes and ignoring control details. The success of this framework is built upon three pillars:

- use of the 'black box'
- implicit boundary definition
- partitioning through employing a hierarchy of DFDs

2.2.1 Black box

A black box is a process with the following characteristics:

- the inputs are known
- the outputs are known
- what the process does is known
- how the process works is not known

Figure 2.1 shows a process called 'ACCEPT ORDERS'. It is a black box because it meets the above criteria. Notice that although something can be inferred about the process by inspecting the inputs and outputs, there is no indication of how this decision is made. This is sometimes referred to as information hiding because some of the information about the process is deliberately not shown. Typically, DFDs contain many black boxes, called processes with the outputs of some processes also inputs to other processes. If all the information known about each process was included on the DFD, then it would become unreadable and therefore its purpose would be defeated.

2.2.2 Boundary definition

It is possible to tell the scope of the DFD by inspecting its boundary. A single DFD can be considered as a window viewing only part of a system.

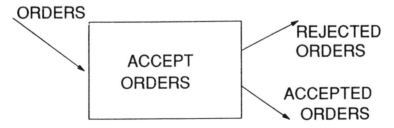

Fig. 2.1. Example of a black box.

Everything within the window is considered within the scope of the DFD. A rectangle is drawn around the DFD to indicate the extent of the boundary. This is an important diagrammatic concept, because since there is much to be described about a system, ways have to be found to split up or partition the problem so that each component is manageable. The use of boundaries helps to achieve this.

2.2.3 Hierarchy of DFDs

DFDs can be used to describe activities at different levels within an organisation. At a high level, one process in a DFD might describe a department's function, such as order processing or invoicing; at a lower level, a process might represent a single task that a clerk carries out, e.g. checking that a customer's credit limit is acceptable for an order. Now, there is clearly a link between credit limit checking and order processing since credit limit checking is a task which is often carried out by the order processing department. So, in order to integrate the different levels of DFDs a hierarchy of DFDs is created. At the highest level (level 0), there is typically only one process (i.e. the system) in the diagram. This is sometimes called a context diagram because it shows the relationship between this system and the rest of the organisation. See figure 2.2.

The context diagram is then expanded into a level 1 diagram which contains, in this case, three major processes (see figure 2.3).

Each process in the level 1 diagram is then expanded into its own level 2 diagram. This is continued until all the diagrams have been exploded into the detail required.

By using a hierarchy of DFDs we are not only able to supply all the details needed for a system, but, perhaps more importantly, we are able to organise the diagrams in a way which enables easy and quick access to the information we require. For example, if we want to see the details concerning credit limit

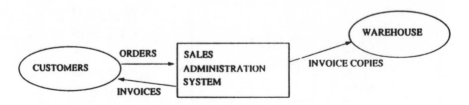

Fig. 2.2. Context diagram for a sales administration system.

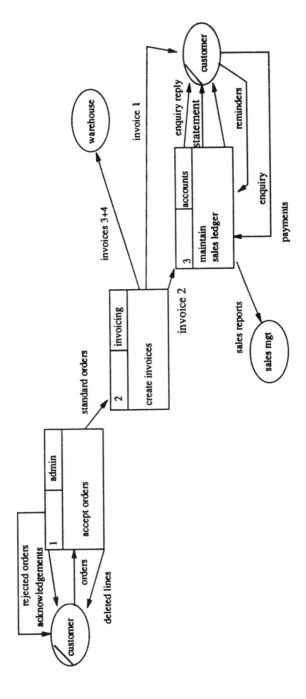

Fig. 2.3. Level 1 diagram for the sales administrative system.

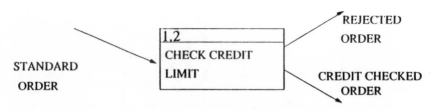

Fig. 2.4. A level 2 process.

checking we merely follow the path down via the 'ACCEPT ORDERS'
process till we find the detail we are after. See figure 2.4.

The use of a hierarchy (or tree) in this manner is a classic example of the
concept of functional decomposition. At the top of the tree the information
is high level, abstract and of a general nature. As we work down the tree the
information becomes more specific and detailed. See figure 2.5. It is no
coincidence that analysts work top-down when they are investigating the
system. At the start, there are very few details about the system; indeed it may

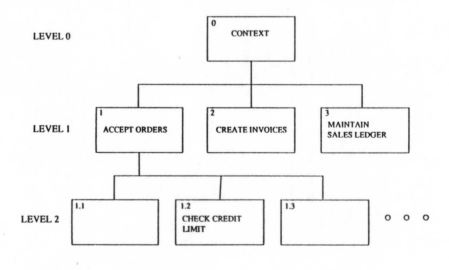

Fig. 2.5. Sample DFD hierarchy.

not even be clear exactly what the scope and therefore boundary of the system are. However, the analyst will be able to attempt to draw the context and level 1 diagrams. As more information about the system is gathered, lower level DFDs are able to be drawn. So the hierarchy of DFDs is a useful aid to the analyst in developing an understanding of the system as well as a means of organising the information. If the scope of the system does need to be clarified, it may be necessary to modify previously drawn higher level DFDs. This is the case with respect to figure 2.2 and 2.3, since inconsistencies exist between them, but this will become clearer once the rules for drawing DFDs are known. This problem illustrates the fact that much of the work done by analysts is iterative, i.e. they have to go back and refine their existing model.

2.3 COMPONENTS AND RULES FOR DFDs

There are four symbols which are used in the construction of DFDs:

- dataflow
- process
- external entity
- datastore

2.3.1 Dataflow

A dataflow is represented by an arrow in a DFD and is defined as a pipeline through which packets of data flow. Perhaps a good example of the concept of a dataflow is an orbiting communications satellite. Messages are sent to earth in short bursts of radio waves. Each burst can be considered a dataflow. In organisations, orders are sent from customers, documents are sent from one department to another. These are dataflows.

However, it is only when one comes to draw the diagram that one's real understanding is tested. Below are presented some of the more common clarifications in this regard.

(1) *A dataflow may be one item or a group of items*
A customer may be in the habit of sending a batch of orders at one time to a company, so the question then is whether the dataflow is one order or a group of orders. The answer lies in the way the order(s) are processed. If orders are processed one at a time (as is likely) regardless of how they are received, then the dataflow is a single order.

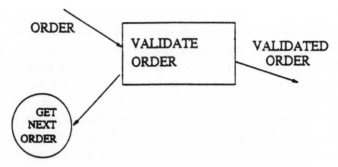

Fig. 2.6. A dataflow is not a control flow.

(2) *A dataflow is not a control flow*

Sometimes there is a temptation to add a 'dataflow' which indicates how the process is carried out. But this is an instruction rather than something which carries data. See figure 2.6. This kind of information simply clutters a DFD. In any case it is not the purpose of DFDs to show this. However it will be recorded elsewhere.

(3) *A dataflow is not a time trigger*

Typically in organisations processes start at certain points in time. For example, the processing of accounts often starts at the end of the month. See figure 2.7. These points in time are known as time triggers. As a deliberate part of the information-hiding philosophy these are not shown on the DFD.

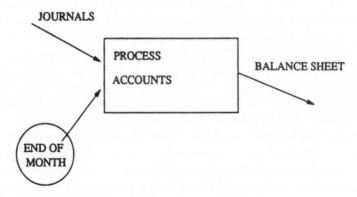

Fig. 2.7. A dataflow is not a time trigger.

2.3.2 Process

A process is defined as a transformation from incoming dataflows to outgoing dataflows. So it can be thought of as a kind of black box. Methods vary in the symbols used to describe a process. In LSDM and SSADM, a rectangle is used to represent a process. In the De Marco approach[1] a circle is used, and in the Gane and Sarson method[2] a soft-box (which is a rectangle with rounded corners) is used. It does not really matter which type of symbol is used as long as it is used consistently. However, from a practical point of view, some people argue that rectangles and soft-boxes are superior because they are easier for adding text. Throughout this book rectangles are used.

When drawing processes it is most important to ensure that the process is feasible. If a process is a transformation from incoming dataflows to outgoing dataflows, then all the data required to create the dataflows must be present in the incoming dataflows or be generated from within the process, otherwise the process could not possibly perform its stated task. If data is generated from within the process there are two possibilities. One is that the output data is in some way derived from the input data. Straightforward examples would include when age is calculated from a date of birth, or when a total is calculated from individual data items. The second possibility is that all or part of the input data is used as a key to access a datastore. Some or all of the data accessed by the key may become the output data.

One basic law for processes is that there must always be at least one input dataflow and at least one output dataflow, otherwise it is not a transformation. A process with no inputs or outputs is not a valid process.

All processes, except in the context diagram, are numbered uniquely. The various levels of DFD are recorded using a decimal catenation system. So, process number 2 would be in a level 1 diagram, 2.3 in a level 2 diagram, 2.3.1 in a level 3 diagram, and so on.

Each process is named as meaningfully as possible. To avoid ambiguity, each name is unique. Typically, process names start with a verb (e.g. TYPE, COMPUTE). This is followed by a meaningful clause (e.g. type INVOICE, compute INVOICE TOTAL). The purpose of naming processes is to aid the reader in understanding the DFD, hence the attempt to name as meaningfully as possible and to avoid relatively meaningless or general phrases like PROCESS INVOICE or worse still HANDLE DOCUMENT. Equally, it should be appreciated that even names which are well thought out are open to some interpretation and therefore there is a limit to what can be conveyed in a process name. At lower levels of the DFD, naming is easier as tasks become more specific.

When drawing DFDs it is sometimes difficult to decide whether to draw a particular activity as one or two (or more) processes. If it is drawn as one process then usually the two sub-processes will appear at the next lower level. Alternatively the two sub-processes could be drawn at the higher level. Unfortunately, there are no detailed guidelines for this except a general rule that no single DFD should contain more than about seven or eight processes. The analyst must decide what is appropriate. This means that two analysts with the same information might draw different DFDs – different at least in that some processes will appear at different levels on the two diagrams. Having said that, if the analysts have done their job properly, the same information about the system can be gleaned from both sets of DFDs. In other words, the criterion for a correct set of DFDs is that all the information about the system will appear somewhere in a set of DFDs.

2.3.3 External entity

An external entity is a person or organisation outside the system being analysed. It is represented here by an ellipse symbol (though both De Marco and Gane and Sarson use a square to represent external entities). External entities appear outside the rectangle which is the boundary of the system being investigated. They are connected by dataflows to processes inside the system boundary and therefore provide information about the source or destination of the data. External entities which supply data are sometimes called sources; those which receive data are sometimes referred to as sinks. Without external entities on DFDs, the reader may be unsure as to the source or destination of the dataflow, so as well as completing the diagram it serves to reassure the reader and reiterate the context of the DFD. Provided there is a dataflow to a specific process, external entities may appear on any level of DFD.

2.3.4 Datastore

A datastore is a temporary repository of data. It may be a computer file or a manual file such as a collection of orders held in a filing cabinet. It is represented by two parallel lines closed at the left-hand end. Each datastore is uniquely numbered and is prefixed by a C or M, where C indicates a computer file and M a manual i.e. non-computer file. In-trays on people's desks and filing cabinets are examples of manual datastores. See figure 2.8. In the diagram, M1 indicates that is data store number 1 and that it is manual.

Fig. 2.8. A manual datastore.

Like processes, datastores can be inspected to confirm that they are feasible. It is not possible to extract data which the datastore does not contain. Note, however, that there may be data which is added to a datastore which is never used (i.e. redundant data).

Some people might question whether datastores ought to be included in DFDs on the basis that, firstly, DFDs are not supposed to be interested in the time dimension (since triggers, for example, are specifically excluded). Secondly, and at a more fundamental level, the issue is whether a datastore adds something to the diagram.

DFDs can be viewed as a set of processes connected by dataflows, where the processes are just transformations performed on the dataflows. A datastore can be considered the antithesis of a dataflow in that it is a place where the data is stationary, i.e. not flowing. Data remains in the datastore for an unspecified period during which it may be accessed or modified and after which it may be removed from the datastore. The argument is therefore that it is acceptable to have a symbol on a dataflow diagram that shows 'non-flow'. This also is confirmed in a practical way when discussing systems with users. It seems natural to annotate datastores (files) on DFDs during discussion; not being able to do so would certainly cause problems during such discussions.

Sometimes when to show a datastore is a problem, i.e. at which level in the hierarchy should it appear. As part of the information hiding philosophy discussed earlier, datastores are shown at the lowest possible level. In other words, the datastore is shown against the specific process which uses the datastore, not against a process which is higher up in the hierarchy.

Another common temptation is for people to connect datastores directly to external entities. This is not appropriate. Whether it is done by computer or by human being, there needs to be some intervening process which moves the data from its resting place to the external entity and it is an oversight not to document this.

2.3.5 Access to and from datastores

There are two basic approaches to datastore access. The first one is called the

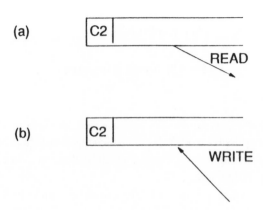

(a)

(b)

Fig. 2.9. The net-flow approach to datastore access.

net-flow approach and appears in De Marco[1]. The idea is that the direction of the arrow indicates the net flow of data. See figure 2.9.

Figure 2.9(a) implies that data is being read from the datastore. This is true even if you first must supply a key to access a particular record in the datastore, because the essential purpose of the task is to take away information. A write, on the other hand, implies you are adding something to the file. This may be when a record is added or when an existing record is modified since new data is added then too. See figure 2.9(b).

A second approach is used by LSDM and SSADM and involves three access symbols. Figure 2.10(a) shows the read access symbol. It is different from the net-flow read, because here it represents the situation where the data is accessed only for the purpose of reading it, i.e. the read has no effect on the contents of the datastore. Figure 2.10(b) shows the insert symbol, which is used when adding data to the datastore. The last symbol is in figure 2.10(c) and shows the modify symbol. The modify symbol covers situations where data is modified or deleted. For brevity this approach will be referred to as the R-I-M technique.

There is some debate over which technique is superior. The net-flow proponents argue that when talking with users one is only interested in whether data is deposited or withdrawn from the datastore, and that it is important not to get deflected from the prime objective of documenting the dataflows by discussing the intricacies of file access. The R-I-M proponents counter this by asserting that for manual access, at least, the user is the one who can provide the details of the access and that this ought to be

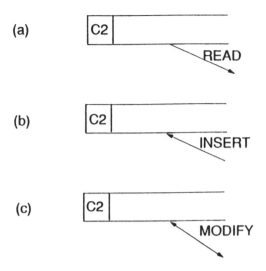

Fig. 2.10. The R-I-M technique for datastore access.

documented. Moreover, many argue that DFDs are not just a tool for documenting user discussions, they are used as an analysis tool to aid decisions on computer file access.

However, in the author's opinion, the R-I-M technique does not go far enough in defining the accesses. The modify symbol is ambiguous because it can represent either modification or deletion. A more precise notation would have four symbols representing read, insert, modify and delete. This we will call the R-I-M-D technique. See figure 2.11. Note that the 'dashed' arrow is used with the read symbol to reflect the fact that a read does not change the contents of a datastore, whereas all 'full-line' arrows do.

But this still leaves the issue of whether to use the net-flow approach or the R-I-M-D technique. In fact, we will use both techniques on different occasions. The net-flow technique is to be used when communicating with users. Here, it is the appropriate medium and allows discussion to take place in terms the user will be comfortable with. Later on, however, a more rigorous analysis needs to take place. Here, it is necessary to consider the accesses more thoroughly and hence the need for the R-I-M-D technique.

2.3.6 Interconnecting diagrams at the same level

Earlier, the philosophy of using external entities to provide a context for the

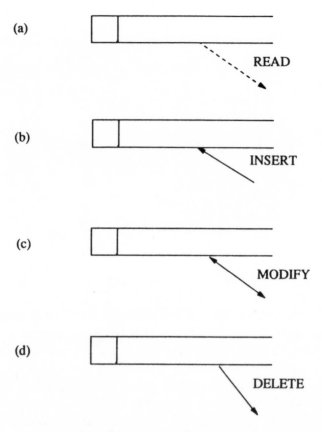

(a)

READ

(b)

INSERT

(c)

MODIFY

(d)

DELETE

Fig. 2.11. The R-I-M-D technique.

diagram was discussed. A similar situation arises when a diagram at a given
level interconnects with another diagram on the same level. For example, in
figure 2.5 it may be that a process in diagram 1 has an output dataflow which
is an input dataflow to a process in diagram 2. In order to provide a context
when drawing exploded diagrams, it is necessary to show the interconnection
as in figure 2.12(a). Occasionally two such diagrams may be interconnected
through a datastore. In this case the datastore would be drawn outside the
boundary line as in Figure 2.12(b).

We are now in a position to understand figure 2.13, which shows the
explosion of process 1 of the Sales Administration System. A detailed
description of this system is given in the appendix.

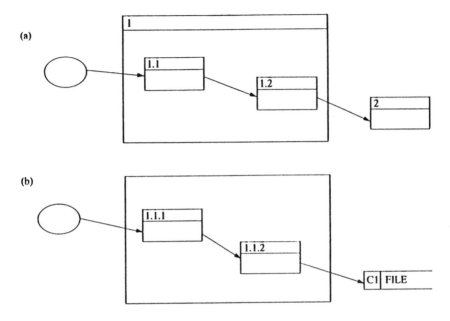

Fig. 2.12. The interconnection problem.

2.3.7 Physical and logical DFDs

What we have been discussing so far has been physical dataflow diagrams. Physical DFDs are DFDs which show physical characteristics of the system. They are 'physical' in the sense that they refer to actual resources such as documents, people, departments, locations or equipment within the existing system. Physical characteristics manifest themselves in the following ways:

Process Name
Process names may have physical characteristics such as TYPE, WRITE, that indicate the physical manner (e.g. by typewriter or by hand) in which the process is carried out.

Process Location
It is possible to annotate the physical location, department, employee name, or job title of employee connected with that process.

Dataflow
Dataflows can contain physical references, e.g. colour as in blue invoice copy

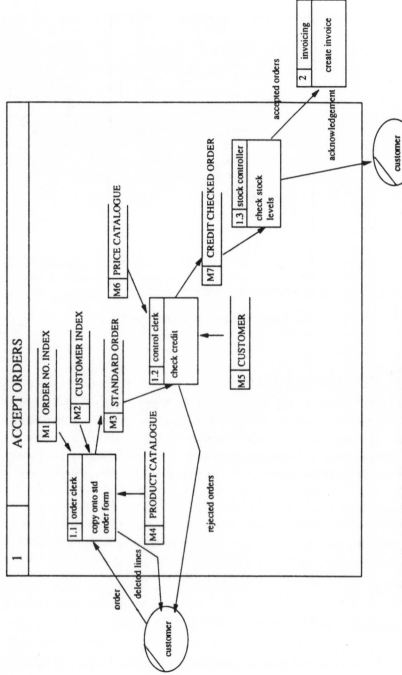

Fig. 2.13. A level 2 for the sales administration system.

or document serial number perhaps. Note that process names may contain physical dataflow references, e.g. STORE BLUE INVOICE COPY.

Datastore
Datastores can take the physical form of filing cabinets or in-trays on someone's desk.

Physical DFDs are a good vehicle for user discussion because the physical references are known to users and so a degree of familiarity and therefore comfort is achieved by using the terms they use themselves. Physical DFD sets extend the usefulness of physical DFDs with users for two main reasons. Firstly, analysts deal with people at all levels in the organisation. When exploring problems or requirements with senior management, it is vital that the discussion is at a fairly high level. Senior managers are often more concerned about wider, interdepartmental issues and the last thing they want is to get 'bogged down' with too much detail on a diagram. Equally, in discussion with staff who work at the operational level it is important to have a suitably detailed diagram to work with. So the use of a hierarchy of DFDs facilitates discussion at any level within an organisation. The second reason is that it is a good way of managing the information that is being collected, i.e. it partitions the processing of the system into discrete units thus enabling the analyst and user to find and focus on a particular aspect of the system very quickly.

In general then the physical DFD set seems the most efficient vehicle for capturing the behaviour of an information system, and indeed that is the role that is recommended for it here. However, for the tasks involved in actually analysing the system, some of the strengths of the physical DFD set turn out to be weaknesses. For example, the analysis task is easier to perform if a single diagram exists containing all detail processes, i.e. if it ignores processes which are exploded. In fact, the physical DFD set is the starting point for a number of transformations. Eventually a new physical DFD set is created; it is new in the sense that it contains solutions to problems and enhancements that have been identified. The transformations reflect the need to go through a series of stages of analysis. Diagrams which aid analysis are often called 'logical' diagrams. These stages are shown in figure 2.14. The detailed rules for creating these intermediate diagrams are described in chapters 9 and 10.

Semi-logical DFD
This is a single DFD containing only non-exploded processes and R-I-M-D accesses. It is used to establish if there are any basic omissions or mistakes in

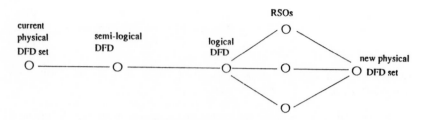

Fig. 2.14. DFD transformations.

the system. Such checking is easier to do with a semi-logical DFD than with a DFD set.

Logical DFD

The semi-logical DFD is refined into a logical DFD. Logical DFDs contain no physical references at all. The processes that are described are absolutely essential for the running of the system and all datastores are converted to their corresponding entities. Entities are discussed in detail in chapter 3. The purpose of the logical DFD is to enable the analyst to concentrate on resolving problems and identifying improvements without being inhibited by unnecessary 'physical' detail. Figure 10.1 shows an example of a logical DFD.

RSOs

RSOs stands for required system options. These are logical DFDs with enough physical processing added to illustrate how a particular solution could be implemented. They are presented to the users so that a final selection can be made. However, they are only outline solutions and therefore are not a full specification of the required system. Figure 10.2 shows an example of an RSO.

So each kind of DFD has its own purpose and each is tuned to meet its purpose. In chapter 15, the use of software to automate software engineering is discussed. Suffice to say there is clearly scope for software to assist the transformation processes discussed above.

2.3.8 General guidelines for drawing physical DFD sets

The most important thing to remember about DFDs is that they are drawn so that they can be read. Readability is therefore a major consideration. Most people tend to work from left to right and top to bottom. This is reflected as

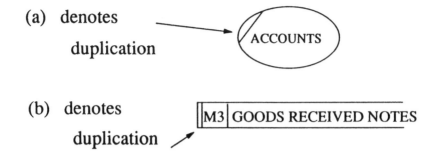

(a) denotes
    duplication

ACCOUNTS

(b) denotes
    duplication

M3 | GOODS RECEIVED NOTES

Fig. 2.15. Duplication on external entities and datastores.

far as possible in the way DFDs are drawn. Typically the earlier processes tend to be placed in the top left-hand side of the diagram.

As a general rule no more than seven processes should appear on the same DFD. It is almost always possible to partition the problem so that this guideline can be accommodated. This improves readability considerably.

Even with a small number of processes it is still possible to have DFDs which look complicated. Two things can be done to make a diagram more readable. Firstly, external entities which are sources appear on the left-hand and, if necessary, top-side of the DFD. External entities which are sinks appear on the right-hand side of the diagram. Obviously, this guideline should be overridden where it is advantageous to do so. Secondly, where the same external entities appear more than once in the same DFD, they are flagged with a mark as in figure 2.15(a) to signal their duplicated nature.

Inside the boundary of the DFD, the same idea can be applied to datastores. Duplicated datastores are as shown in figure 2.15(b).

2.4 DEFINING THE STRUCTURE OF DATA

For our purposes, there are two types of data. These are elementary data and composite data. Elementary data is 'basic' data which does not need to be subdivided any further. A data item representing someone's age or salary would be an example of elementary data. In order to answer questions about elementary data, certain characteristics of the elementary data item have to be identified such as:

• What is the name of the data item?

BANK STATEMENT

ACCOUNT-NO	ACCOUNT NAME	DATE
10067307	D McDERMID	31/5/90

TRANS-NO	TRANS-TYPE	AMOUNT	BALANCE	STATUS
D101756	D	50	101.50	
D101759	D	25	126.50	
17005576/W	W	150	-23.50	

Fig. 2.16. A simplified bank statement.

- Is it known by any other name?
- How many characters does it contain?
- Does it restrict itself to a range or a set of acceptable values?

and so on.

In businesses, however, it is much more usual to see data items constructed into groups. For example, any document will contain one, or, more likely, many data items built up in a particular way. A document is one example of a composite data item because it is composed of individual elementary data items. In a DFD, both dataflows and datastores are likely to be composite data items. In addition, screen layouts, computer reports, files and databases are composite data items and therefore can make use of the notation about to be described.

Consider the simplified bank statement in figure 2.16. Let's try to define it in terms of elementary data items. The notation used here is broadly similar to that found in De Marco[1], but readers familiar with Backus-Naur Form should have no difficulty with the principle.

2.4.1 Sequence

Looking at the top line of the statement, it can be seen that there are three different elementary data items, one occurring after the other. If this was all that was on the bank statement it could be written as:

STATEMENT = BANK-ACCOUNT-NO + ACCOUNT-NAME
+ DATE-OF-ACCOUNT

This is an example of SEQUENCE, which means that individual data items must always occur in a certain order. The '+' is used to separate one data item from the next.

2.4.2 Repetition

The bank statement is, in fact, more complicated. In the main body of the statement, we see there is a series of lines. On each line the individual elementary data items are repeated. This is referred to as REPETITION or a repeating group. The bank statement now becomes:

STATEMENT = BANK-ACCOUNT-NO + ACCOUNT-NAME
+ DATE-OF-ACCOUNT + {TRANSACTION-NO
+ TRANSACTION-TYPE + AMOUNT
+ BALANCE + ACCOUNT-STATUS}

Here the curly brackets denote a group of items which are repeated. Note that the following is not equivalent to the above:

{TRANSACTION-NO} + {TRANSACTION-TYPE} + {AMOUNT}
+ {BALANCE} + {ACCOUNT-STATUS}

What this is saying is that there is a series of transaction numbers followed by a series of transaction types, followed by a series of amounts, etc. The convention, however, is to define the composite data item starting at the top left-hand corner of the document and then work along to the right and then start on the second line and so on – just as one would read the document.

Sometimes the upper and lower limits of a repetition are known and these may be documented as follows:

2{item}	lower limit only known
{item}5	upper limit only known
2{item}5	both upper and lower limits known

A common alternative to the above notation is to use superscripts to indicate an upper limit and subscripts for the lower limit. This can sometimes cause problems if these definitions are being recorded in a computerised data dictionary and the editor has difficulty with superscripts and subscripts.

2.4.3 Selection

If we inspect the transaction-no more closely, it can be seen that there are two different types of transaction – a deposit and withdrawal. Each has their own codification system (they do not even contain the same number of characters). What is clear is that the transaction-no is either a withdrawal-no or a deposit-no. This is known as SELECTION since only one of a number of possibilities can be true (in our case there were only two possibilities) and in the example is annotated in the following manner:

```
STATEMENT =  BANK-ACCOUNT-NO + ACCOUNT-NAME
             + DATE-OF-ACCOUNT + {[WITHDRAWAL-
             NO| DEPOSIT-NO] + TRANSACTION-TYPE
             + AMOUNT + BALANCE
             + ACCOUNT-STATUS}
```

2.4.4 Optionality

One more refinement is required because there is a problem with the ACCOUNT-STATUS field. When the account goes into the red an asterisk appears under ACCOUNT-STATUS. If the account is in the black then nothing appears. This is not the same situation as selection, because in selection there MUST be one of a set of possibilities.

OPTIONALITY therefore means that a data item may or may not appear and is indicated using ordinary brackets. The bank statement now becomes:

```
STATEMENT =  BANK-ACCOUNT-NO + ACCOUNT-NAME
             + DATE-OF-ACCOUNT + {[WITHDRAWAL-
             NO| DEPOSIT-NO] + TRANSACTION-TYPE
             + AMOUNT + BALANCE
             + (ACCOUNT-STATUS)}
```

2.4.5 Intermediate composite data items

What we have above is a perfectly acceptable way of meeting the objective of defining composite data items in terms of elementary ones. However, it can be worthwhile to use the tactic of intermediate definitions to avoid repetition elsewhere. For example, suppose we had defined the bank statement as:

$$STATEMENT = TOP + BODY$$

We could then go on to describe both TOP and BODY as composite data items. The potential benefit here lies in the possibility that TOP or BODY may be definitions which are reusable in describing other composite data items, and so if chosen and named wisely this may save time and effort, as well as making things clearer for the reader.

2.4.6 Data dictionary

Elementary and composite data item definitions are stored in a data dictionary which may be computerised. Composite data items can be put into sections such as dataflows, datastores and entities to enable quick access, i.e.:

DATA-DICTIONARY	=	ELEMENTARY + COMPOSITE
COMPOSITE	=	DATAFLOW + DATASTORE + ENTITY
ELEMENTARY	=	NAME + (ALIAS) + TYPE + SIZE + (COMMENT)

2.5 SPECIFYING PROCESSES

In this section we will look at techniques for specifying processes. Ideally, a specification should define *what* a process does, without defining *how*. In other words, the specification should contain the essence of what a process has to do but no more. Indeed there may be many different ways of implementing a specification. For a number of reasons any one way may have advantages or disadvantages, hence the quest for pure specification. However, as we shall see, pure specification is not always practical.

We will discuss three techniques for specifying processes. These are:

- decision trees
- decision tables
- structured English

2.5.1 Decision trees

A decision tree is a tree-like structure which identifies the decision paths at each mode. See figure 2.17. Here each node represents a question regarding acceptance for a mortgage plan. Movement from one node to the next is dependent on whether the answer to the question at the node is true or false.

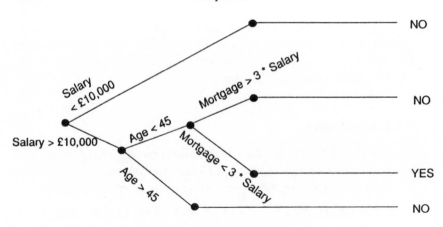

Fig. 2.17. Sample decision tree.

2.5.2 Decision tables

The decision table for the same problem is shown in figure 2.18. In this example, only if the answer to each of the questions is YES is the mortgage granted, as indicated by the tick in the 'grant mortgage' row. If the answer to any of the questions is NO, then the mortgage is denied. A dash against a question indicates that it does not matter whether the answer is YES or NO to that particular question.

Salary > £10,000	Y	N	-	-
Age < 45	Y	-	N	-
Mortgage < 3 * Salary	Y	-	-	N
Grant Mortgage	✓			
Deny Mortgage		✓	✓	✓

Fig. 2.18. Sample decision table.

2.5.3 Structured English

The third technique for specifying processes is called structured English. It has been proven that any process can be described using a combination of three basic 'constructs' (i.e. types of sentences). Both structured English and structured programming use this to advantage by limiting the way that logic is allowed to be expressed. Basically, the only constructs permitted are the three constructs of sequence, selection and iteration. We have just seen something very similar when we considered the notion of sequence, selection and repetition in relation to data structures. However, here they will be used as 'constructs' to build up the procedural logic necessary to define any particular problem.

(1) Sequence

Sequence is the first and most basic construct. In sequence, one statement simply follows another. Figure 2.19 is a diagram which shows the sequence of statements to be executed. It is called a flowchart (or control-flow graph) and here it indicates that statement 2 is executed after statement 1. Only very simple problems can be defined using the sequence construct, e.g.:

SUM   = A + B + C
AVERAGE = SUM DIV 3

(2) Selection

Selection is where either one set of statements or another set is to be executed, depending on whether a boolean expression is true or false. See figure 2.20. The diamond symbol denotes a question (boolean expression). As an

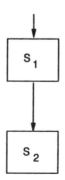

Fig. 2.19. A sequence statement.

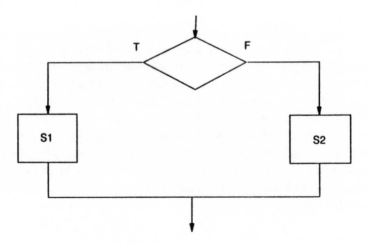

Fig. 2.20. A selection statement.

example, the structured English for the control-flow graph in figure 2.20
might be:

```
if      mark > =  40 then
        passes  =  passes + 1
else
        fails    =  fails + 1
endif
```

Note the use of indentation to make the structured English more readable and

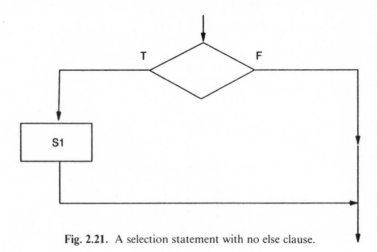

Fig. 2.21. A selection statement with no else clause.

the use of the 'endif' to clearly delineate the end of the selection clause.

Sometimes the problem to be described is such that there is no statement to be executed under the else condition. For example, suppose we did not wish to calculate the number of fails. See figure 2.21.

The structured English for this situation is:

```
if      mark > =  40 then
        passes  =  passes + 1
endif
```

On other occasions, it is necessary to have a sequence of statements embedded within a condition as illustrated in figure 2.22.

The structured English for this might be:

```
if      mark > =  40 then
        passes  =  passes + 1
else
        fails    =  fails + 1
        write student name
endif
```

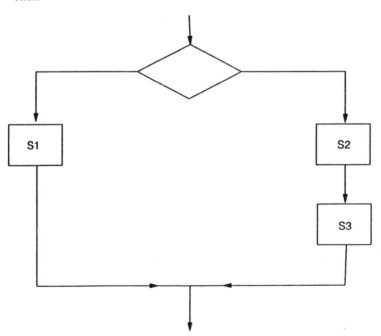

Fig. 2.22. A selection statement with an embedded sequence clause.

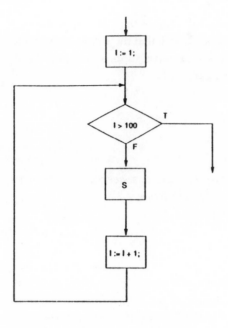

Fig. 2.23(a). The FOR construct.

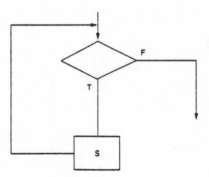

Fig. 2.23(b). The WHILE construct.

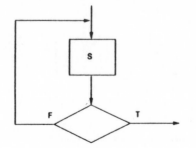

Fig. 2.23(c). The REPEAT construct.

(3) Iteration

Iteration is used where you want to execute a statement (or statements) many times. There are three variants of this construct. The first is where the number of executions is known; the FOR construct is used for this. The second is the WHILE construct; here a number of statements are executed while an expression is true. The last construct is the REPEAT construct, which executes a number of statements until a certain condition is met. The difference between the WHILE and REPEAT constructs is that the test for the WHILE is made at the start of the construct, whereas the test for the end-condition of a REPEAT is done at the end of the construct. This means that it is possible for the WHILE construct to be executed zero times (if the WHILE condition is not true upon the first execution) whereas the statements within the REPEAT construct must be executed at least once. See figures 2.23(a), (b) and (c).

Now, the object of structured English is to describe processes. With iterative processes there is often a choice as to which construct to select. For example, suppose we wish to describe a process which sums up marks in a row for each student on a marks sheet. We could use any iterative construct.

The FOR construct would be:

```
for each student on the marks sheet do the following:
    sum = a + b + c
    put sum in total column
endfor
```

The WHILE construct would be:

```
while students on the mark sheet
    sum = a + b + c
    put sum in total column
endwhile
```

The REPEAT construct would be:

```
repeat
    sum = a + b + c
    put sum in total column
until no more students on marks sheet
```

(4) Nesting

The three basic constructs of sequence, selection and iteration only allow a limited degree of complexity in specifying processes. Clearly, processes can be

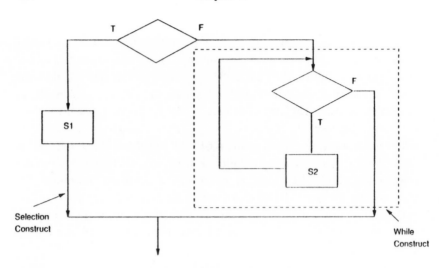

Fig. 2.24. Nested construct.

and often are far more complex than any one construct can reflect. Examination of each of the constructs shows that each construct has only one entry point and one exit point. This is highly significant because it allows constructs to be embedded within other constructs and yet still preserves an overall consistency and predictability of approach. Embedding constructs within others is known as nesting and is illustrated in figure 2.24. Here a WHILE construct is embedded within a SELECTION construct. Each construct can therefore be viewed as a building block which as a nested set allows us to describe more complex processes.

(5) The CASE construct
A particularly common nested construct is the 'nested if'. Suppose a variable 'a' can have four possible values from 1 through 4. If you wanted to take different actions depending on the value of 'a' then the structured English would be:

```
if a = 1 then b = b + c
    else if a = 2 then b = b – c
        else if a = 3 then b = b * c
            else b = b/c
        endif
    endif
endif
```

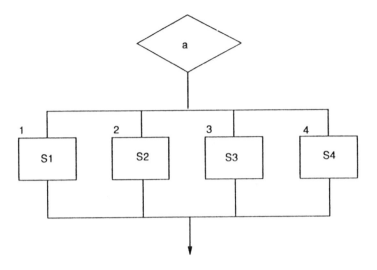

Fig. 2.25. Case construct.

There are two problems with this. Firstly, the logic is not particularly easy to follow. Secondly, if there are many nested ifs then the amount of indentation becomes impractical to document.

Although the three basic constructs (with their variants) are sufficient to describe any problem, the CASE construct is a useful additional construct to structured English because it improves readability and understandability. Figure 2.25 shows the control-flow graph for the nested if example above.

The structured English for the example would be:

```
Case a of
    1: b = b + c
    2: b = b - c
    3: b = b * c
    4: b = b / c
endcase
```

2.5.4 Choosing specification techniques

Perhaps the purest specification technique is the decision table since it gives no indication as to how the process should be implemented. Even the decision tree gives a hint to implementation in the sense that there is a sequence in the questions asked as one proceeds down the nodes of the tree, though the

```
for each item-line on the standard order form, do the following:
        obtain unit-cost for line-item from price catalogue
        multiply by quantity to obtain line-item cost
endfor

sum line-item costs and add VAT to obtain order-cost
obtain customer-credit from customer file
if order-cost <= customer-credit

        then reduce customer-credit by order-cost
                send credit-checked order to stock control
        else stamp standard order form as rejected
                indicate order-cost and current customer-credit
                send rejected order form to customer
endif
```

Table 2.1. Structured English for process 1.2 in the sales administration system.

implementor is not obliged to follow that sequence.

But a more fundamental concern of both decision trees and decision tables is that they do not lend themselves well to describing iterative constructs. Having said that, if the nature of the process only deals with selections then they are both excellent media for communicating this type of problem.

As a general strategy, structured English is recommended as the default approach, with decision tables or decision trees being used where the situation permits. Table 2.1 shows the structured English for process 1.2 in the Sales Administration System.

2.6 SUMMARY

This chapter introduced dataflow diagrams and data dictionary techniques.

2.6.1 Review of dataflow diagrams

Dataflow diagrams are a network of dataflows and corresponding processes (black boxes) with external entities providing the relationship to the rest of the system and datastores allowing data to be deposited and withdrawn. Explicit boundaries delimit the scope of a DFD. DFDs have the following qualities:

- They only provide some facts about the system. DFDs do not show the internal details of processes, neither do they provide a breakdown of the data that make up the dataflows or that are held in the datastores. This information hiding philosophy is necessary to avoid overcrowding the DFD and to improve readability.

- They are a tool for user communication. A characteristic that typifies information systems is the need to extract information about the existing or proposed system from users. Experience has shown that most users readily take to DFDs and find them a comfortable vehicle in discussion.
- They are useful as an analysis tool. DFDs are not just for recording user statements. The DFDs are later refined in ways which aid the analysis process. The ability to use essentially the same tool in different stages of the development process has significant advantages.
- They are semi-rigorous. They are not rigorous because different analysts may draw slightly different hierarchies of DFDs with perhaps different numbers of processes at some levels, although essentially the same information about the system is being captured. Also, the naming of processes is subjective and therefore the meaning implied is open to interpretation. Yet DFDs are rigorous to some extent. They have definite symbols to describe the various objects used as well as rules and guidelines to aid their drawing.
- Hierarchies of DFDs permit partitioning. With some thought given to the way the system is partitioned into levels of DFDs, analysts and users will find it easy to access the part of the system they want, which makes it a practical and convenient technique for managing a large amount of information. It also makes the system more maintainable, since quick access is facilitated.

2.6.2 Review of data dictionary techniques

(1) Data definitions
The decomposition technique for describing composite data items in terms of elementary ones is a simple but powerful way of storing definitions of any composite data item. It can be applied to any document, to dataflows, datastores and so on. Its main features are that:

- It uses sequence, repetition, selection and optionality to identify the main structure of the data.
- It permits 'intermediate' data items to be defined so that they can be reused.
- repeating groups can indicate upper and lower limits.

(2) Specification techniques
Three techniques were introduced as ways of specifying processes. Decision

tables are probably the purest form, followed closely by decision trees, yet neither have the widespread applicability of structured English. However, structured English is not ideal as a specification technique because it is procedural and therefore in an important sense describes HOW the process should be implemented. Of course, the designer or programmer is not obliged to implement the process in the way it is described, but nevertheless it does suggest a method for implementing the process.

Because structured English uses the three basic constructs, it is able to describe any process which means that it can be used in any circumstance. Traditionally, processes have been specified using standard English which can often be long-winded and open to misinterpretation. Structured English is an improvement over standard English in the following ways:

- It uses a limited set of the English language. Indeed, an installation may adopt a set of standard words with standard meanings and only these would be permissible when writing structured English.
- There is a fixed structure to sentences. For example, sequence sentences always start with a verb (e.g. MOVE) followed by an object (e.g. A to B). Selection and iteration constructs have 'reserved' words.
- It uses indentation to show nesting. This gives structured English a kind of two-dimensional aspect, which makes the logic much easier to see.
- The use of ENDIF, ENDFOR, ENDWHILE, UNTIL and ENDCASE act as markers to delimit the end of a construct. Again, this improves readability.

So, there is some structure to the use of structured English. Yet it is not fully rigorous. For example, it is not necessary to declare variables used (though meaningful names are always helpful and in any case most variables would already be defined in the data dictionary). Neither would it be considered mandatory to initialise variables. The object of structured English is to communicate a process specification. As long as it meets that criterion, anything else is superfluous.

2.7 FURTHER READING

1   DeMarco, T. (1979) *Structured Analysis and System Specification*, Prentice-Hall, New York, is a good account of how dataflow diagrams and data dictionary techniques can be used to put structure on information systems problems.

2 Gane, C. and Sarson, T. (1979) *Structured Systems Analysis: Tools and Techniques*, Prentice-Hall, New York, is another interesting exposition of the problem domain. They present, at times, contrasting approaches to DeMarco. Behind these differences lie alternative philosophies about the nature of the software engineering problem. Both books are highly recommended to the serious software engineering student.

2.8 EXERCISES

1   Figure 2.3 contains a much more comprehensive set of dataflows to its external entities than its context diagram figure 2.2. Draw a new context diagram on the basis of the information available in figure 2.3.

2   The appendix contains the case study for the Sales Administration System (SAS) in a company called Superior Builders Merchants (SBM). So far, figures 2.2, 2.3 and 2.13 have been drawn using the information contained in the case study. Draw the remaining DFDs in the DFD set. Hint: there is no more real information for the invoicing department, so no explosion is possible, but it is now necessary to add any datastores to the lowest level invoicing process; process 3 (maintain sales ledger) needs exploding to a lower level as does process 1.3.

3   The appendix contains 3 documents used by the Sales Administration System. Using the decomposition technique, decompose each into elementary items. Also, document at least 10 elementary items.

4   Select 3 unexploded (i.e. lowest level) processes from your DFD set and write the structured English for each.

5   Convert the net-flow accesses in figure 2.13 to R-I-M-D accesses.

Chapter 3
Data Modelling

An important feature of information systems is the need to share the same data with other users of the system. Although this characteristic can occur in other types of system, it is not the overriding consideration that it is in information systems. Only recently has the software industry begun to grasp fully that different types of software have different problem domains and that different strategies for approaching and resolving problems are required.

Since the 1960s, much has been learnt about the problems associated with information systems and it is worthwhile briefly reviewing some of these lessons in order to set the background for the rest of the chapter.

3.1 TRADITIONAL FILE-BASED SYSTEMS

The creation of files is a natural response to many information system problems. For example, take a system required to process customer orders for a company (i.e. an order processing system). Orders arrive daily and they have to be entered into the computer. If a batch system is being used then a batch of orders will be transferred onto a computer readable medium such as disk and then presented to a program which validates them to ensure all mandatory fields are present and no typing errors have crept in. Valid orders have to be held somewhere for subsequent processing, e.g. perhaps to check if the required items are in stock. So a file is used as an intermediate storage vehicle. Storing data in files is a natural and arguably sensible tactic which assists in achieving the objectives of the system.

A major problem arises because of the proliferation of these files and the data they contain. If a system is also required by the invoicing department to prepare invoices then clearly an invoice file will contain much of the information contained in the order processing file. Further, if the accounts department wish to hold a computerised sales ledger, then some duplicate information will be held in the sales ledger file also. The problem of duplication goes back to the days before computers when armies of clerks were employed to process documents and keep internal records in personal filing cabinets. Duplication was accepted then because there was no real alternative.

With duplicated data comes the problem of inconsistent data, which is apparent in manual and traditional computer systems alike. There are two kinds of inconsistency. The first kind arises because data is not necessarily held in a standard way. If two departments hold data say on customers, the first department may refer to a particular customer as 'Smith, A.B.', whereas the second department may record the name as 'A.B. Smith' or just 'Smith'. Further complications can arise through simple misspelling of names. Basically, this is because there is more than one record of the same customer.

The second kind of inconsistency arises because each occurrence of duplicated data is not updated simultaneously. Imagine a company has a payroll system which is updated and run weekly and a personnel system which is updated and run monthly. As people join, leave and transfer within the company this information will be reflected in the information produced by both systems. However, since the personnel system is run only once a month, reports produced by the personnel system will become more and more inconsistent with the payroll information as each week, and therefore update of the payroll system, passes. Worse still is the possibility that because updating these two separate systems will require two separate actions perhaps initiated by different staff, one will not be actioned leaving these two files permanently inconsistent.

The concern with inconsistent data is obvious – it wastes precious time. However, if everyone in the organisation uses the same information then many misunderstandings, disagreements and so on are avoided. Imagine how much time, effort and money is spent in organisations all over the world just resolving problems created by inconsistent data.

Duplicate data, apart from wasting storage space unnecessarily, brings problems for the computing department if the characteristics of the duplicate data items such as size or format have to be modified. Every file which contains those data items has to be modified. Changes like this occur more often than one would like to think and the number of files can become significant. The work involved creates significant political, managerial and technical problems for the computer department, perhaps the worst of which is that the computer department is seen as slow and unresponsive to business changes.

3.2 DATABASE SYSTEMS

Instead of having separate files containing duplicate and sometimes inconsistent data, it would be ideal to have one centralised store of data which contains no duplicate data items. This is, in effect, a database. Clearly, because there would be only one occurrence of any data item, there would be no duplication and therefore less maintenance headache. Also, there would be no possibility of inconsistency. Unfortunately, it is not always possible to have no duplication of data in a database. This is to do with the need to link different parts of the database together, but what we can do is limit such duplication to key fields. In other words, database systems aim to contain no duplicate data items outside of key fields. Departments within organisations must be prepared to share data with other departments or staff by permitting access where appropriate. Databases also cut down the volume of trans- actions that need to be processed since, for example, two transactions which delete an employee from the payroll and personnel files respectively can now be performed in one single transaction on the database.

So adopting a database philosophy is an important step in recognising the nature of the information systems.

3.3 DATA ANALYSIS

Behind the database philosophy is a commitment not just to building one computer system, although it can be used for that, but also to creating a database which will meet, as far as it is possible to anticipate, the future needs of all computer systems the organisation will require. This is data analysis. To do this one has to analyse the underlying structure of the data thoroughly in order to identify the nature of the data and relationships between data. There is an assumption here that the underlying structure of the data remains relatively static over time. However, unlike data, the business processes which operate on the data are liable to change much more frequently over time. For the remainder of this chapter, we will examine one fundamental technique in data analysis. It is called data modelling and it is a technique for identifying and describing data.

3.4 THE DATA MODELLING TECHNIQUE

A data model is a conceptual model of the data required by the system and of the relationships between data. The deliverable from data modelling (also known as entity modelling) is a 'first-cut' data model. There are two stages to the data modelling process. Firstly, an unrefined first-cut data model is created; this is then refined into a refined first-cut data model. An unrefined first-cut data model may contain aspects which are not implementable on a database (e.g. see recursive relationships later on); however the refined data model is more directly implementable on a database, though it will still require a degree of conversion to suit individual database software characteristics, after which it is known as a final data model. Some basic terminology of data modelling is now introduced.

entity
An entity is something of interest or relevance to the organisation about which data is likely to be stored. Entities may be physical entities like CUSTOMER, SUPPLIER, EMPLOYEE, or more abstract like ORDER, INVOICE, or some event that takes place, e.g. BREAKDOWN, PROJECT. An entity name is always singular, never plural.

entity occurrence
An entity occurrence is an instantiation or example of an entity. So customer 'ABC' is an entity occurrence of entity CUSTOMER. It may help at this stage to consider an entity as a file and an entity occurrence as a record in a file.

attribute
An attribute is a piece of data about an entity. Often this will be a property or characteristic of the entity. For example, for an EMPLOYEE entity, likely attributes would be name, address, date of birth and so on. Each attribute is unique, i.e. it only occurs once in one entity occurrence and should not appear in another entity save for key fields. Note, however, other entities may have similar attributes, e.g. CUSTOMER may also have a name and address. Here the attribute names ought to be qualified into customer-name, employee-name and so on. This is called its role name. An attribute may be considered equivalent to a field in a record.

key
A key is an attribute or group of attributes which uniquely distinguishes one entity occurrence from all others. The concept is identical to that of a key in a file.

Entities can be identified in a number of ways depending on the circumstances. If one is interviewing users then appropriate questions to the user can help identify candidate entities. Typical questions might be:

- What does the department process?
- What inputs and outputs do you have?
- What things are your department interested in?
- What aspects of your work do you consider important?

Departmental manuals, job descriptions and so on can be a useful source of entities, as can computer files if there is already an existing system. Also, any documents and computer files used by the department are useful in the identification of possible attributes too.

This information is documented in a formalised way; firstly the entities are identified and then the key and attributes for each entity are recorded. At this stage it is understood that what is recorded may not be the final version; indeed the process is an iterative one and it may be necessary to review the data model to iron out problems, inconsistencies or omissions found.

A list of entities is prepared with a definition for each entity as in figure 3.1(a).

For each attribute of an entity, a significant amount of information needs to be collected, but for the moment assume that the information in figure 3.1(b) is stored where it is known.

entity name	alias	definition
EMPLOYEE	WORKER	a person currently paid a salary or weekly wage by the organisation

Fig. 3.1(a). An entity definition.

attribute name	alias	type*	size**	value/meaning***
stock-no	part-no	a/n	5	a code which distinguishes one stock item from all others. First two characters are alpha followed by a three-digit running number.

* type is the format of the attribute eg. numeric, alphabetic etc.
** size is the number of characters it takes up on paper or on a screen.
*** value/meaning is any helpful commentary on the attribute.

Fig. 3.1(b). An attribute definition.

This information is recorded in the data dictionary. If it is a computerised data dictionary, then access is typically quick and easy. At this stage not all information about the data is known, so the data dictionary must be able to accommodate situations where only some information is known. As more becomes available, it can then be added to the data dictionary.

3.4.1 Relationships between data

The next stage is to identify relationships between data.

relationship
A relationship is a meaningful association between entities. For example, where an employee works in a department, the relationship is 'EMPLOYEE WORKS FOR DEPARTMENT'.

relationship occurrence
A relationship occurrence instantiates a relationship by identifying related entity occurrences, e.g. 'MR JONES WORKS FOR ACCOUNTS', where Mr Jones and Accounts are respective entity occurrences.

degree of relationship
The degree of relationship is an important aspect about the nature of the relationship between two entities. It tells us about the number of occurrences that one entity occurrence has with respect to its counterpart in the other entity. There are three degrees of relationship.

(1) One-to-one relationships (1:1)
A one-to-one relationship is where there is only one occurrence in one entity for one occurrence in another. A good example of a one-to-one relationship is the relationship IS MARRIED TO, which is an association between entities MAN and WOMAN as in figure 3.2. In most Western societies, at any rate,

Fig. 3.2. One-to-one relationship.

one man may be married to, at most, one woman at any one time and vice versa. Note, however, that the relationship does not imply that for every man in the MAN entity there will always be a wife and equally for every woman in the WOMAN entity there will be a husband. What the relationship is saying is that where there is a 'IS MARRIED TO' relationship occurrence it is a one-to-one relationship.

An example of where one-to-one relationships occur in information systems would be where a business always fulfils customer orders immediately. Here, there is a one-to-one relationship between order and invoice. Note that time here has a strong influence. The order will always be produced before the invoice; in other words, there may be orders for which there are no invoices but there should never be invoices for which there are no orders.

(2) One-to-many relationships (1:n)
A one-to-many relationship is where one entity occurrence is related to many entity occurrences in its counterpart. The entity with the single entity occurrence is called the MASTER; the other is called the DETAIL. Sometimes they are referred to as OWNER and MEMBER respectively. Consider the relationship IS FATHER OF in figure 3.3.

The crow's foot symbol is used to signify that the 'many' is on the CHILD entity. Arrows may be used instead of crow's feet, but to avoid confusion with arrows on DFDs, crow's feet are used throughout this book.

The relationship indicates that a single entity occurrence MAN (i.e. one man) may have many children, each one of which is an entity occurrence in

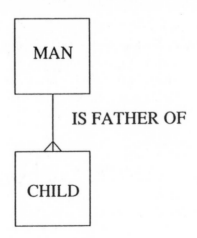

Fig. 3.3. One-to-many relationship.

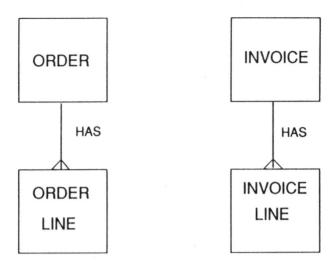

Fig. 3.4. Examples of one-to-many relationships in businesses.

CHILD. As in the previous example, it is possible that a man may have no children and hence no entity occurrences in CHILD are associated with that particular man. So a one-to-many relationship means that there may be zero, one, or more than one entity occurrences in the DETAIL entity for each MASTER entity occurrence. One-to-many relationships occur frequently in data models of information systems applications. They often occur where a document contains header information followed by many lines of detail information. Typical examples are order and invoice – see figure 3.4.

Here, the attributes in the MASTER entity contain general information which is pertinent to all DETAIL entity occurrences. For ORDER, typical attributes would be order-no, order-date, etc.

Note that in this kind of relationship, the DETAIL entity occurrence cannot meaningfully exist without a MASTER entity occurrence. This is not exclusively the case however. For example, if the MAN entity in figure 3.3 contained only living men then it would be possible to have DETAIL entity occurrences without a corresponding MASTER entity occurrence.

(3) Many-to-many relationships (m:n)
A many-to-many relationship is one where an entity occurrence in the first entity is related to many entity occurrences in the second, and where an entity occurrence in the second entity has many in the first. In figure 3.5 there is a many-to-many relationship between STUDENT and ASSIGNMENT (one

Fig. 3.5. A many-to-many relationship.

student undertakes many different assignments and one assignment is done by many students). Here, crow's feet are placed against both entities to signify a many-to-many relationship. Many-to-many relationships are harder to visualise than the others; however, identification is achieved simply on the basis of the definition provided above, i.e. that two one-to-many relationships in different directions exist. In many-to-many relationships, it is possible that individual entity occurrences have no corresponding occurrences in the counterpart entity. Also, some entity occurrences may have only one occurrence in the other entity. However, as long as one occurrence has or may have many occurrences in the other entity and this is true in the opposite direction, then it is a many-to-many relationship.

One way of visualising the degree of relationship is to sketch a few entity occurrences and some relationship occurrences, as in figure 3.6. The student-nos and assignment-nos have been added to make each entity occurrence uniquely identifiable (names are notoriously ambiguous and should be avoided as keys where possible). Note that McGregor has no entity occurrences in ASSIGNMENT (perhaps through non-submission, illness or exemption). However, all ASSIGNMENT entity occurrences have at least one occurrence in STUDENT. So, in this example, it is reasonable for

STUDENT   ASSIGNMENT

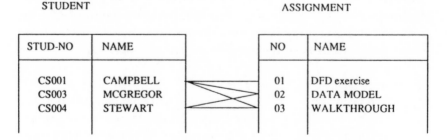

Fig. 3.6. Relationship occurrences in a many-to-many relationship.

STUDENT entity occurrences to have no corresponding occurrences in
ASSIGNMENT, yet all ASSIGNMENT occurrences have at least one
STUDENT occurrence. To illustrate the time dimension again, suppose
entity occurrences for assignments were added to the ASSIGNMENT entity
at the start of the year and as students submitted their work (or as it was
marked) the specific relationship occurrence was established. In this case it
would be reasonable for ASSIGNMENT entity occurrences at the start of the
year to have no corresponding STUDENT entity occurrences, although of
course the degree of relationship has not changed.

It is entirely possible that two entities could have two or more relationships
between each other. In such a case these relationships are simply drawn as
separate relationships in a diagram. See figure 3.15(a). Here the two
relationships are mutually exclusive since any man who is already a brother
to a woman cannot, by law, be married to her. In other situations the
relationships need not be mutually exclusive.

The above discourse illustrates the value of data modelling. It causes the
analyst to consider and review the underlying structure of the data and its
relationships. Perhaps questions are identified which require the analyst to re-
interview users, re-read operating procedures, etc. More is learnt and
understood about the data. In short, data modelling is a vehicle for
understanding the data as well as describing it.

3.4.2 Relationship matrix

A triangular matrix can be used to ensure that all possible combinations of
entities have been considered as potential partners in a relationship. Boxes
with each entity's name are listed alongside both rows and columns; see figure
3.7.

If there is a relationship between say MAN and WOMAN then an X is
entered in the appropriate box; otherwise O is entered to indicate that this
pairing has been considered but rejected. If there are two distinct relationships
between two entities then XX is entered in the box and so on. Where a
relationship exists, the relationship name and degree are recorded in an
accompanying list.

3.4.3 Drawing the unrefined first-cut data model

The drawing of the first-cut data model is now a trivial matter since all the
necessary preparation has been done. A rectangle is drawn for each entity and

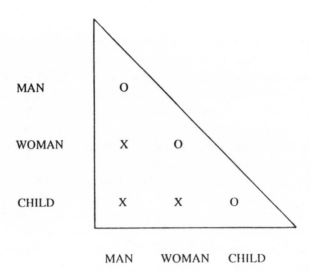

Fig. 3.7. Relationship matrix.

relationships are drawn for each box with an X, according to the relationship name and degree in the accompanying list. See figure 3.8.

3.4.4 Refining the first-cut data model

The model can now be refined in a number of ways before continuing with the

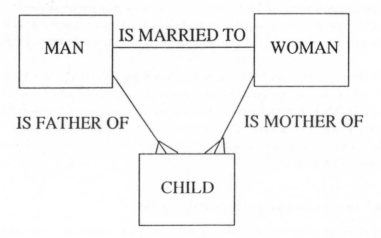

Fig. 3.8. A data model.

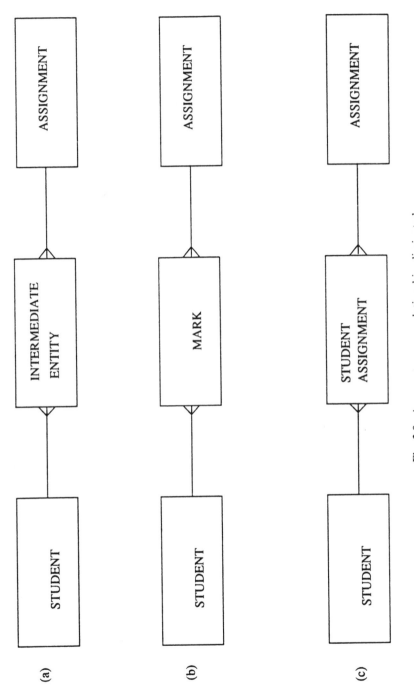

Fig. 3.9. A many-to-many relationship eliminated.

rest of the analysis. The order suggested here, provides the minimum amount
of wasted time on rework.

(1) Eliminate m:n relationships

Many-to-many relationships are probably not a true representation of the
problem. On first inspection they may seem to represent a valid view of the
data, albeit that they are difficult to visualise; yet often the more the data and
relationships are examined, the more a feeling grows that the relationship
model is not quite right or that there is something missing. In fact, many-to-
many relationships can always be substituted by adding an intermediate
entity and redefining relationships to the intermediate entity. Figure 3.9(a) is
a substitute model for figure 3.5. Note that the crow's feet are on the
intermediate entity rather than the original entities. The intermediate entity is
given the keys of both the original entities; this makes each entity occurrence
of the intermediate entity unique. In most cases, one finds that there is useful
data that can be held in the intermediate entity. For example, the logical place
to store a student's mark for an assignment would be in the intermediate
entity. In fact, an appropriate name of the intermediate entity would be, in
this case, MARK. The model in Fig. 3.9(b) now looks far more sensible than
before. It is often the case that once the substitution has been made the analyst
is more comfortable with the model. However, sometimes naming the new
entity is not so straightforward, because it is not easy to find a name which
encapsulates all the data held. If, by inspection of the attributes, an
appropriate name does not suggest itself, then use the associated entity names
to construct the entity name as in figure 3.9(c).

(2) Eliminate recursive relationships

A recursive relationship is a relationship where an entity has a relationship

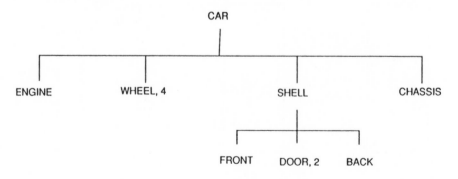

Fig. 3.10. Simplified bill of material for a car.

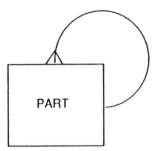

Fig. 3.11. A recursive relationship.

with itself. Perhaps the most common example of this is the bill of materials problem. Parts may be split into components which are parts themselves. These in turn may be decomposed into further parts. Figure 3.10 shows the breakdown of a car, which has been simplified to illustrate the problem.

When drawing the data model for a bill of material one might be tempted to draw it as in figure 3.11, which is, in effect, saying that one PART occurrence is related to many other PART occurrences. On examining the bill of material requirement the following becomes clear:

• There is a need to know the components of each part.
• There is a need to know what the part is assembled into.

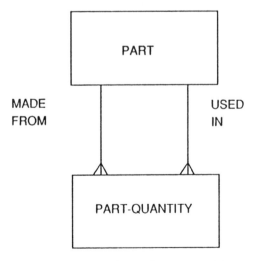

Fig. 3.12. A bill of materials data model.

- The quantity required of a particular component is needed in order to calculate the bill of materials (i.e. only required when there is a need to know the components of each part).

The problem is that the model is a poor approximation of reality. Figure 3.12 presents a better model which meets all the needs of the bill of material model problem.

Entity PART-QUANTITY will contain attributes part-no and quantity. Where occurrences exist in PART-QUANTITY for the MADE FROM relationship, the quantity attributes will contain the number of components required, e.g. 4 wheels. Where entity occurrences exist in PART-QUANTITY for the USED IN relationship, the quantity attribute is not of interest because the aim of the interrogation is to determine the identity of part(s) in which this particular component is used and therefore the quantity attribute is not

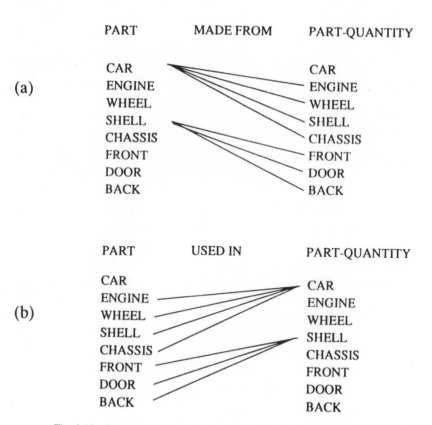

Fig. 3.13. Relationship occurrences for bill of materials problem.

PART-QUANTITY

PART	QUANTITY
CAR	1
ENGINE	1
WHEEL	4
SHELL	1
CHASSIS	1
FRONT	1
DOOR	2
BACK	1

Fig. 3.14. Entity occurrences for PART-QUANTITY.

meaningful. Figure 3.13(a) shows the relationship occurrences of the MADE FROM relationship; figure 3.13(b) shows the relationship occurrences for the USED IN relationship and figure 3.14 shows the entity occurrences.

Importantly, the integrity of the rules for entities has been preserved, which are that each entity must have a key and each entity must contain unique attributes (except for its key(s)).

(3) Eliminate redundant relationships

A relationship is redundant if the same information can be obtained through other relationships. Perhaps in figure 3.8 one could argue that the IS FATHER OF is a redundant relationship since by supplying the man's identity the woman's identity can be obtained, and by using the woman's identity the children's identities can be obtained. This is a false argument for two reasons. Firstly, the parents may not be married, or the father may be married to someone else who is not the mother (or vice versa), so there would not be an appropriate relationship occurrence in the first place. It is most important to examine the meaning of relationships before redundancy can be confirmed. Secondly, the hypothesis takes no account of a father who has children from previous marriages. The time dimension of relationships is a key factor when assessing redundancy.

(4) Eliminate unnecessary relationships

Sometimes one-to-one relationships can be merged into a single entity.

Identifying entities in the first place is a hit or miss business, so it is not unreasonable to expect to create new entities, as seen previously, or merge existing entities in order to obtain a better model of the data. The strength of data modelling is that the technique has steps where these points are explicitly reviewed.

Perhaps in an organisation it is not important to have the entity MAN distinguished from the entity WOMAN as in figure 3.2. Instead the organisation merely needs to know whether an employee is married or not. So one entity called EMPLOYEE is all that is required. In order to accommodate the informational needs, the EMPLOYEE entity would have an attribute called spouse. Sometimes it will be appropriate to rename the entity, as in this case; in others it may not be necessary. In subsuming one entity within another the overriding consideration is what perspective is important to the organisation. The effect of this subsumption is that an entity has been removed, a relationship has been eliminated and an attribute has been added to an entity.

Another kind of unnecessary relationship can be said to exist in figure 3.15. Here two relationships exist between MAN and WOMAN. It is possible to combine these into a single relationship IS RELATED TO. The WOMAN entity would need to contain an attribute called, say, relationship-type which would indicate whether the man was husband or brother. Again, the view of what the organisation thinks is important, and this is the overriding consideration. It may be that informational needs are such that one relationship is sufficient. Here, two relationships have been combined into

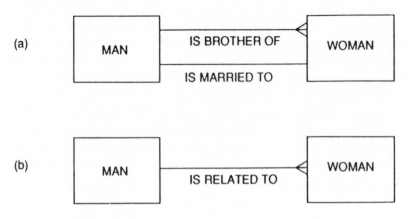

Fig. 3.15. Removing an unneccessary relationship.

one and an extra attribute added to an entity. Redundant relationships are distinguished from unnecessary relationships as follows. Removing redundant relationships implies no change in the number of entities and no addition of attributes within entities; removing unnecessary relationships almost certainly implies new attributes and for a one-to-one relationship reduction in the number of entities.

(5) Review data model
A full data model for an organisation may contain upwards of 100 entities and perhaps 500 attributes or more. Even if one is dealing with relatively few entities, say 10 or 15, then the refined first-cut data model may differ significantly from the unrefined. This last review of the data model is required in order to confirm that the implications of any refinements have not affected other parts of the model. Three aspects are important:

redundant key attributes
Check any multiple-key entities (i.e. entities which have more than one attribute in their key) to determine if all key attributes are still required. During refinement it is possible that the continued need for multiple keys has been overlooked.

entity names
Having made modifications to the model, the essential purpose and hence the name given to entities may have become clearer and therefore they should be renamed.

relationship names
The same point applies to relationship names as entity names. In addition, the relationship names should be reviewed in terms of practicality. For example, the relationship IS FATHER OF is probably quite a difficult one to prove. In many cases, for legal or financial reasons, the organisation is really interested in the registered or adopted father, which is a fact that can be much more easily established, e.g. from a birth certificate or adoption papers. So the relationship name should then become IS REGISTERED/ADOPTED FATHER OF.

3.5 DATABASE NAVIGATION

The refined first-cut data model is refined later on to become the blueprint for the database. So as well as serving an important function as a vehicle for understanding the data, it also provides the basis for creating the database itself. Most of the time, information is required which probably resides in several entities. Access is achieved by moving from one entity to another via the relationship lines. This is called navigation. In figure 3.4, if all the detail of an order is required, the order-no (key) is supplied to the ORDER entity and its attributes are picked up. Then, by following the relationship HAS to ORDER-LINE, all the order-lines for that particular order can be accessed. Entities are accessed directly by simply supplying the key, or indirectly by moving from one entity to another via relationships.

3.6 REVIEW OF DATA MODELLING

Data modelling is an interesting technique. It has no clear starting point, since identifying entities from interviews, documents and so on is necessarily vague and unstructured. Yet, by following the steps provided, a good understanding of the data important to an organisation can be achieved.

It is an example of an iterative process. As one works through the stages, new entities or relationships may be discovered, necessitating return to an earlier stage for rework. Indeed it is a characteristic of ill-defined problems generally that they require iteration.

It is clear, too, that in order to perform data modelling, some knowledge about the organisation is required. Some data modelling experts argue that is it possible to perform data modelling just by analysing the nature of the data, i.e. with absolute disregard as to how the organisation chooses to use that data. For example, consider the relationship between entity PART and entity STORE. One company may use its stores to hold different kinds of materials, e.g. it may have a wood store, paint store, etc. Here no part is stocked in more than one store. So STORE has a one-to-many relationship with PART. In another company, however, the same items of stock may exist in different stores, so the relationship would be many-to-many. One school argues that it is impossible to divorce the data from how it is used. The other school would counter by pointing out that the concept of a store is in fact different in the two companies. And so the debate continues. In practice, it is quite difficult to separate data and how it is used; human beings build mental models based on all the knowledge they have at their disposal. Perhaps a more practical model is one where data is said to be relatively static and business functions relatively dynamic (some business functions such as producing balance sheets have not changed much, if at all, over time). As long as analysts strive to create the best data model they can and are aware of the dangers of considering current business functions in data modelling, this seems the most pragmatic compromise.

3.7 PRACTICAL DIFFICULTIES IN DATA MODELLING

When people first meet the concepts of data modelling, it is often considered a 'mind-blowing' experience. Having thought that they understood the theory and terminology of data modelling, when presented with a practical problem they find they do not know where to begin. 'Just what is an entity?' is a very popular question.

(1) Identifying entities
The most common misunderstanding is that people do not really appreciate the simplicity of an entity and its attributes. Let's review the facts.

(i) Entities, attributes and relationships are there to support the operation of an information system. So, anything that appears as an output of an information system, must either be stored in its database or generated by it. This is perhaps a slight over-simplification, but it will do for now.

(ii) A data model organises the data required by an information system into a simple non-composite format. This means that:
  (a) An attribute required by the information system may only occur once in the data model, i.e. it is not legal for the same attribute to appear in two different entities (except for keys). Having recognised this, the problem is really one of identifying in which entity the attribute most properly belongs.
  (b) Any attribute may occur only once within an entity occurrence. For example, there may be a temptation to create an entity called ORDER which contains order header information and detail information, i.e. a number of lines of items to be ordered. However, the detail information is really a repeating group, as discussed in chapter 5. If it were to be stored within one entity occurrence then several attributes would have to occur more than once, e.g. one entity occurrence would contain many occurrences of part-no, part-description and quantity. It would require one set of these for each line on the order. This is how variable-length records operate, but in

data modelling it is not acceptable. Where repeating groups arise, these need to be separated and held in different entities, such that one entity occurrence contains attributes which are all different.

Once people really understand the above, they are often far more able to see the solution and are not so often diverted into unproductive directions or, worse still, stuck not knowing where to begin. So the acid test for data modelling is 'can the data model generate the outputs required?'.

(2) Identifying too many relationships

Another temptation for the inexperienced data modeller is to 'see' relationships between virtually all entities. When the relationship matrix is drawn, it is not uncommon to see nearly every box containing an X!

Obviously this will vary from one situation to another, but in most situations there are likely to be far fewer relationships than this. What often happens is that the data modeller does not appreciate that the same information can be arrived at by navigation rather than by direct relationship, i.e. that a redundant relationship exists.

Now, before further discussion, there are two points that must be remembered. Firstly, the eventual physical database implemention may well reintroduce the direct relationship for reasons of efficiency. Secondly, the refinement phase will eliminate redundant relationships. But here the problem is that the first-cut data model is virtually useless because the over-identification of relationships takes away any real value from the first-cut data model.

An approach that can work is as follows. The explosion in relationships seems to occur when the relationship matrix is being constructed. (The previous stage, identifying relationships and their degree, tends to throw up essential relationships such as order header has many order-lines.) Before beginning the relationship matrix it is suggested that small clusters of related entities are identified. When the relationship matrix is then attempted, it should become clearer that only one relationship is required to access the cluster rather than a relationship for every entity within the cluster. Done sensibly, with due care, this can produce a better first-cut data model.

3.8 SUMMARY

Data modelling is a technique performed very early in situations where data is shared across the organisation. In fact, data analysis can be a separate function within a computer department and performed in advance of any systems analysis activity. But the important thing to recognise here is that the need to share data has overwhelming implications in deciding the kind of method to select. Indeed, giving data such a dominant role in a method will be unfamiliar territory for many software engineers, but it is a contrasting perspective on the problem and needless to say a most important one.

3.8.1 Create unrefined first-cut data model

This is the first attempt at creating the data model and assumes that it has not been previously attempted. The emphasis is on capturing the big picture, i.e. the major entities and important attributes and relationships. It is an iterative process, so if, for example, new entities present themselves during the latter steps of this task then rework of earlier steps needs to take place. Equally, it is an unrefined model, so certain modifications can be postponed to the next task. The major steps are:

- identify entities
- identify attributes
- identify relationships and their degree
- construct relationship matrix
- draw unrefined first-cut data model

3.8.2 Refine first-cut data model

The main focus here is to improve the initial data model. This is done by verifying the data model against a checklist of quality guidelines. The impact of using the checklist is to improve the correctness of the data model with respect to the analyst's understanding. Again, insights may be obtained during this task which necessitate reiteration. Often, experienced analysts will perform some of the refining in the unrefined first-cut data model. For example, there is no real point in drawing a many-to-many relationship only to have to convert it later on. That said, it is still vital to work through the refinement process to ensure that all opportunities for improvement are taken. The steps in the checklist are:

- eliminate many to many relationships
- eliminate recursive relationships
- eliminate redundant relationships
- eliminate unnecessary relationships

- review data model with respect to:
  - redundant key attributes
  - entity names
  - relationship names

3.9 FURTHER READING

Howe, D. R. (1983) *Data Analysis for Data Base Design* Edward Arnold, London, provides a well-rounded introduction to the whole area of data modelling and in fact databases generally. Although the notation is different to that used here, it provides a justification for the need for a database approach as well as a discussion of data modelling.

3.10 EXERCISES

Using the material in the case study go through the stages of data modelling, i.e. identify an unrefined first-cut data model then refine it. (Figure 9.3 shows the model solution to this question.)

Chapter 4
Entity Life Histories and the State Dependency Diagram

4.1 INTRODUCTION

The DFD is one model of the system. Together with data dictionary techniques, it can tell us about the processes, dataflows and so on in the system. What it does not convey is the notion of time or rather of time-dependent relationships. For example, somewhere in a DFD set, there may be a process which creates, say, a stock entity occurrence; in a totally different place there may be a process which deletes the stock entity occurrence. Now clearly these two processes are related – an entity occurrence cannot be deleted unless and until it has been created. But that kind of checking is not easily obtained from the DFD.

The data model is another useful model of the system. But it is a static model in the sense that it contains no real concept of time – the entities, their attributes and relationships just seem to exist in a vacuum.

Both these models are cornerstones of sound software engineering practice. But there is still something missing, something at the heart of an information system which is to do with the underlying logic of the system, something which has to do with time-dependent relationships.

This chapter will explore this area in some depth. Specifically, we will look at the entity life history and the state dependency diagram. The idea behind the entity life history (ELH) is that each entity in the data model has stages or events in its life which it can go through. These stages plot its life history. For example, every entity occurrence must be created and eventually deleted and most will be modified in certain ways during their life. The ELH therefore starts to tell us something about those time-dependent relationships, but not everything, unfortunately, because the problem is more complicated. Specifically, other entities and their respective statuses have an effect on what can happen to a particular entity. For example, should an order be accepted for a customer if that customer does not yet exist? The state dependency diagram addresses this problem. It takes the ELHs and from them constructs a model of the system which shows time-dependent relationships across entities, i.e. across the whole system.

4.2 DRAWING THE ENTITY LIFE HISTORY

This task is repeated for each entity in the data model and consists of the following steps:

- draw a simple life
- add complexity
- refine the ELH
- add state indicators

4.2.1 Draw a simple life

Although ELHs are dependent on the data model to provide the basic entities, ELHs are essentially a third perspective of the system, because they are created from the analyst's raw understanding of the system. Each stage in

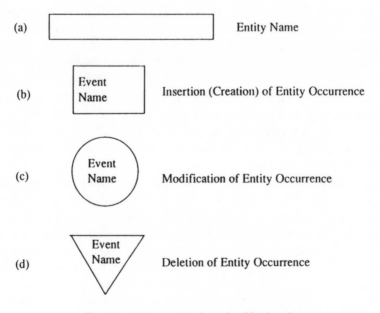

Fig. 4.1. Main symbols in entity life histories.

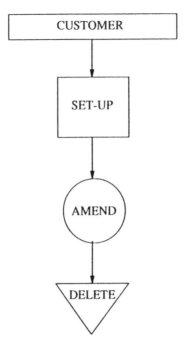

Fig. 4.2. A simple entity life history.

the life of an entity must be preceded by an event which enables the stage to come into being. The purpose of the ELH is to record these events. Figure 4.1 shows the main symbols used in the ELH diagram. The entity name is placed in a rectangle at the start of the sequence of events and each symbol is connected to its successor by an arrow. Figure 4.2 represents a very simple life for a customer entity. A new customer is set up, some details are amended and then at some later point in time it is decided that the customer is no longer a customer and is deleted.

4.2.2 Add complexity

Unfortunately few entities are that simple, so let's add some complexity to illustrate the rest of the notation. Assume a customer can be created in one of two ways, that is, either by standard set-up or by default when the first order is accepted. Also, it would be more realistic if customer details could be amended several times. Figure 4.3 shows the additional complexity. The double arrow shows a selection constuct which means that the customer

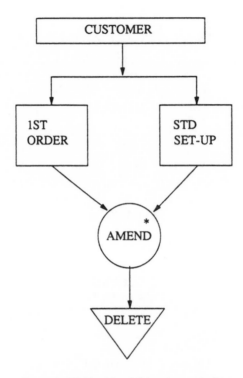

Fig. 4.3. ELH with additional complexity.

entity (occurrence) is created either by a first order or the standard set-up, but not both. The * symbol represents iteration, which means that an amendment may take place zero, once or many times. If it is required to indicate that an amendment can take place once or many times then a normal amendment symbol is drawn followed by an iteration amendment symbol.

One further situation can arise when one of several alternatives has to be selected. This is analogous to the case statement in programming. Imagine there is a third route to becoming a customer, say by the company mail-shotting prospective customers. Figure 4.4 shows the case construct.

Assume that when customers are first accepted they are allocated a provisional status until they have proven their ability to pay. Thereafter, they are made permanent customers. Permanent status has many grades. So it may be necessary to amend permanent status. If they default on their payments after being made permanent, they may be reallocated a provisional status until they once again prove themselves. See figure 4.5. The problem here is

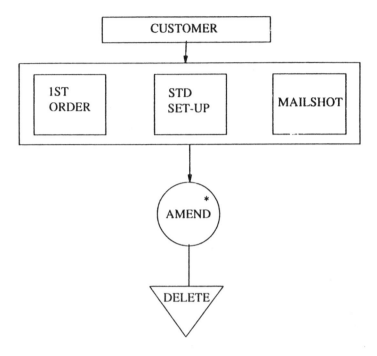

Fig. 4.4. ELH with CASE construct.

that a group of amendments is to be iterated. The use of the rectangle is to enable the group to be identified. The iteration symbol against the group signifies that it is the group that is to be iterated. Note that since it is possible that a permanent customer might need to be deleted, the additional arrow is required to go straight to deletion.

4.2.3 Refine the Entity Life History

This step is included for two reasons. Firstly, in creating ELHs, there is a tendency to overspecify the ELH by including additional states. The criteria in this step therefore serve the purpose of reviewing the ELH to confirm that all states are necessary. Secondly, the ELHs are the precursor of the State Dependency Diagram which requires that the ELHs are refined in a certain way. The goal of this refinement step is to obtain ELHs which are directly related to logical system events. This is because the SDD is in fact a model of the logical system itself.

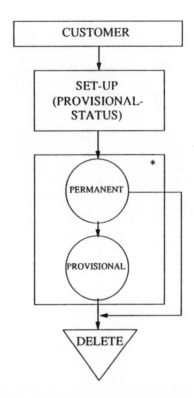

Fig. 4.5. ELH with ITERATION construct.

(1) Only show states which are owned by that entity
Experience in drawing ELHs shows that states declared in one entity often refer to other entities. For example, suppose an ORDER entity is given a state which permits many part-payments for that order, yet on the data model ORDER and PAYMENT are two separate entities. The PAYMENT entity itself will have a state which permits the receipt of a part-payment, so it is argued it is superfluous to also have a state in the ORDER entity.

(2) Avoid too many alternative lives
An alternative life occurs when the entity has many different routes it can follow. Usually the sequence of events is quite different or separate from an entity's normal life. This is not unusual in organisations. For example, a rush order may not go through the many stages that an ordinary one goes through. As a general rule, alternate lives are valuable documentation in an entity life history as long as readability is not compromised. Where the entity has too

many alternatives, say in excess of 3 or 4, then it is better to document these as separate entity sub-types with separate entity life histories, e.g. normal order and rush order. If there are so many alternative lives that it becomes impractical to document all of them, then one solution is to simplify the ELH by not attempting to document all possible combinations. Clearly, this would be reviewed with the user and would ultimately depend on how important the separate identification of these alternate lives was to the quality of the system.

(3) Only show states which are non-redundant
The purpose of ELHs is to provide a third model of the system (after dataflow diagrams and data models). Here the task is to try to identify all the stages in the life of an entity from a consideration of the entity and its chronology. However, some of these states may be redundant as states which affect the processing of the system, particularly intermediate amendment states which, although arguably legitimate in terms of the entity's life, have no bearing on system processing.

Now it is possible that having drawn the first-cut ELHs, the analyst will realise there is a superfluous state in the ELH, so this refinement step allows the modification to be made. Equally, it may only be later when the SDD is being drawn that the analyst realises the problem, in which case it is necessary to return to this step and make the required adjustment.

(4) Only show states which are distinct
In first-cut ELHs, it is common to see a range of alternative ways in which an entity's life can be moved from one state to the next. This is the selection construct and is often seen at entity creation. However, if these alternative states are analysed in terms of the processing of the system, some of these may be identical. For example, suppose a customer entity can be created either through a normal set-up or when the first order is received. Provided the operations on the database are identical (in this case it can be assumed that they are both straightforward inserts), there is no need to show them separately. Alternative set-up states such as these are just alternative triggers to the same event in the system.

(5) Only show 'natural' lives on the ELH
Figure 4.5 shows the life of a customer entity which is suggested as being typical of current practice in drawing ELHs. Here a customer may be deleted if his status is permanent or provisional. However, there is a difference between the two states. For a permanent customer, deletion is likely only to follow the payment of all outstanding debts, whereas for a provisional

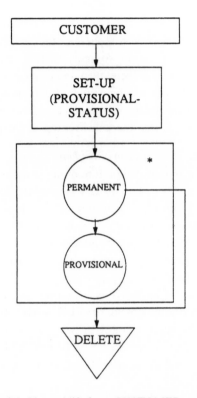

Fig. 4.6. Natural life for a CUSTOMER entity.

customer additional action may need to be taken, such as writing off any bad debt in a general ledger. The point is that deletion from provisional customer status is an abnormal life and not consistent with the natural termination of an entity. The ELH shown in figure 4.6 shows a natural life for entity CUSTOMER.

4.2.4 Add state indicators

Once the basic ELH is drawn, state indicators are added. State indicators are shown after each construct. The state of an entity has a one-to-one correspondence to a particular stage in its life. Numbering each stage (i.e. the state indicator) is a mechanism for uniquely identifying the state of an entity. The convention for state indicators is to show the valid pre-condition(s) for entrance to the state followed by the state indicator upon exit from that state. See figure 4.7. Here, there is no pre-condition to the set-up event, so this is

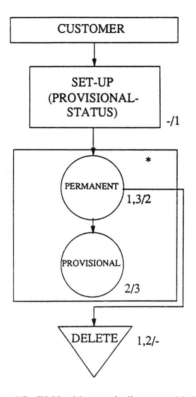

Fig. 4.7. ELH with state indicators added.

shown with a dash. The output state to this event is state 1. Amendment to permanent status can arise from either having been just set-up with provisional status (i.e. from state 1) or from the provisional state itself, i.e. state 3. The iteration symbol on the rectangle allows the return to the permanent status. The output state of permanent status is state 2. Amendment to provisional status is achieved only after permanent status, so the input state is 2 and the output state is 3.

Lastly, a deletion can occur either from the set-up status, i.e. state 1 (remember the asterisk symbol can have zero iterations), or from permanent status, i.e. state 2. The output state is a dash, since this post-condition affects nothing else.

Readers familiar with the notion of finite state machines or Petri nets will detect a similarity in concept with Entity Life Histories. In fact, with some adjustment to the graphical notation ELHs are easily converted to such diagrams. The refined ELHs for the SBM case study are shown in figure 4.8.

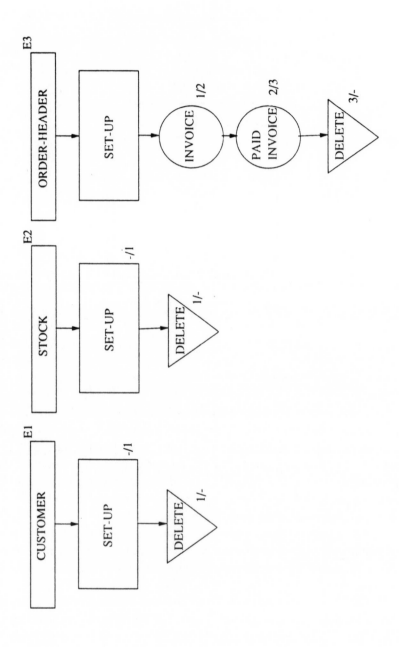

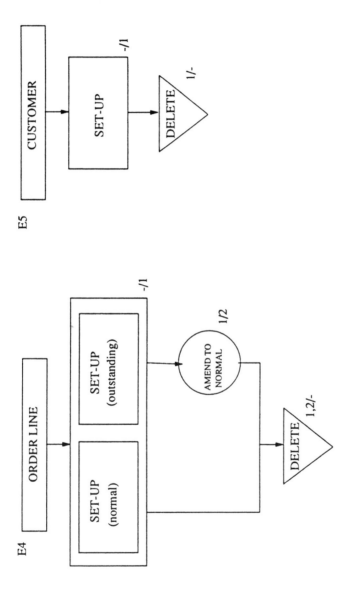

Fig. 4.8. Entity life histories for case study.

Before reading the next section, the reader should attempt the questions on drawing ELHs at the end of the chapter.

4.3 THE STATE DEPENDENCY DIAGRAM (SDD)

As stated earlier, one problem with ELHs is that, on their own, they are not powerful enough to provide answers to questions which begin to present themselves. For instance, when the ELH is drawn and refined, the analyst may have questions like:

• If incorrect information has been added to an entity at what stages can it be corrected?
• What effect does premature termination have on an entity's life?
• Can events happen out of sequence? If so, which ones are permissible?

These questions show the level of understanding the analyst is beginning to have about the system, but they are probably not the first set of questions about ELHs – those are asked as the ELHs are drawn. Nevertheless, they are vital questions that must be answered. Indeed they are often the sort of question which, if not considered, precipitate the downfall of a system. However, in order to answer such questions satisfactorily, the analyst may have to look wider than just that ELH. For example, take the first question. Suppose an incorrect quantity of say 100 rather than 10 was entered on an item of an order. If the mistake had just been made and nothing else had happened in the system then presumably it could be corrected immediately since nothing else would be affected. However, suppose the invoice was already generated, or worse still suppose payment had been received for that order. The point is that if further related events have taken place other adjustments may have to take place, and these could affect other entities. In order to determine this, a model of the system is required which shows dependencies between entities.

We will now draw the SDD for the case study. Figure 4.8 shows the entity life histories for each of the entities in the SBM data model. These are used to create the SDD, although they will have to be modified slightly.

4.3.1 NOTATION FOR SDD

The symbols for set-up, modification and deletion are those used in an individual ELH.

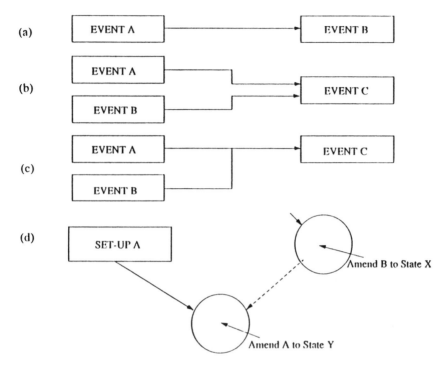

Fig. 4.9. Notation for SDD.

Now, the essence of the model is to capture the dependencies between significant events in the system regardless of which entity is affected, so precedence in the model implies that event A (the predecessor) must have taken place before event B (the successor) can begin. See figure 4.9(a).

Events may have more than one direct predecessor, as shown in figure 4.9(b). This means that both events A and B must have taken place before event C can begin. Figure 4.9(c) shows the situation where only one of two (or more) events need take place before a successor event may begin.

There is a need to allow for the situation where an entity occurrence may or may not exist. This is called contingent dependency. See figure 4.9(d). If it does not exist then, in the example, the only prerequisite is that A is set-up. If it does exist then entity B must be in a prescribed state.

4.3.2 Create the prerequisite table

Creating the prerequisite table is where all the 'thinking' is done. Readers who

1.	set-up customer
2.	delete customer
3.	set-up order-header
4.	amend order-header to invoice
5.	amend invoice to paid-invoice
6.	delete order-header
7.	set-up normal order-line
8.	set-up outstanding order-line
9.	amend outstanding order-line to normal order-line
10.	delete order-line
11.	set-up credit-note
12.	delete credit note
13.	set-up stock
14.	delete stock

Table 4.1. List of all states.

are familiar with creating critical path networks should have little difficulty with the concept.

1 Create a single list of all states in all entities and number each state uniquely. See table 4.1. Because, for example, the event 'DELETE' occurs in many different ELHs, it is necessary to qualify the name with its role name, e.g. 'DELETE CUSTOMER'.

2 Scan the data model to identify entities which have no owners. These are used as the starting point in step 3. In the case study, entities CUSTOMER and STOCK have no owner.

3 Using the entities identified in step 2 as a starting point and then progressing in a general direction into the data model to entities which have no members, identify any prerequisite events.

Table 4.2 shows the first few entries made in the prerequisite table. Since 'SET-UP CUSTOMER' and 'SET-UP STOCK' have no prerequisites, a dash is entered. The prerequisite for 'SET-UP ORDER-HEADER' is that a CUSTOMER entity occurrence must exist before it would be reasonable to set-up an order for that customer. So the number 1, which represents the event 'SET-UP CUSTOMER' is made a prerequisite of event number 3. The event 'SET-UP NORMAL ORDER-LINE' is dependent upon two prior events. These are that the order-header for it must be set-up and, secondly, that a

No.	Events Name	Prerequisite
1.	set-up customer	
2.	delete customer	
3.	set-up order-header	1
4.	amend order-header to invoice	
5.	amend invoice to paid-invoice	
6.	delete order-header	
7.	set-up normal order-line	3, 13
8.	set-up outstanding order-line	
9.	amend outstanding order-line to normal order-line	
10.	delete order-line	
11.	set-up credit-note	
12.	delete credit note	
13.	set-up stock	
14.	delete stock	

Table 4.2. First year entries in the prerequisite table.

stock-item must exist for it. The numbers representing these prerequisite events are placed appropriately in the table and are separated by commas. Table 4.3 shows the completed prerequisite table.

4.3.3 Draw the State Dependency Diagram

It is a straightforward task to convert the prerequisite table into the SDD using the notation described earlier. See figure 4.11. The duplication symbol (as used in DFD external entities) is used to identify identical functions as discussed in note 5 of table 4.3. Also notice that there are no iterative cluster boxes on the SDD. Although they can be used to improve readability with ELHs, it is felt that they have the opposite effect on the SDD and therefore their use is avoided. Instead, arrows are used.

4.3.4 State indicators and the SDD

State indicators are a good way of showing unambiguously the state of a particular entity and their use is recommended here. However, since many different entities are involved, the notation has to be amended to qualify the reference to a specific entity. Also, further changes are required to signify that

Chapter 4

Event No	Event Name	Prerequisite	
1.	set-up customer	-	
2.	delete customer	6	
3.	set-up normal order-header	1	
4.	amend order-header to invoice	[9I7]	(see note 1)
5.	amend invoice to paid-invoice	4 (,11)	(see note 2)
6.	delete order-header	10 (,12)	
7.	set-up normal order-line	3, 13	
8.	set-up outstanding order-line	1, 13	(see note 3)
9.	amend outstanding order-line to normal order-line	15	
10.	delete order-line	5	
11.	set-up credit-note	4	
12.	delete credit note	5 (,11)	(see note 4)
13.	set-up stock	-	
14.	delete stock	10	
15.	set-up outstanding order-header	8	(see note 5)

Note 1   The notation here shows that the prerequisite to this state is either state 9 or state 7 but not both. The selection construct is used to denote this.

Note 2   The optionality construct describes contingent dependency i.e. there may or may not be credit notes for this particular order.

Note 3   Remember the reason for this event. In the case study, if there is insufficient stock for an ordered item, that order item becomes outstanding until sufficient stock becomes available. Until that time it is "owned" by entity CUSTOMER as the separate relationship on the data model indicates. (See Note 5.)

Note 4   Because of the nature of a delete it makes no practical difference whether prerequisite 11 is contingent or not.

Note 5   Here is a situation which the ELHs on their own just didn't detect. When outstanding order-lines are converted to become a "normal" order, two things must happen. Firstly, an order-header has to be set up. Secondly, the relationship occurrences have to be transferred from CUSTOMER to ORDER-HEADER. Now the ELH for ORDER-HEADER as originally identified contained only one set-up event, but what the above implies is that there are actually two separate set-up events - one for a normal order and one for an outstanding order. Although, these events are identical in terms of the "program code" required to perform them, they are different in that they have different prerequisites. To maintain consistent documentation it is necessary to modify the ELH for ORDER-HEADER as in figure 4.10 which also implies the addition to event 15 to the prerequisite table and modification of the name of event 3.

Table 4.3. Completed prerequisite table.

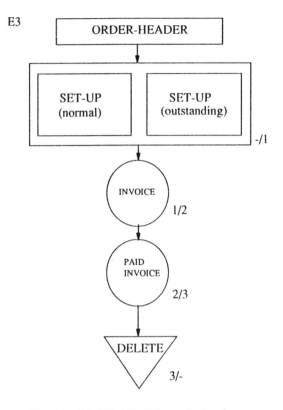

Fig. 4.10. Modified ELH for order-header.

many pre-conditions hold. The state indicator for 'SET-UP OUTSTANDING ORDER-LINE' would be written as 'E1 = 1 and E2 = 1 / E4 = 1'. Alternatively, the state numbers in table 1, the prerequisite table, could be used in which case the state indicator would read '1 and 13 / 8'. But because of the maintenance implications the earlier solution is the preferred one.

4.4 ANALYSING THE SYSTEM USING THE SDD

Hopefully it can be seen that the act of creating the SDD has brought with it useful insight into the nature of the information system. Yet the final purpose of the SDD is achieved once it has been constructed, because if it does represent the essential logic of the system, it should assist in providing answers

Chapter 4

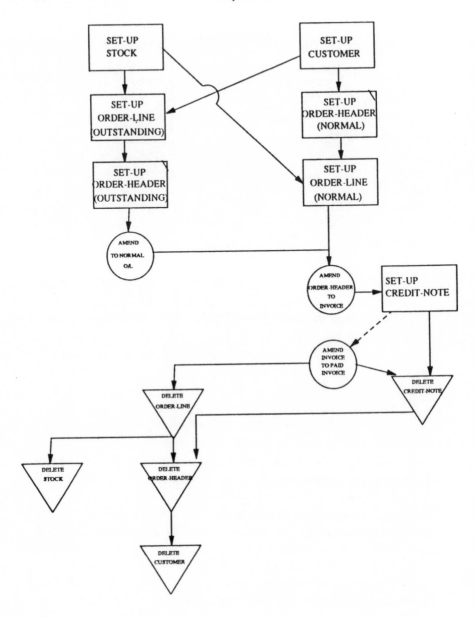

Fig. 4.11. State dependency diagram.

to fundamental questions about the system. These are questions which can only be answered by a model whose elements are related in a time-dependent fashion.

In Part B the method outlines a systematic way in which these questions can be addressed, however in order to illustrate the benefit to be derived from creating the SDD, a summary of the analyses performed is described below.

(1) Trigger analysis

Each state in the state dependency diagram has a corresponding event in the system. Each event will be triggered by some agent either external to the system, such as the arrival of an order from a customer, or internal such as a decision to review outstanding orders. These triggers should be consistent with the corresponding processes in the dataflow diagrams and process specifications. Any inconsistencies so identified require further investigation.

(2) Delay analysis

Some events in the SDD may be performed immediately after their prerequisite(s). An example would be the setting up of order-header followed by the setting up of order-line (typically many order-lines). By analysing the triggers of events, it is possible to detect ones which need no time delay after their predecessor(s). Often, as in the example, it makes sense to group such operations together. The state dependency diagram assists in identifying the opportunity.

(3) Constraint analysis

In addition to its dependence on prerequisite states, an event may have other constraints. Nearly all events will need to meet validation criteria, e.g. 'set-up stock' will require that a valid stock-no, stock-qty and so on are supplied. However, some events could have further constraints. Two examples from the case study are given here. The first is when setting up a normal order-line, the ordered quantity must be less than or equal to the stock quantity. The second example is to do with the trigger for amending order-header to paid invoice. Here, the constraint is that the payment value for that invoice plus the sum of any credit notes equals the sum of the value of order-lines.

The above are examples of where constraints have some algorithm. Sometimes it is not possible to specify an algorithm, e.g. the decision to change a customer from bad customer status to good customer status may depend on a number of parameters which are not easily specified. Businesses often leave such subjective matters to the appropriate human decision-maker. In effect, such constraints are really just internal triggers and therefore are not considered constraints under this heading.

Any constraints identified should be consistent with their corresponding process specifications.

(4) Abnormal life analysis

The state dependency diagram limits itself to the logic of natural lives. It does not attempt to depict dependencies which exist in abnormal lives. An abnormal life is an exception to what would be a legitimate sequence of events. In the SBM case study, it is expected that orders may be set up as normal or outstanding, so these lives are not abnormal. However, if it is decided that a customer is to be deleted, say because bills have not been paid and debts are to be written off, this would be considered an abnormal life because a natural customer deletion would only take place if all outstanding orders were paid.

This is why only natural lives are integrated into the SDD. For the purpose of this discussion, it was recognised that a normal customer deletion would imply that no corresponding order-headers (and therefore order-lines, payments or credit-notes) would exist for that customer, hence the deletes immediately prior to the delete customer in the SDD.

The abnormal termination of the customer entity would require that a contingency is identified for state 3 in figure 4.7. If state is 3 then it is possible that several unpaid invoices exist, in which case these need to be deleted before the customer occurrence is deleted.

Each entity in turn is analysed in this fashion and so a comprehensive list of 'housekeeping' transactions is methodically built up.

(5) Attribute amendment analysis

The state indicators identified in the ELHs are ones which are crucial to the underlying logic of the system, i.e. changes in states alter what is permitted to be performed on that entity and perhaps other entities. However, most information systems will require other kinds of amendments, ones which do not or at least should not alter states, e.g. changing a customer's address or, more contentiously, changing the quantity on an order-line. If such amendments have no real impact on the system, they may be termed 'state insignificant' amendments.

The state dependency diagram can be used to determine the impact of these amendments on the system. The example of a change in customer address is a relatively trivial one with little impact on the system save for the 'engineering change' decision as to when to implement the change of address. However, consider that change of quantity on order-line (assume quantity is to be reduced). Examine the events between the setting up of an order-line and its deletion. What should be done if the order has become an invoice? It will need to be decided (a) if it is not permitted to make such a change after an order becomes an invoice, or (b) if some other action must ensue, e.g. the setting up of a credit-note equivalent in value to the reduction in quantity. Clearly, if route (b) is chosen, this amendment has an impact on the system and therefore becomes a 'state significant' amendment.

In the method defined in Part B, there will be a list of all transactions in the system (i.e. transactions which actually change the database in some way). Some of these will already be in the state dependency diagram. The remainder are dealt with here under attribute amendment analysis. Without the aid of the state dependency diagram, it will be difficult for the designer to see the implications of amendments with respect to the rest of the system and decide what course of action can be taken.

(6) Error condition identification

The SDD can be used as a source for identifying certain kinds of condition. Since it defines the states that entities must be in to permit an event to take place, it follows that invalid states, i.e. error conditions, can easily be identified. So, in a mechanical fashion certain kinds of error messages are derived from the SDD.

4.5 SUMMARY

The use of ELHs and the SDD is a significant advance in the quality of systems analysis that can be performed. This is because they allow examination of important and fundamental aspects of the system, which hitherto have been more or less ignored.

The starting point is the data model, which provides a list of entities. For each entity an ELH is drawn and subsequently refined against criteria discussed earlier. The act of drawing and refining ELHs can provide the analyst with the following:

- A set of questions that need to be resolved.
- A better understanding of the nature of the system and what is important in it.
- A basis for further analysis through using the ELHs to create the SDD

The creation of the SDD takes the depth of analysis one stage further. The 'logic' contained within the SDD is an important statement of precedence in the system and as such can act as a source of knowledge when the analyst is faced with questions about the consequences of certain circumstances. The SDD is a model which has been constructed from a knowledge of the system and therefore can be cross-referenced against other models, in particular the DFDs and process specifications. Inconsistencies identified may shed new light on the system. The benefits of creating the SDD include:

- Identifying inconsistencies through cross-referencing triggers with DFDs and process specifications.
- Identifying transactions which can be grouped together because there need be no delay between them.
- Permitting focus on constraints in a methodical fashion so that they can be validated and checked for inconsistencies with respect to process specifications.
- Analysing abnormal lives in a structured way.
- The identification of the impact of amendments to attributes on the system.
- Identifying error conditions in a structured manner.

4.6 FURTHER READING

1 Cutts, G. (1987) *Structured Systems Analysis & Design Methodology*, Paradigm, London, discusses entity life histories. In addition it shows how to draw ELHs using a hierarchical notation and using Petri Nets.
2 Peters, L. (1988) *Advanced Structured Analysis and Design*, Prentice-Hall, Englewood Cliffs, New Jersey, recognises that there is a need for a model which shows the underlying logic of a system. He uses 'event diagrams' to try to capture the logic of a system, though these are not generated from ELHs.

4.7 EXERCISES

1   In societies in which one partner may only be married to one other at any one time, there are a number of marital states. These are single, married, widowed and divorced. Draw the ELH for this assuming that the initial state is single and the final state is death.

2   A person's educational and work career may be as follows. A person

may attend a nursery school; or they may proceed directly to primary school. After primary school, secondary education takes place; both primary and secondary education are compulsory. After secondary school they may go on to higher education or straight to work; clearly, if the higher education route is chosen the expectation is that they will eventually join the workforce though this may be after a number of qualifications have been obtained. Higher education is carried out at either a college or university. A person may have a number of jobs over their career; a work career may be interspersed with periods of higher education. Regrettably some people may never obtain a job at all. Draw the ELH for the above assuming that the creation state is birth and the final state is death.

3   Assume that the case study had an additional requirement which was that part-payments of invoices are permitted.

The following is now required:

(a) Modify the data model to include a PAYMENT entity.
(b) Draw the ELH for the new entity and check to see if other ELHs have to be modified.
(c) Modify the SDD to accommodate the existence of the new entity.

Chapter 5
Normalisation

5.1 INTRODUCTION

This chapter describes the technique of normalisation, sometimes referred to as relational data analysis. Much of what is discussed is based on the work of Dr Edgar Codd whose ideas underpin relational database technology. The technique itself however plays a part in confirming the data model.

Normalisation is a technique for examining dependencies between data items, so that data items which are found to be related in certain ways can be grouped together. Unlike data modelling which can be regarded as a top-down technique, normalisation is a bottom-up technique since it starts by utilising existing documents or whatever and synthesises them into what are called relations. Given that a data model has already been drawn, this technique can be used to confirm its correctness and that there is no ambiguity in the definition of data items.

Firstly, some terminology:

relation   A relation is a two-dimensional table of data.
tuple   A tuple is a row in the table.
domain   A domain is a column in the table.

PRODUCT

key   domain
↓   ↓

PART-NO	DESCRIPTION	QUANTITY	LOCATION	
A135	$\frac{1}{2}$ inch bolt	20	BIN1	
A150	Washer	10	BIN3	← tuple
B222	$\frac{3}{4}$ inch bolt	15	BIN7	
C750	Flange	5	BIN9	

Fig. 5.1. A relation.

Figure 5.1 shows a simple relation.

key	A key is a domain or domains which uniquely distinguish all tuples in a relation, i.e. for each key there is only one tuple
simple key	A simple key is a key requiring only a single domain to establish identity
compound key	A compound key is one where more than one domain is required to establish identity
composite key	A composite key is a compound key in which at least one domain of the key is not a unique identifier of its domain and therefore needs to be catenated with other domains. For example, an invoice line number is non-unique since many invoices may have a line-number of 1. Invoice-no + invoice-line-no could be a composite key
foreign key	A foreign key is domain of one relation which is a key in another relation. For example, in figure 5.1, location is a domain of the relation PRODUCT. If another relation existed called, say, STORAGE-LOCATION in which location was the key, then location would be a foreign key in PRODUCT. A foreign key may itself be part of a key (i.e. an attribute in a compound key).

The properties of a relation are straightforward to establish. A table is said to be a relation if the following is true:

(1) Each domain must be a unique data item and have a unique name
Suppose two domains in a relation represented the same data item, e.g. they represent the time it took an athlete to run a certain distance. This would mean that by supplying the key of the relation, say athlete-no, one could obtain two pieces of similar information, i.e. the times for two different races. This is inconsistent with the purpose and idea of a relation. What we have here is two different tuples representing two different races. We would need a compound key to distinguish the different races.

A practical problem arises in naming domains. Domains which contain dates or people's names are often simply called 'date' or 'name'. This is acceptable as long as there is no other domain in this or any other relation identified which is also a date or name. Where duplication can arise, the domain name should be qualified to distinguish these different domains. This is called a role name.

ATHLETE-NO   TIME

ATHLETE-NO	TIME
10	1.58
5	2.01
7	2.05
3	2.10

Fig. 5.2. Results of athletes in a race.

(2) No two tuples are identical
This means that there has to be at least one domain containing a different value from any other tuple.

(3) The sequence of tuples and domains should not be significant
Figure 5.2 represents the results of athletes in a race. The first tuple, i.e. row 1, represents the athlete who finished first. It is important that there is no implied relationship between one tuple and another in a relation since that is a piece of information that cannot be gleaned by inspecting a single tuple. The solution here is to create an additional domain which contains the athlete's position in the race.

5.2 THE NORMALISATION TECHNIQUE

Normalisation can be performed on any set of data. Typically, several key documents are selected such that their attributes in aggregate cover all the attributes in the data model. Each document is normalised separately, then each set of relations is integrated with the sets of relations from the other key documents. This is known as synthesis and allows us to construct in effect a data model from analysing the relationships between the attributes themselves and to compare the resultant model with the previously derived data model.

The steps in normalisation are as follows:

1 Convert the document (or other data source) into an unnormalised table, i.e. unnormalised form or UNF.
2 Convert the unnormalised table to first normal form (1NF).
3 Convert 1NF relations to second normal form (2NF).
4 Convert 2NF relations to third normal form (3NF).
5 Synthesise 3NF relations into a data model.

6 Check synthesised model is in 3NF.

The invoice used in the SBM case study is used here to illustrate the first four steps in normalisation.

5.2.1 Convert into an unnormalised table

An unnormalised table is not the same thing as the document itself. One of the main benefits of normalisation is in the avoidance of redundant or duplicate data, but in order to achieve this, the data must firstly be expressed in a form which allows redundancy and duplication to be identified.

(a) Each attribute on the document becomes a domain in the UNF table. Sample data is then added to populate the table. Where the invoice header information is common to all lines on the invoice, as in this case, it is only shown once since this serves to highlight the underlying relationship between the two parts of the invoice. Attributes which are derived or calculated directly from other attributes on the document are not shown in the table, as they will be dealt with separately.

(b) More than one instance of an invoice is shown in the table as this aids the identification of key fields. Also, as far as possible try to populate the table with data which covers the spectrum of combinatorial events which can arise across all documents. This will help when deciding on the transition between one normal form and the next.

See figure 5.3.

5.2.2 Convert the unnormalised table to first normal form (1NF)

By convention, all attributes within each normal form are listed in a single column as this aids analysis. Keys are underlined and foreign keys denoted by an asterisk.

(a) The first task is to identify a key for the unnormalised table. A problem arises immediately in that, strictly speaking, we cannot find a key for tuples, many of whose attributes have been left blank. What we really have here is a table of invoices whose format currently does not quite fit the rules of a relation. So, we ignore for the moment tuples with blanks in them and identify the key as invoice-no.

Note the identification of a key will not always be as simple as in this case. It may be a compound key or perhaps there is more than one candidate key.

INVOICE

Invoice-No	Invoice-Date	Order-No	Order-Date	Cust-No	Cust-Name	Address	Prod-Code	Description	UOM	Qty Del	Unit Cost
018758	24.10.88	017321	15.10.88	0324	J SMITH	....	PA129	PAINT ...	5 LTR	100	7.5
							CM002	CEMENT	CWT	50	5.5
							BR031	BRICK	100	2000	440
018760	31.10.88	017324	12.10.88	0125	A JONES	....	PA129	PAINT ...	5 LTR	50	7.5

Note that derived domains are not shown in this table.

Fig. 5.3. Unnormalised table for SBM invoice.

Sometimes it may even be necessary to generate a key, say a serial number so that a document can be uniquely identified. However, as long as a valid key is identified the normalisation process will work.

In choosing a key, the following guidelines may help:

1 Avoid keys containing text, if possible. Domains containing codes or serial numbers are much more practical since they are less prone to misspelling or improper abbreviating.
2 Given a choice between more than one candidate compound key, choose the candidate key which is inherently more appropriate. Sometimes there may be little choice between candidates, in which case choose the key with the smallest number of domains.

(b) The main task of this step is to remove all repeating groups. A repeating group is a group of domains (or indeed one domain) that may occur with multiple values for a single occurrence of the key. Now this is why at an earlier stage the invoice header data was only listed once in the table. If it is not obvious that a repeating group exists, a simple way of checking is to look at the data dictionary definition for invoice which is:

INVOICE = INVOICE-NO + INVOICE-DATE + ORDER-NO
+ ORDER-DATE + DATE-DUE + CUSTOMER-NO
+ CUSTOMER-NAME + CUSTOMER-ADDRESS
+ {PRODUCT-CODE + DESCRIPTION + UOM
+ QTY-DEL + UNIT-COST + AMOUNT}
+ TOTAL-AMOUNT + TOTAL-VAT + TOTAL-DUE

The braces clause tells us that we have a repeating group of the domains representing the invoice line. The repeating group along with the original key is moved to a separate relation. In doing so, a new key has to be found for the new relation. Here the key is invoice-no plus product-code. (For the purpose of this example we have assumed there is no order line number.) The original relation is now reduced to the invoice header information. See table 5.1.

Sometimes there may be more than one repeating group or indeed repeating groups within repeating groups. A set of relations is in 1NF only if there are no repeating groups. In such cases the rules are applied iteratively until no repeating groups remain.

Another perspective on normalisation comes from appreciating that in practice, except for very small relations, one normal form takes up less space than the previous one. For argument's sake say there are 1000 invoices with an average of 5 invoice lines per invoice. Using the estimates for the size of

1NF

Invoice-no	(6)
invoice-date	(8)
order-no	(6)
order-date	(8)
cust-no	(4)
cust-name	(20)
cust-address	(90)

invoice-no	(6)
prod-code	(5)
description	(20)
uom	(4)
qty-del	(5)
unit-cost	(6)

Table 5.1. First normal form for SBM invoice.

each domain as shown in table 5.1, the size of each tuple is 182 characters. This comes to 910,000 characters in total, although it includes the blank domains discussed earlier. In first normal form there are 1000 invoice headers at 142 characters each, which gives 142,000 characters plus $5 \times 1000 \times 46$ characters which is 230,000 characters giving 372,000 characters in all. Clearly, the major saving in 1NF is through the non-use of the blank domains in the relation. Note that invoice-no appears in both relations, which is an overhead.

5.2.3 Convert 1NF relations to second normal form (2NF)

The transition to second normal form involves examining whether domains are dependent on the whole key or just part of it. In other words the question only applies to 1NF relations with compound keys. 1NF relations with simple keys are automatically in 2NF.

If a particular domain depends more on part of the key than the whole key then that domain with that part-key should be moved to a separate relation. So, the question is posed to each non-key domain in turn and through these questions one or more new relations may be identified. Where the key contains several domains each combination of domains making up the key must be considered as candidate part-keys for the question.

As in the first step, relations are in 2NF only if no part-key dependencies remain, so it may be necessary to repeat this step on new relations created during this step. It therefore makes sense to try to identify part-key dependency on each single domain of the multiple-key first, since this will avoid unnecessary iterations of this step.

So, for the invoice example, the invoice header relation goes straight into 2NF. For the order-line relation, part-description, unit-of-measure and unit-cost all depend more on product-code than they do on the concatenation of invoice-no and product-code. So a new relation is created containing product-code as key with product-description, unit-of-measure and unit-cost as domains. See table 5.2.

The total size of 2NF relations is sometimes difficult to calculate. The invoice header relation remains the same at 142 000 characters. The invoice-

2NF

invoice-no	(6)
invoice-date	(8)
order-no	(6)
order-date	(8)
cust-no	(4)
cust-name	(20)
cust-address	(90)
invoice-no	(6)
prod-code	(5)
qty-del	(5)
product-code	(5)
description	(20)
uom	(4)
unit-cost	(6)

Table 5.2. Second normal form for SBM invoice.

line relation now takes up $5 \times 1000 \times 16$ characters making 80 000 characters. The difficulty lies in identifying how many product tuples there will be, since it depends on the number of distinct product-codes quoted across all of the invoice-lines. It is highly likely that most products will appear several times across 1000 invoices which would reduce the size requirement considerably. For calculation purposes in this kind of situation, take the number of products held in stock, say 800: the size of the product-code relations is 800 $\times$ 35 characters which is 28 000 characters. The total size of 2NF relations is then 250 000 characters, which is still significantly smaller than 1NF.

5.2.4   Convert 2NF relations to third normal form (3NF)

Conversion to third normal form is similar to conversion to second normal form, except that it deals with dependencies between non-key domains and compares these to the domains that make up the key.

For each pair of non-key domains in the relation the same question is asked, namely 'does the domain depend more strongly on the other domain in the pairing than it does on the key?'. If the answer is yes then a new relation is created.

In the invoice example it can be seen that order-date depends more on order-no than invoice-no and also customer-name and customer-address depend more on customer-no than on invoice-no. So two new relations are created, i.e. the order relation with order-no as key with order-date as a domain and the customer relation with customer-no as key and customer-name and customer-address as domains. See table 5.3.

Sometimes the conversion can be quite tricky. For example, suppose that the invoice had two further domains, i.e. customer-rating and discount-code. Upon investigation it was discovered that the discount-code is determined by a combination of the customer-rating and the volume of business usually done with this customer. Therefore one customer-rating could generate many discount codes. So, discount-code would depend on customer-rating and such a relation would have customer-rating as part-key with discount-code as domain. In other words, make absolutely sure you understand the nature of dependencies – do not just assume them.

With regard to space utilisation, again there can be some difficulty in precisely calculating the total size of 3NF relations. The invoice relation is 1000×24 giving 24 000 characters. Suppose there is one invoice for every order then the order relation is 14 000 characters. Note that since the degree of relationship between order and invoice is one-to-one, it actually increases

3NF

	<u>**invoice-no**</u>	(6)
	invoice-date	(8)
*	order-no	(6)
*	cust-no	(4)
	<u>**order-no**</u>	(6)
	order-date	(8)
	<u>**cust-no**</u>	(4)
	cust-name	(20)
	cust-address	(90)
*	<u>**invoice-no**</u>	(6)
*	<u>**prod-code**</u>	(5)
	qty-del	(5)
	<u>**product-code**</u>	(5)
	description	(20)
	uom	(4)
	unit-cost	(6)

Table 5.3. Third normal form for SBM invoice.

the space requirements to separate out an order relation. This is because of the overhead of incurring an order-no key in the relation.

For calculation purposes taking all 500 customers, the customer relation is 500×114 which is 57000 characters. This makes a total requirement of 203000 characters for the 3NF relations.

5.2.5 Synthesise 3NF relations into a data model

Once all the identified documents or whatever have been normalised individually, the results need to be merged together to obtain a composite view of the total data being used. This literally means identifying relations whose keys are identical. A composite relation is created out of domains from both relations.

5.2.6 Check that synthesised data model is in 3NF

Sometimes synthesised relations are not in 3NF. For example, suppose we have two 3NF relations, one with a domain of part number, the other with a domain of part description. When these are merged, then the combined relation clearly will not be in 3NF, because part description will depend more on part number than it will on its original key. So a new relation containing part number and part description will need to be created (assuming one does not already exist).

Another problem arises where relations do not represent the same entity. For example, there may be two relations, say customer and delinquent customer, with the same key and domains. However, a straightforward merged approach is inappropriate because the relations represent different things. So it is always necessary to review the synthesis activity to ensure that mistakes of this nature do not creep in.

5.3 GUIDELINES FOR PERFORMING NORMALISATION

A set of rules for performing normalisation is one thing, but actually performing normalisation is sometimes quite another. However, there are a number of practical hints which can help in easing one through the transformations.

5.3.1 Identifying data sources for normalisation

There is clearly the possibility that one will identify the same data items over and over again across the different sources identified. The other likelihood is that some data items may be omitted from the normalisation problem. So it is worthwhile surveying all possible data sources to identify a minimum set of sources which includes all data items but keeps to a minimum the number of sources to be normalised. Potential sources include:

* documents used by the current system
* existing manual records
* existing computer transaction, master and history files
* reports and screens

If a computerised analysis data dictionary is being kept then this easily provides a list of all data items defined during an analysis. A data item/ document matrix can be constructed by listing all data items vertically and all documents, files, and so on horizontally. If a data item is used in a particular document then an 'X' is entered at the intersection on the matrix. Once completed the data item/document matrix is a good way of identifying a minimum set of documents for normalisation. Note too that it is possible for the matrix to be produced automatically from a computerised data dictionary.

5.3.2 Aliases

Sometimes domains have more than one name, e.g. customer number might be an alias for account number. When investigating the system it is important to document any aliases, since otherwise this may lead to confusion. It is probably best to try to use one name as far as possible. Beware, however, that aliases may not always be true aliases. For example, part number may not be the same thing as stock number. Part number may refer to items which may be stocked or bought-in specifically for assembly, whereas stock number only refers to items which are stocked anyway. So it is important to analyse carefully each alias to determine its validity.

5.3.3 Processing codes

When analysing input documents or file specifications, there are often data items which have no bearing on the data analysis. These would include data codes, record size counts, print indicators, etc. Any data item which is clearly a manifestation of the physical processing should be ignored in normalisation.

5.3.4 Implied domains

One of the major benefits of normalisation is the opportunity to analyse critically the structure of and interdependencies between data. That analysis often causes the analyst to go back to the user with more detailed questions concerning his understanding of the data.

The problem is that documents in the so-called 'real' world do not necessarily have to obey the rules of structure or even common sense. Often an important data item upon which others depend is for some reason (e.g. brevity, political or confidential reasons) omitted from a document. During normalisation, the analyst may make assumptions about the relationships between the data, which in fact are not true. However, had the omitted data item been present, a much clearer and more logical insight would have been gained. Examples of implied domains include:

(1) Absent key

In this situation the key does not appear in the document at all. Suppose that a bonus is paid based on an employee's grade, but the grade itself does not appear on the employee's payslip. The analyst might infer that the bonus is dependent on the department or the hourly rate or whatever. If there is enough data, there will probably be no logical pattern and so return to the user is necessitated.

(2) Generated key

This is where no proper key exists to identify a relation, so one needs to be invented. This can occur in orders or invoices where there are many lines of items. Sometimes the product on each item line may not be unique within the order. So an order line number is invented to guarantee uniqueness.

(3) Sequence data

One of the properties of a relation is that the sequence of tuples must not be significant. If it is significant, as in the case of positions in a race or, more pertinently, in the sequence of tasks in manufacturing, then an additional domain is created which defines its sequence, i.e. a sequence number. The sequence number may well form part of the key of the relation.

(4) Hidden domains

Often reports contain titles or headings which may hold data which is a domain for the relation. For example, a delinquency report tells the reader about, say, all customers who have not paid their debts on time. This is a property or characteristic of these customers which distinguishes them from the rest and therefore in relational terms becomes a domain. Report date may also be a domain. In this case, it depends very much on whether the date plays a part in classifying the information on the report. In other words, if it is required to keep multiple versions of data which are essentially distinguished by time, then date has to be a domain.

5.3.5 Calculated fields

Another problem arises when dealing with reports containing calculated fields, especially totals and subtotals. Because total fields may represent aggregates of the individual tuples in the relation, it will often happen that extra, possibly many extra, relations will be generated just to hold these totals and subtotals. The alternative would be to calculate such fields from the raw figures when the report is produced.

This is clearly a difficult decision to make at this stage, since computer processing time to perform the totalling is being traded off against additional storage space, increased data model complexity and navigation. It is quite possible that the particular software to be used may not yet be chosen so there is little hope of quantifying the problem absolutely.

It is recommended that calculated fields be ignored for the purposes of normalisation and that a separate list be maintained to hold such fields. At a later stage this list can be reviewed and possibly some fields incorporated into the data model.

5.4 DRAWING THE DATA MODEL

This a mechanical task. Each relation becomes an entity. A relationship is established between a foreign key and its counterpart entity. See figure 5.4. In some cases it will be clear what the degree of relationship is, e.g. the degree of relationship between PRODUCT and INVOICE-LINE is one-to-many, because the key of PRODUCT is prod-code and the key for INVOICE-LINE is 'invoice-no + prod-code'. In other cases, such as the relationship between CUSTOMER and INVOICE, the tuples in the relations will have to be inspected to identify the degree.

5.5 SUMMARY

Normalisation is an important technique when developing information

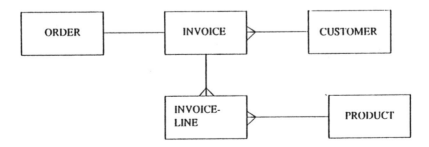

Fig. 5.4. Data model for SBM invoice created by normalisation.

systems. Compared to its counterpart technique, data modelling, it is a far more mechanical procedure, though the discussion in this chapter has illustrated that it is not totally mechanical and demands that the analyst think very carefully about the nature and structure of data being dealt with.

In Part B, it will be proposed that normalisation be used to confirm and perhaps build on the data model produced by the data modelling technique. And it is suggested that this is its proper role. The importance of getting the data model absolutely right cannot be emphasised enough, and therefore rather than asking the analyst to choose between using one of two approaches to identifying the data model, it is submitted that the additional workload in using both is a small price to pay for the improved integrity of the data model. The benefits of normalisation include:

- A fairly mechanical process for producing a data model.
- The identification of attributes overlooked in the data modelling process.
- The possible identification of entities overlooked in the data modelling process.
- A structured opportunity for gaining insight into the nature of the data.
- An increased confidence that the data model is correct.

5.6 FURTHER READING

Howe, D. (1983) *Data Analysis for Data Base Design*, Edward Arnold, London, which was previously mentioned also contains a comprehensive discussion of normalisation.

5.7 EXERCISES

1   In this chapter we have just 'walked through' the normalisation of the SBM invoice in the case study. The SBM order form is a simpler document. Try normalising the order form. At each normal form, calculate the space utilisation making appropriate assumptions where necessary.

2   The third document in the case study is the statement of account, which is a bit more complicated. Normalise this document. Hint: the remittance advice note section is actually a copy of fields on the main part of the document. What should be done about these fields?

3   Take the SBM invoice and, without ignoring the calculated fields, normalise the document.

4   Create a synthesised set of 3NF relations for the SBM order form, original invoice (i.e. without calculated fields) and the statement of account. Draw the data model for this.

Chapter 6
The Structure Chart

One the most important lessons learnt in solving many kinds of problem is the 'divide and conquer' strategy. This approach applies in a very fundamental way to designing, writing and testing computer programs. The computer community has now begun to realise that programs which are split up into modules in a sound way have significant advantages over the alternative, which is a single monolithic program containing little or no use of partitioning. The size and intricacy of a typical monolithic program is just too big for the human mind to fully comprehend.

Monolithic programs are difficult to read, difficult to understand, difficult to debug and difficult to maintain. Fortunately, there is no need to have to live with this. If a program is broken up into modules which perform significant tasks within the program, we, in effect, divide and conquer many of our problems. In reality, we are just decomposing the problem into smaller units, but given that these smaller units are all within a programmer's ability to understand, we have a most acceptable alternative to the monolithic solution. The diagram of the program architecture, i.e. the modules within the program and how they relate to one another, is known as the structure chart. The details of the notation are shown in figure 6.1.

Because of the nature of information systems, especially with regard to the requirement for continued maintenance, there is a need to construct programs which are easy to read, understand, debug and maintain. When designing a program it is essential to build in these characteristics. The central question is how to do so. The problem facing software engineers is not dissimilar to some problems faced and overcome by other engineers whether it be in constructing integrated circuits or building ships. The solution has two facets:

- The entity under construction should be made up of components which are as independent as possible with respect to other components. This is known as coupling.
- Components should be simple to understand and be as reusable as possible. This is, in effect, cohesion.

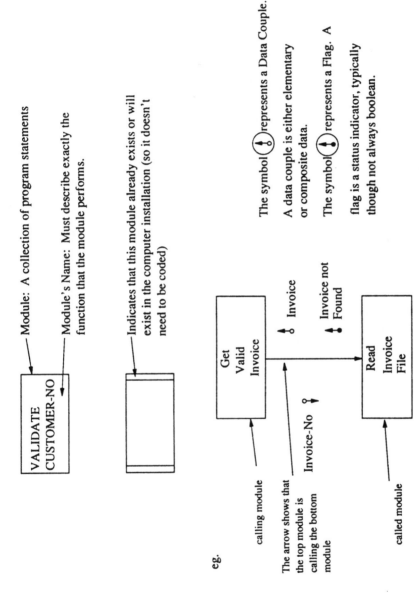

Module: A collection of program statements

Module's Name: Must describe exactly the function that the module performs.

Indicates that this module already exists or will exist in the computer installation (so it doesn't need to be coded)

The symbol ⊕ represents a Data Couple.

A data couple is either elementary or composite data.

The symbol ⊕ represents a Flag. A flag is a status indicator, typically though not always boolean.

eg.

calling module

The arrow shows that the top module is calling the bottom module

called module

Invoice

Invoice not Found

Invoice-No

Fig. 6.1. Graphic notation for the structure chart.

First of all, we will define what is meant by coupling and cohesion and then look at how to construct structure charts. A fuller discussion appears in Page-Jones[1].

6.1 COUPLING

Coupling is the degree of interdependence between two modules. Because it is desirable to be as independent as possible (so that they can be understood and maintained easily), low coupling is considered good and high coupling bad. Low coupling is good because:

• The fewer connections there are between the modules, the less chance there is for what is called the ripple effect (an error in one module causing errors in another).
• We want to be able to change one module with minimum risk of having to change another module and we want each change to affect as few modules as possible.

Two modules are data coupled if they communicate by parameters, which since modules must communicate, is unavoidable and harmless.

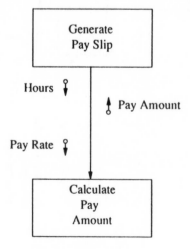

Fig. 6.2. Data coupling.

Two modules are stamp coupled if they refer to the same composite data (e.g. a record)

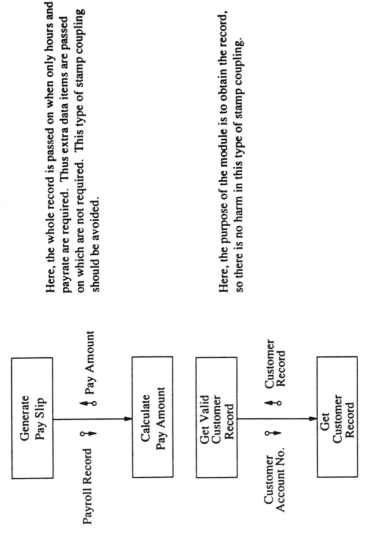

Here, the whole record is passed on when only hours and payrate are required. Thus extra data items are passed on which are not required. This type of stamp coupling should be avoided.

Here, the purpose of the module is to obtain the record, so there is no harm in this type of stamp coupling.

Fig. 6.3. Stamp coupling.

Two modules are control coupled if they have a flag.

Here, however, the subordinate module is telling the boss module what to do. This type of flag is called a control flag, because it is trying to control another module.

This should be avoided.

Here the subordinate module is passing a message back to the boss module. This type of flag is called a descriptive flag. This type of control coupling is better than the other, but try to choose modules so that control coupling is minimised if possible.

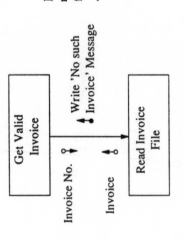

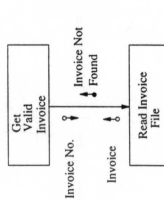

Fig. 6.4. Control coupling.

- While changing one module we do not want to worry about the internal details of other modules. We want the program to be as simple as possible to understand.

There five main kinds of coupling. From low to high they are:

- data
- stamp
- control
- common
- content

Figures 6.2, 6.3 and 6.4 define and show examples of data, stamp and control coupling respectively. Common coupling is the name given to describe the situation where two modules refer to the same global data area, e.g. in languages such as Fortran a variable may be declared in the main program and a subroutine may refer to that variable. Common coupling is considered so bad that there is no way of drawing this on the structure chart. In any case, it can always be avoided by adding a parameter to the procedure call. Content coupling occurs when one module refers to the inside of another module, e.g. if you branch or jump into another module or change the data owned by another module. Not all languages allow this to be implemented and again there is no way of showing this on a structure chart.

Lastly, it is important to remember that two modules may be coupled in more than one way, in which case the coupling is the highest (i.e. worst) coupling found.

6.2 COHESION

Coupling is the degree to which two modules are independent. Another way of looking at the problem is to look within a module and establish how related the tasks within one module are. This is cohesion.

Cohesion is the measure of the strength of functional association of elements within a module. So, highly-cohesive modules are good because their elements are strongly related. There are seven kinds of cohesion:

- functional
- sequential
- communicational
- procedural

A functionally cohesive module contains elements which are related to one single task.

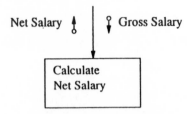

Fig. 6.5. Functional cohesion.

A sequentially cohesive module is one where the output data from one activity in the module is the input to the next activity in the module.

Example

A sign that it may be sequential cohesion is if the word "and" appears in the module name.

Sequentially cohesive modules usually have good coupling. The only disadvantage is that they tend not to be as useful elsewhere in the program, e.g. it might be that a "validate record" module is required elsewhere but not a "read and validate" module.

Fig. 6.6. Sequential cohesion.

A communicationally cohesive module is one whose elements use the same input or output data.

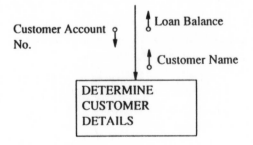

Maintainability is improved if you split them into separate (functionally cohesive) modules.

Fig. 6.7. Communicational cohesion.

A procedurally cohesive module is one where the elements of the module are linked by flow of control (not flow of data as in sequential cohesion).

Example

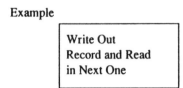

They tend to have strong links with other modules.

Fig. 6.8. Procedural cohesion.

A temporally cohesive module is one where the elements are related in time

Example

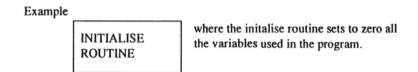

where the initalise routine sets to zero all the variables used in the program.

Maintenance is very difficult because there is so much that is probably not relevant to the maintenance task. Also, it is unlikely to be able to be used elsewhere.

Fig. 6.9. Temporal cohesion.

A logically cohesive module contains a number of activities of the same kind

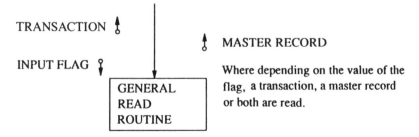

Where depending on the value of the flag, a transaction, a master record or both are read.

Maintenance and re-usability are terrible.

Fig. 6.10. Logical cohesion.

A coincidentally cohesive module is where there is no relationship between the
elements of module.

Example

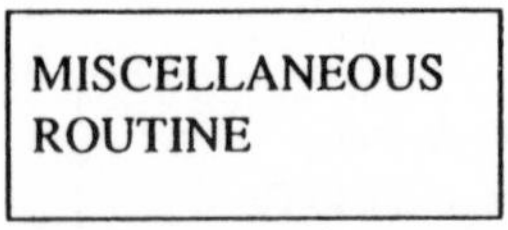

```
┌─────────────────────┐
│ MISCELLANEOUS       │
│ ROUTINE             │
│                     │
└─────────────────────┘
```

Fig. 6.11. Coincidental cohesion.

- temporal
- logical
- coincidental

Figures 6.5 through 6.11 define and show examples of the various kinds of
cohesion.

Maintainability is important. Modules which are highly-cohesive are easier
to maintain because the job is easily understood, whereas modules which are
at the other end of the scale are generally poorly defined, contain many
unrelated tasks, and are therefore much more difficult to maintain.

Modules low down on the module diagram are easily identified as
functionally cohesive because they are so simple. However, higher up in the
module diagram you must also create functionally cohesive modules which
are more 'complicated', e.g. 'validate customer no' might do several things. It
might check that the first two characters are numeric and then that a record
exists for that customer-no on the masterfile. The point is that it needs to do
all these things in order to 'validate customer-no'. In fact, it will probably call
up other modules to do part of this job. The phrase used to describe the
module should sum up all the activities it does, e.g. 'validate customer-no'
should not also update the masterfile.

6.3 THE DESIDERATA OF STRUCTURED DESIGN

There are wider issues to be addressed which coupling and cohesion by
themselves do not deal with. Typically these issues look at more than just the
coupling between two modules or the cohesion within a module; they are
concerned more about the structure chart as a whole and indeed issues
spanning many different structure charts.

6.3.1 Create reusable modules

A more detailed discussion of reusability occurs later in the chapter, but a great strength of structure charts is the potential for identifying modules which can be used time and time again. This saves not only development time but also maintenance time, since often only one module will require maintenance instead of several programs. The trick is in identifying modules which have as wide an application as possible, yet do not compromise too much on efficiency, understandability, etc. There are basically two concepts:

(1) Searching for generic modules
In figure 6.12(a) the top module calls up a module which checks whether any 6-digit field is numeric. Stepping back for a moment, one should realise that there will be many similar needs across all computer systems in the company, though sometimes the need might be to validate a 4-digit number, 8-digit number or whatever. By identifying a slightly more complex module, it is possible to deal with a whole class of problems. What is required is to add an extra variable to indicate the number of digits in the field to be validated. See figure 6.12(b). This task calls for an ability to abstract the problem and see it in more general terms. The impact on workload can be dramatic.

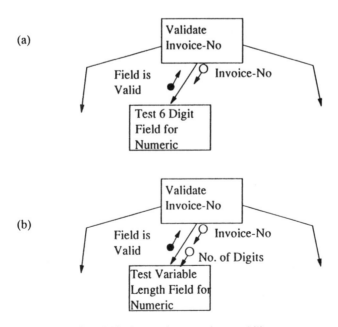

Fig. 6.12. Improving generic reusability.

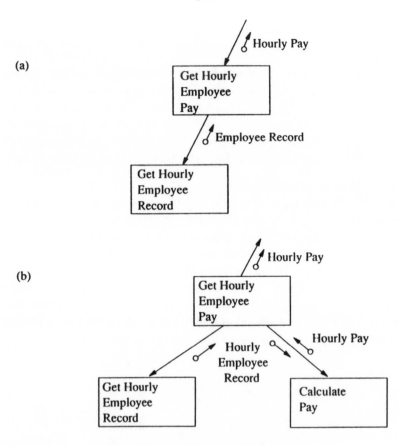

(a)

(b)

Fig. 6.13. Identifying reusable modules.

Another use of the idea is where a generic task is embedded in a function. See figure 6.13(a). The top module is doing two things, firstly getting the data required, and secondly performing the pay calculation (i.e. this is sequential cohesion). Clearly, a task which calculates pay is likely to be needed elsewhere, so it should be made a separate module as in figure 6.13(b).

(2) Constraint avoidance
The tasks involved in validating a field include checking the field against the rules, constructing the text of an error message and writing out that message on some medium. In figure 6.14(a) the module 'TEST 6-DIGIT FIELD FOR NUMERIC' prints an error message on a printer. This is a restriction or constraint on the use of a validate module at two levels. Firstly, it is not a test module's job to decide what is done about an invalid field. Secondly, it must

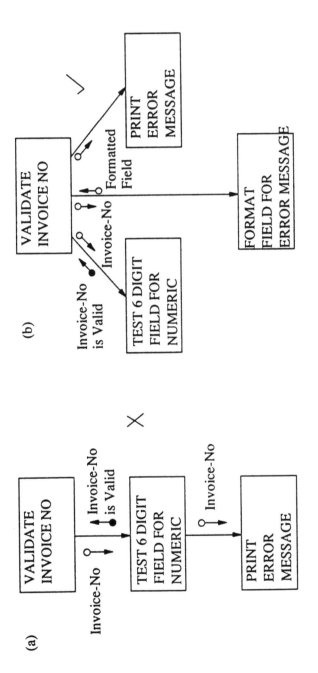

Fig. 6.14. An example of constraint avoidance.

always print the error on a line printer. Figure 6.14(b) has a much better solution. The test module can be used anywhere. A generic module which formats the error message has been identified and the print module is called from the top module.

It is important that the software engineer has a positive attitude towards finding reusable modules. The productivity gains achieved by structured design help to reinforce this.

6.3.2 Strive for a balanced architecture

The architecture of a structure chart should be a balanced one. There are two ideas which contribute to a balanced architecture.

(a) The first one is logical versus physical considerations. By 'logical' is meant that modules will typically make decisions and call up other modules. The word 'physical' on the other hand relates to basic tasks like reading, writing, etc. There is a general expectation that logical modules will appear towards the top of the structure chart and physical modules towards the bottom. In its purest form this guideline would ban the inclusion of physical tasks in logical modules, preferring them to be delegated to lower levels of the structure chart, though this needs to be tempered by a degree of pragmatism particularly when issues on reusability and efficiency are confronted. A useful parallel here is that of a business organisation. The person at the top of the organisation would not be expected to perform tasks which could be delegated to lower-level staff within the organisation.

(b) The second concept of a balanced architecture is that, moving left to right across the structure chart, you would expect to see a sequence of 'input-process-output'. Firstly, there will be modules dealing with the input of data and the associated cleaning up of the data that goes with it. Secondly, modules will be concerned about processing the data, for example updating entities or performing some algorithm. Lastly, on the right-hand side, modules will typically be involved in output activities such as writing success messages, printing out results, etc. Again, it must be stressed that this is a desired characteristic for which there will be exceptions, e.g. a write error message appearing on the left-hand side as data is validated.

Continuing the organisational analogy further, the second concept is similar to the notion of departments in an organisation each of which has its place in the scheme of things. Each department can be said to 'own' tasks and one should not expect to see tasks which belong to one department being

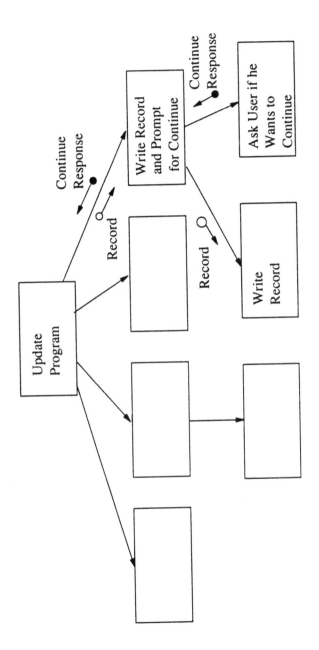

Fig. 6.15. An example of tramp data.

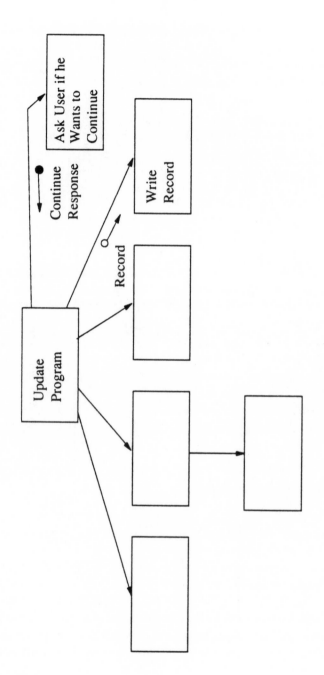

Fig. 6.16. Tramp data removed.

performed in another. One difficulty that often occurs when designing structure charts is the naming of logical modules. This is because they represent a group of related tasks and if you think about this in terms of cohesion it is difficult to arrive at a functionally cohesive name. A solution, which is expanded on later, is to use standardised names for certain logical tasks, e.g. 'GET VALID CUSTOMER DATA' is a module whose job is to get customer data from the screen and validate each item. If any item is invalid, an error message is produced, and the data re-input.

6.3.3 Avoid tramp data

Tramp data is the name given to describe the situation where the same data couple(s) or flag(s) travels round the structure chart unnecessarily. See figure 6.15. The key point here is whether the use of the continue response flag is unnecessary.

In nearly all cases, unnecessary tramp data is caused by a module being put in the wrong place in the structure chart. Consider figure 6.15 again. The continue module really should not be where it is currently placed. Also, the module 'WRITE MODULE AND PROMPT FOR CONTINUE' has temporal cohesion. Figure 6.16 shows where the prompt module should be placed. Note that there is now no tramp data.

On the other hand, there are occasions when tramp data is unavoidable. For example, sometimes flags are passed two levels up, because the top module needs to know an outcome to make a decision on what to do next. So, the guideline is if couples or flags appear to be tramp data, check them to see if their use is strictly necessary.

6.3.4 Avoid state memory

State memory is the name given to describe the situation where a called module has to remember something from the last time it was called, so it does not start with the same initial values each time it is executed.

In figure 6.17, the module 'GET VALID ADDRESS LINE' has the job of returning a valid address line each time it is called. Now the first time it is called it has to 'GET ADDRESS LINES FROM SCREEN', say four lines in all. The next and subsequent times it is called, it already has obtained the lines from the screen and only needs to remember which is the next line to be validated and then passed upwards. This is state memory. This is just a poor

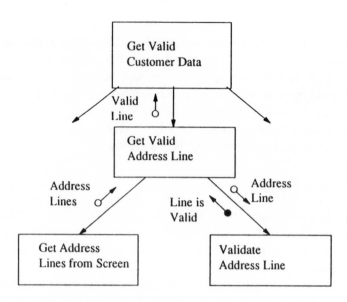

Fig. 6.17. An example of state memory.

way to solve the problem. Figure 6.18 shows an alternative which avoids state memory altogether.

6.3.5 Avoid initialisation and termination modules

Some programmers with a traditional background are tempted to use old and inappropriate ideas when developing structure charts. Of particular note is a

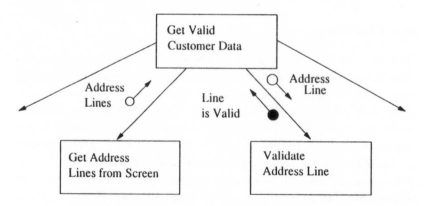

Fig. 6.18. State memory removed.

view that all initialisation of variables and opening of files should take place at the same place in a program. With structure charts they might be tempted to do this in a single module. Similarly, they might also have a termination module in which all files are closed. Such modules have, of course, temporal cohesion and are not recommended anyway, but note that any variables so initialised will have to be passed to the modules where they are actually used, causing significant tramp data.

6.3.6 Keep span of control within reasonable limits

The span of control is the number of modules called up by another module. If the span of control is too high, then clearly that module may be overworked. Equally, if the span of control is too low, then it must be questioned whether there is a need for such a module in the first place. As a working guideline, an upper limit of about ten and a lower limit of two are suggested. Modules with a span of control between four and six seem about right, although this is a matter of preference and if there is a good cause then this rule should be ignored.

6.4 DEVELOPING AN ON-LINE STRUCTURE CHART

Understanding the meaning of the notation is one thing; knowing how to put together a structure chart is quite another. Remember we are concerned about the architecture of the program we are writing, i.e. its component modules and how these modules are related to one another.

(1) Display transaction

First of all will look at a simplified on-line transaction which displays the attributes of a customer entity occurrence when the key of customer-no is input. We assume that once the customer-no is input, it is validated to see if there is an error in the customer-no. If there is no error then the entity is read so that the contents of the matching occurrence can be displayed. If there is an error, then an error message is displayed and the customer-no is re-input until there is no error in the customer-no. The corresponding input and output screens for the transaction would be as in figure 6.19(a) and (b).

The approach taken in creating a structure chart is called functional decomposition. A high-level statement of the problem (e.g. display customer details which is the name of the program) is decomposed into its major parts.

(a)

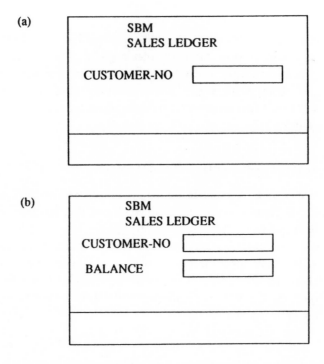

(b)

Fig. 6.19. Input and output screens for a simplified read customer program.

Our first attempt at this can be done by scanning the dialogue descibed above. Here we see that there are four components:

- display customer-no skeleton
- enter customer-no
- an iteration of displaying error message and re-inputting customer-no
- display customer data

The first attempt at a structure chart might be as in figure 6.20. If we think about the second and third component modules in figure 6.20, we see that they are really concerned with the same task, i.e. about getting a valid customer-no input. So figure 6.20 can be converted into figure 6.21, with the proviso that beneath 'GET VALID CUSTOMER-NO' other modules will deal with the re-input problem. So far we have only looked at the user interface for the transaction. One item that is clearly missing is the accessing of the customer entity occurrence, not forgetting that although the customer-

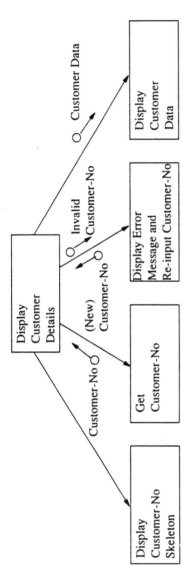

Fig. 6.20. First level structure chart for 'display customer details'.

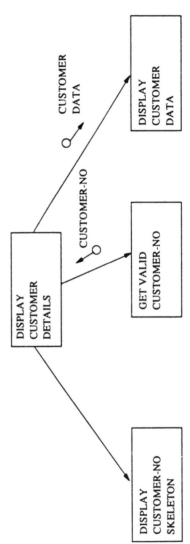

Fig. 6.21. Refined structure chart (to include a single task of getting a valid customer-no.).

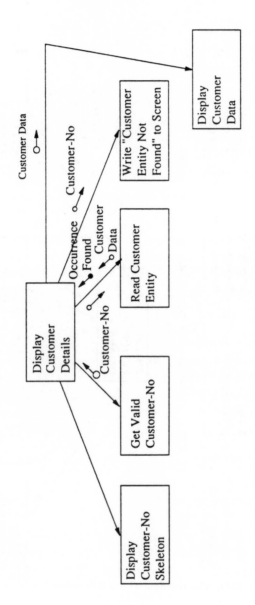

Fig. 6.22. Refined structure chart to include accessing customer entity.

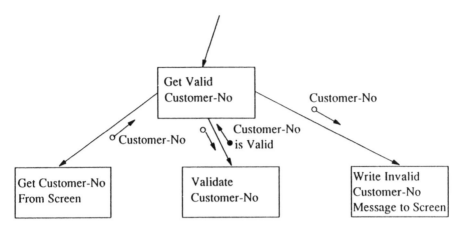

Fig. 6.23. Second level refinement for 'get valid customer-no' module.

no may meet the validation rules, there may not be a corresponding customer-no on the database. So we have figure 6.22.

The 'GET VALID CUSTOMER-NO' module can be decomposed further. Clearly we need to input the customer-no. Next the customer-no has to be validated. If it fails to meet the validation rules then an error message is written. See figure 6.23.

If we review the coupling and cohesion of the modules, we see that modules are data, stamp or control coupled and that all modules are functionally cohesive except for the write error message modules which are sequentially cohesive because there are, in fact, two tasks involved here. The first task is to format the error message. Since the data couple is to be embedded into the error text, e.g. 'CUSTOMER-NO 1234 DOES NOT EXIST IN DATA-BASE', the second task is to write the string of text to a message area on the screen. This can be made functionally cohesive by creating two separate modules as in figure 6.24.

Now a large proportion of any on-line system is taken up with basic transactions on the database such as the display of an existing entity occurrence which has just been examined. The others are insert, delete and modify occurrences on the database. There is a one-to-one correspondence with the R-I-M-Ds discussed in chapter 3 and, of course, it is usual to see these four transactions occurring as a family and applied against most, if not all, entities in a database.

Each of these basic transactions is likely to follow a characteristic pattern. For example, to display a stock occurrence, a stock-no (instead of a customer-

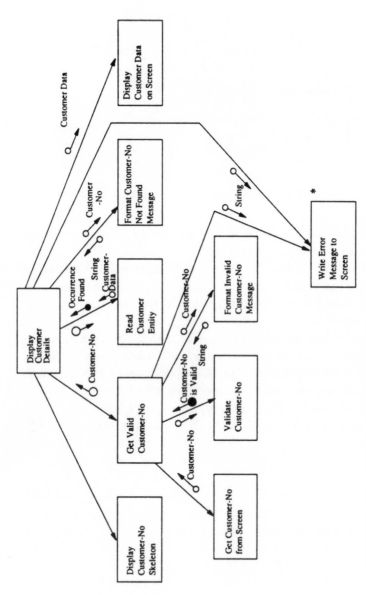

Fig. 6.24. Further redefined 'display customer details' program.

*   Note the use of the "fan-in" instead of the more common "fan-out". This is
    to indicate that the module is called in this case by two different modules.

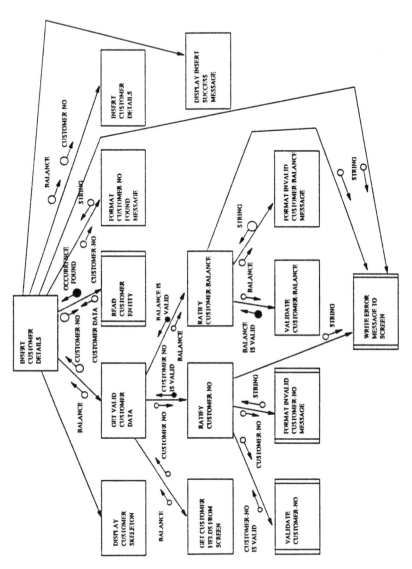

Fig. 6.25. Structure chart for 'insert customer details'.

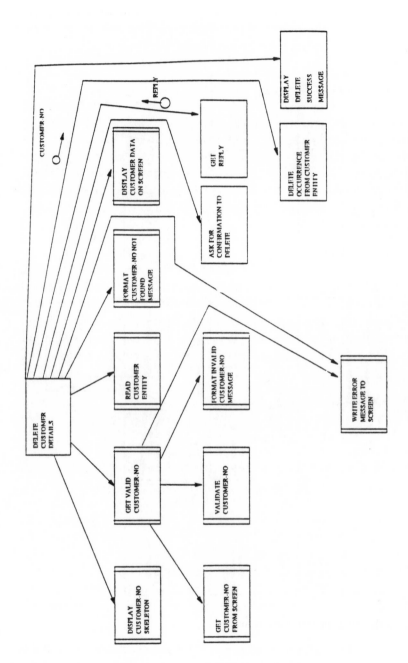

Fig. 6.26. Structure chart for 'delete customer details' (previous couples and flags omitted).

no) will be input, then validated, then checked for existence against the stock entity and so on. This means that each basic transaction type can be used as a template for constructing similar transactions of the same type.

(2) Insert transaction

An insert transaction might follow a pattern of enter all attributes, validate all attributes, check that an occurrence does not exist in the database (since this is an insert transaction) and write the occurrence to the database ending with a success message. Figure 6.25 shows an insert transaction for the customer entity. For brevity, it is assumed that customer entity has only one other attribute which is customer-balance. Note that the 'READ CUSTOMER ENTITY' module is the same one as used in the display structure chart. This is because it is the 'boss' module which decides what to do depending on the status of the flag.

(3) Delete transaction

The pattern for a delete transaction is likely to be to enter the key attribute(s), validate key attribute(s), check that the occurrence exists on the database, display all attributes on screen, allow user to confirm that a delete is to take place, and then delete the occurrence from the database followed by a success message. See figure 6.26. Because the act of display forms such a substantial part of a delete transaction there are only a few modules to be coded; the rest was done in the display transaction.

(4) Modify transaction

The last basic transaction is modify. Here, modify is taken to mean modification of non-key attributes only. If it is required to modify a key attribute then that occurrence should be deleted from the entity and inserted elsewhere, since it will almost certainly occupy a different physical location in the database. The pattern for modify is again to display the whole occurrence, by inputting the key attributes, then to validate all non-key attributes since one or more may have been amended, and finally updating the occurrence and displaying a success message. See figure 6.27. Note the use of an additional piece of notation on the module entitled 'DISPLAY CUSTOMER DETAILS'. This means that there are pre-existing modules underneath this one which are not drawn on this diagram. To find these modules the designer will need to refer to another structure chart; however it does save considerable time in drawing the structure chart.

Structure charts are produced as part of the documentation of the design process along with structured English for each module in the structure chart.

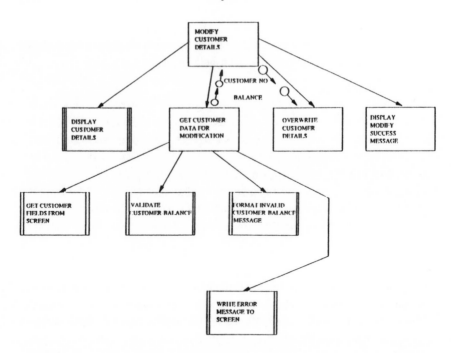

Fig. 6.27. Structure chart for 'modify customer details' (previous couples and flags omitted).

Structure charts are a graphic architectural description of a program and as such are the starting point for understanding the program or investigating a problem. For example, they enable the software engineer to locate the source of a problem – perhaps only the code of one or two modules will have to be consulted. This is much preferable to, as well as quicker than, poring over a single monolithic program.

6.5 REUSABILITY

The power and impact of reusability cannot be emphasised enough in the context of structure charts. In addition to the above benefits in readability, understandability and maintainability, the ability to reuse modules already coded is very important. This dramatically reduces development time and maintenance time. The customer transaction example used in this chapter is clearly over-simplified; a more realistic example is likely to have included more attributes, more detailed individual error messages, help facility modules, extended quit facilities, transaction log, an error message for invalid reply responses, and error messages for detailed input/output problems such as 'databases not open' and 'database full'. This would tend to lead to even more reusability. But even in this example of only four basic on-line transactions, there are (if you include the effect of 'fan-in') 61 modules that would in other circumstances require coding. Because of reuse, there are only 29 modules to be coded. Productivity gains of around 50 per cent are not unusual if the use of structure charts is deployed. There are also advantages in testing and in organisation of work which are discussed later. However, there are a number of design issues which will affect the final structure chart and these are discussed in the next section.

6.6 STYLE, STANDARDS AND SOFTWARE

The structure charts constructed earlier in this chapter are examples of well-designed structured charts. However, they have been created based on a number of assumptions about the environment in which they will work. Broadly, these assumptions fall into three categories which are to do with the style or preference of the designer, the standards policy within the installation and the nature of the software which will be used to generate the code. These assumptions affect the structure chart in fundamental ways. The following, although not exhaustive, is a representative list of some of the issues involved.

6.6.1 Recommended sequence of testing

In figure 6.25, the customer-no and customer-balance (i.e. all attributes of the entity occurrence) were first validated, before going to the database to check if the occurrence existed on the database. An alternative approach would have been to check for existence as soon as customer-no was validated and before checking customer-balance. Arguably, such an existence check would be done as a module underneath 'RATIFY CUSTOMER-NO' although its more general reusability would perhaps be lost. In fact a number of different checks can be done. The sequence of checking recommended is as follows:

(1) Attribute checking
This is the basic validation of the attribute as seen so far. Note, however, that there may be several reasons why an attribute does not pass the validation rules, e.g. 'alpha character in expected numeric field' or 'attribute not in range'. So there could be several different error messages generated. This

would also mean that the flag returned from the validation module could have several states.

(2) Consistency checking

This check confirms that two different attributes are consistent with each other. For example, if only certain staff grades are permitted to be on certain salary scales, then these two attributes can be checked for consistency before proceeding further. This ensures a higher quality of information added to the database.

(3) Existence checking

Existence checking merely confirms if a corresponding occurrence exists on the database. Remember that for display, modify and delete it would be expected that an occurrence existed on the database. For an insert, an occurrence should not exist.

(4) Sensibility checking

As an example, suppose a transaction's task is to reduce the number of items in stock by a specified amount and further that insufficient items exist in stock to achieve that purpose. Here it is not sensible to perform such a task and an appropriate error message would be generated.

6.6.2 Screen input and output

Depending on a combination of style, standards and software, data may be passed to and from screens on the basis of individual fields/strings, complete lines on the screen, or even whole screens. This affects the structure chart in the following way. If it is possible to read from and write to specific locations on the screen, then an alternative strategy would be to include the get module under the ratify module as in figure 6.28.

One advantage of this approach would be that if the attribute were invalid, 'RATIFY CUSTOMER-BALANCE' could easily go back and obtain a new customer-balance by calling 'GET CUSTOMER-BALANCE FROM SCREEN' again. On the other hand, one is tied to always picking up customer-balance at exactly the same position in the screen every time 'RATIFY CUSTOMER-BALANCE' is called. The alternative of having a separate module which picks up the data from the screen makes this family of modules more flexible. Also, an implication of having a separate module for all input data is that when an error is detected and data re-input, all the data attributes are re-validated. Although inefficient it ensures all data is always valid.

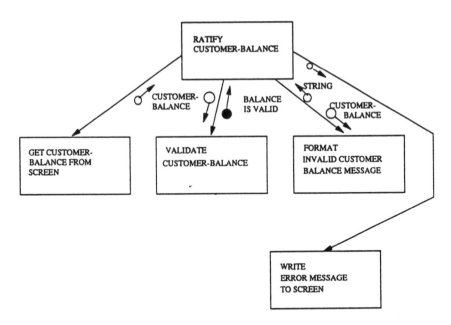

Fig. 6.28. Obtaining data, a field at a time.

6.6.3 The pursuit of reusability

Reusability can be pursued to varying degrees. Again, the extent to which this is practised depends largely on style, standards and what the software will permit.

6.6.4 The use of the RATIFY module

The ratify module is simply a module whose task is to handle the validation of a particular attribute and its associated implications. By comparing figures 6.24 and 6.25, we can see that its existence is not strictly necessary. However, when dealing with large numbers of attributes it is convenient to partition the structure chart so as to use such modules as 'collection points' for more detailed tasks. Remember, in our example, there is no design overhead involved, since it was defined in the insert transaction. Such families of modules should be viewed as 'off the shelf' commodities which have been well designed, implemented, tested and documented and are available for immediate reuse. One last point is that choice of module names such as ratify or validate is relatively arbitrary. What is important is that the department adopts a naming convention which is standard across all systems. This makes examining a structure chart for the first time so much easier.

6.6.5 The separation of logical and physical activities

Ideally, logical or decision-making activities should appear at the top of a structure chart and physical activities such as reading and writing towards the bottom. So, there is a general reluctance to see display skeleton modules, format modules and write error message modules being called from the top module. Consider the display skeleton module. One might argue for placing such modules under for example, 'GET VALID CUSTOMER DATA' in figure 6.25. If that were done it would lead to a problem. As the structure chart currently stands, if there is a matching occurrence in the database, then an error message is written and the top module will want to go back and pick up a new customer-no, revalidate it and so on. But now 'GET VALID CUSTOMER DATA' will firstly call the display skeleton module, so the user will have to retype all the data in instead of only correcting customer-no. This problem can be resolved by moving 'READ CUSTOMER ENTITY' and 'FORMAT CUSTOMER FOUND MESSAGE' to under 'GET VALID CUSTOMER DATA', and admittedly there is some merit to this solution as it saves the top module from dealing with these modules directly. However, it does add to the number of modules 'GET VALID CUSTOMER DATA' deals with and, in any case, the top module still has to deal with other modules which do reading and writing, so the solution is still not ideal. The reader should recognise that the broad templates shown in the above figures represent an approach which aims to achieve a balance in span of control on key modules, but it is only one approach to this problem and other solutions might be just as good.

Whatever approach is used, it is important that it is adopted right across the installation by everyone involved, so that all software engineers are familiar with the rationale behind the approach and are therefore able to develop structure charts within the spirit of the approach.

6.6.6 The use of DISABLE

Most software nowadays permits specific parts of the screen to be disabled, which means the user cannot enter data into that area. This can assist the search for reusability.

Consider the modify and insert transactions in figures 6.27 and 6.25. The

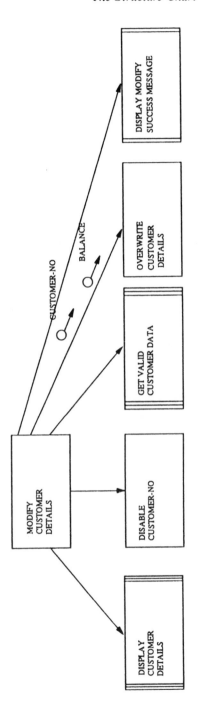

Fig. 6.29. The use of DISABLE.

work done in inputting data for the two transactions is identical, except that it is not required to revalidate the customer-no in the modify transaction under 'GET CUSTOMER DATA FOR MODIFICATION'. Indeed, it is not wise to do so, because the user could have changed the customer-no and therefore the transaction could rewrite the occurrence into the database in the wrong position. However, if the customer-no attribute were disabled as in figure 6.29 then it would not be possible to change the value in customer-no, either inadvertently or otherwise. More significantly, the same family of modules could be used as in the insert transaction.

The remaining issues make a smaller contribution to the design of structure charts. However, they are included here, because they provide the reader with an insight to the design process and also the trade-offs that have to be struck in structured design.

6.6.7 General screen I/O routines

If the software permits, it is possible to create a general read and a general write module, in which the position and length of the string to be read or written as well as the string itself are passed as parameters. Figure 6.30 shows

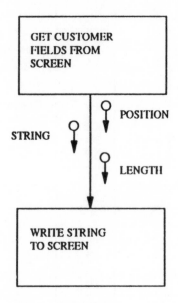

Fig. 6.30. Example of generic write module.

the 'GET CUSTOMER FIELDS FROM SCREEN' module taken from the insert transaction.

The advantage of this tactic is debatable, but it does remove the software engineer from the detailed I/O instructions. The generalised read module could read all input fields including reply responses, confirmations and so on, and the generalised write module would output the writing of headings, data and error messages.

6.6.8 The use of common messages/screens

There is scope for using common success messages. For example, when a transaction has completed its work it is reasonable to display a success message. The message could be reusable in the extreme, e.g. 'SUCCESSFUL COMPLETION OF TRANSACTION'. Alternatively it could be more specific, but of course less reusable, e.g. 'DELETE TRANSACTION COMPLETED SUCCESSFULLY'. Clearly both the above transactions could be used in all systems within an organisation.

The use of common screens is a more complex issue and one which goes to the heart of the trade-off between reusability and user-friendliness. It would be possible, for example, to have only one skeleton screen for the four basic transactions discussed earlier. Currently, there are two skeletons, one to pick up customer-no only and one to pick up all attributes in the customer occurrence.

Here, user-friendliness is good because the user must always fill in all fields on the screen. If a standard skeleton containing all attributes were used then there may be doubt in the user's mind as to how much to enter which might lead to confusion. A compromise would be to retain a standard skeleton and add an instruction as to what to complete, but this would increase the number of modules required and buy us nothing.

6.7 DEVELOPING A STRUCTURE CHART FOR BATCH PROGRAMS

On-line transactions are ideal candidates for structured design because the heavy use of input and output lends itself to modularisation. Traditionally, because of the need to consider efficiency as a top priority, batch programs have tended to be programs in which a number of temporally cohesive tasks are performed, e.g. updating a file and producing a summary report.

Before technology gave the choice of on-line or batch, batch programs had to perform all the tasks within a system. When the above two factors are put together, it is not so surprising to see why a monolothic style of programming had become so common.

The first task is to examine the nature of the batch program, i.e. the tasks that it must perform, so that the structure chart can be developed. Because transactions are 'batched' in batch programs, there tend to be more iterative constructs, i.e. one execution of a loop for each transaction. A slightly different principle can be used to create the structure chart, although in practice the result is the same. This principle is called stepwise refinement and is discussed in more depth in chapter 7. The idea of stepwise refinement is to convert a high-level statement of a problem (say in structured English) to a form which can be easily translated into program code. This is done by successively restating the problem in more and more detail. So at each stage (step) you are refining the problem. Clearly, in the context of structured design, once each stage is refined, candidates for modules are identified and in this way a structure chart is developed.

The difference between stepwise refinement and functional decomposition is as follows. In stepwise refinement, the intermediate steps may contain constructs which may or may not be modules on the structure chart. A corresponding intermediate step in functional decomposition would be when the problem was decomposed say one level down. Here clearly all modules would appear on the final structure chart, barring the effect of refinements for coupling, cohesion, etc. However, because of the strong influence of iteration mentioned above, stepwise refinement can be used to advantage in decomposing batch problems.

Figure 6.31 shows the structure chart for the batch program discussed earlier. Note that six modules are found reusable from the previous on-line transactions. Although in a real system this batch program would probably replace the on-line transaction, it should be clear that generally speaking there is scope for reuse across the batch/on-line boundary.

6.8 SUMMARY

The use of structure charts in design is an important advance for a number of reasons. Probably the most important is the move away from the assumption that the monolithic program is an acceptable response to any information system problem. The use of structure charts implies that the problem will be broken up into small manageable units which make the overall program

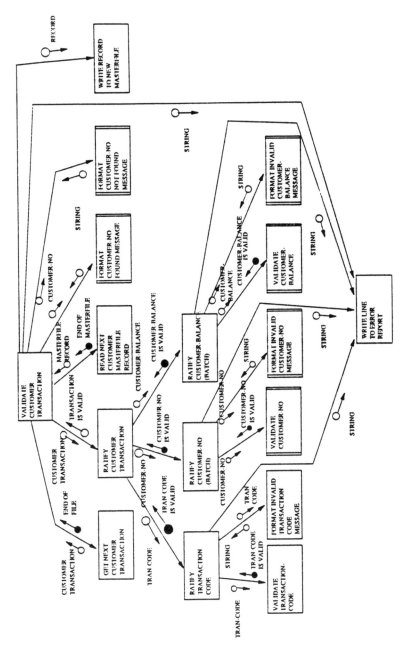

Fig. 6.31. Structure chart for batch program.

easier to design, program, test and document. When it comes to maintenance, structure charts are better at indicating the extent and implications of the modification required.

Like any technique there are ramifications to its use. For example, there are criteria (e.g. coupling and cohesion) for assessing the quality of the design and there are decisions to be made concerning style, standards and the priority given to issues such as reusability. Such ramifications should be considered as opportunities to address what is important in designing computer programs. The benefits of using structure charts are summarised below:

- Programs are able to be partitioned into small manageable units. This reflects a view that readability and understandability are important in design. The use of a diagram to describe the structure chart is significant, because humans are able to absorb information from diagrams more readily than from narrative and also they can 'home in' quickly on parts of the diagram that are of interest.
- Structure charts are developed in a structured way by functional decomposition, which means that they carry the advantages of the structured approaches generally. These include the ability to train staff in the technique, to reduce risk and to obtain more predictable estimates for the length of time to perform tasks.
- Fairly objective criteria exist for measuring the goodness of design. These criteria can be applied at any stage during the design and so are an aid to developing structure charts as well as a means for final assessment. The criteria are tests for coupling, cohesion and a list of desiderata such as avoidance of tramp data, state memory and so on.
- There is scope for identifying reusable modules in structure charts. The simplified example in this chapter demonstrated that the number of modules that need to be designed, coded, tested, documented and maintained can be halved by embracing the opportunity of reusability. This is clearly a significant saving.
- The use of structure charts allows a flexibility of approach in terms of meeting the requirements of house style, standards and software. This is a necessary ability since computer installations vary somewhat in these parameters.
- An advantage not possible with monolithic programs is the opportunity to allocate and distribute parts of the program to different members of the project team to construct and test.

6.9 FURTHER READING

Page-Jones, M. (1980) *The Practical Guide to Structured Systems Design*, Yourdon Press, New York, is a must for anyone who has to design programs for a living.

6.10 EXERCISE

The entity CUSTOMER in the case study contains occurrences of attributes which will require to be maintained on-line, i.e. will require to be displayed, added, modified and deleted. In addition, a special program is required which just alters the customer-balance and nothing else. Design the structure charts for these 5 transactions with an eye to optimising reusability.

Chapter 7
Module Construction

The great strength of the approach described in Part B is that the design stage breaks the problem into small modules. Many would argue that the modules are too small! However, in doing so they overlook the advantage that very small modules have over larger ones, and that is that they are so much easier to construct and test. Many of the modules from the structured design process will have less than 20 statements, which means that the logic within them is likely to be relatively straightforward. Equally, it has to be recognised that for reasons of efficiency or cohesion there will be occasions when modules are bigger than 20 statements, say 50 or 100 statements. Such modules are much more difficult to construct and it is therefore more likely that they will not be correct in some way.

7.1 STEPWISE REFINEMENT

What is required is a process which converts a module specification into a set of executable program statements. To do this we will use a process called stepwise refinement. Stepwise refinement is a top-down technique which converts a module specification into successively more detailed versions until eventually the program statements in the target language are defined. For the majority of modules, because they are small, only one or perhaps two refinements are necessary, but for the occasional complex module resulting in many more statements, several refinements may be required. Stepwise refinement can be applied to any target language, including fourth generation languages or, for that matter, machine code or assembly languages. Clearly, the number of refinement stages will depend on the level of the target language. For brevity, the examples shown will relate to target languages which are third generation.

Each refinement stage has four steps:

- visualisation
- identification of construct

- codification
- verification

It will be proposed later that codification and verification are done in parallel.

7.1.1 Visualisation

The process of visualisation involves two things. Firstly, a knowledge of the target language is required. This is necessary in order that the programmer can determine that the end-point has been reached. Secondly, some insight into the problem is required so that the programmer can 'see' how the specification can be converted to something closer to the target language.

It is important to recognise that the complete specification for a module may reside in different parts of the data dictionary. Obviously it depends on what the module has to do, but the following illustrates some of the places in a data dictionary where part of a specification may reside:

- Clearly the module process specification itself is an important source of information. This may be a structured English narrative, decision table or decision tree. Sometimes modules will be so trivial that inspection of inputs and outputs is all that is required, e.g. 'READ CUSTOMER ENTITY OCCURRENCE'.
- The structure chart defines the incoming and outgoing couples and flags.
- Composite data dictionary entries can describe:
  - Dataflows
  - Files/entities/datastores
  - Screen and report structures
- Elementary dictionary entries supply the validation rules for attributes.
- In addition to screen and report structures it is still necessary to have a picture of the intended screen or report, so that headings and positions are known.

Wherever the source of the specification resides, it is necessary to inspect the specification components to begin the visualisation process. Some modules will be so trivial that conversion to program statements is a simple matter. Others, as will be seen later, require the use of tools to assist visualisation.

7.1.2 Identification of construct(s)

There are three basic constructs to choose from. These are sequence, selection

NAME	:	CUSTOMER-NO
ALIAS	:	ACCOUNT-NO
TYPE	:	ALPHANUMERIC
SIZE	:	4
FORMAT	:	A999
RANGE	:	"999 PART" IN RANGE 100 TO 500 INCLUSIVE

Table 7.1. Specimen data dictionary entry.

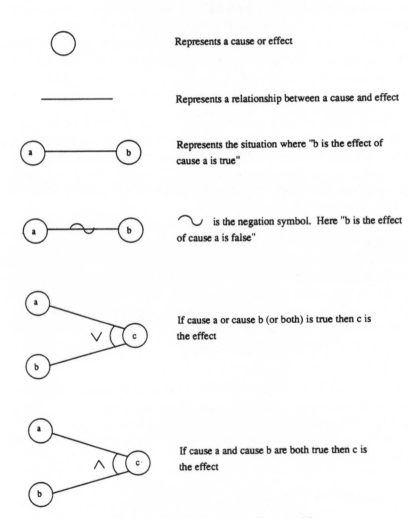

Represents a cause or effect

Represents a relationship between a cause and effect

Represents the situation where "b is the effect of cause a is true"

$\sim$ is the negation symbol. Here "b is the effect of cause a is false"

If cause a or cause b (or both) is true then c is the effect

If cause a and cause b are both true then c is the effect

Fig. 7.1. Notation for cause-effect graphing.

and iteration. However, recall that selection may be IF-THEN, IF-THEN-ELSE or CASE, and iteration may be a WHILE, REPEAT-UNTIL or fixed loop. So, given that the target language has implementations of these constructs, the most suitable constructs may be chosen to fit the purpose. It is a question of formalising the visualisation into a set of appropriate constructs.

Sometimes the order in which constructs should appear is not obvious. A technique called cause-effect graphing, which has been used in creating test data[1], can be used to advantage here. Consider the validation specification in table 7.1.

A cause-effect graph maps causes onto effects in a manner which highlights the dependencies between causes and effects. Figure 7.1 shows the notation for the cause-effect graph.

The tasks in cause-effect graphing are as follows:

• List the causes (on left-hand side, starting at no. 1).
• List the effects (on right-hand side, starting at no. 100).
• Link the causes to effects.

For the validation problem, the causes are:

1 1st character is alphabetic
2 2nd character is numeric
3 3rd character is numeric
4 4th character is numeric
5 number spanned by characters 2 through 4 must be in range

Suppose the effects are:

101 customer-no is valid
102 1st character of customer is not alphabetic
103 digit in customer-no is not numeric
104 invalid range for customer-no

Figure 7.2 gives the cause-effect graph for the customer-no validation. Note that intermediate effects are generated such as effect 51. Intermediate effects are important because they can provide a clue as to the order in which the tests should be made, which is the point of the exercise. Also, where causes have negations, it is clear that the IF-THEN-ELSE construct will apply. From the cause-effect graph, it can be much easier to identify the order of constructs.

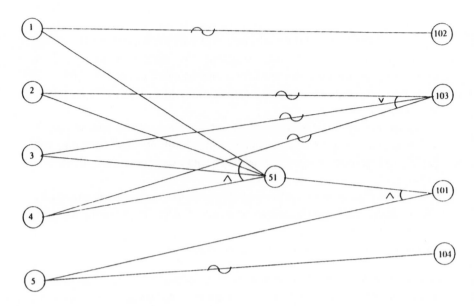

Fig. 7.2. Cause-effect graph for customer-no.

7.1.3 Codification

Codification takes place whether or not the refinement has reached the target language, that is to say that where there is more than one refinement, all but the last refinement will be expressed in some form of structured English. It is simply the formalisation of the processes of visualisation and identification of construct(s). The verification process, which takes place next, needs a formal statement to work upon.

The decision whether to have one or more than one refinement is discretionary, it being largely a matter of the intellectual distance between specification and target language and also a matter of confidence on the part of the programmer. Strictly speaking the verification process, which can be time-consuming, should follow every codification, e.g. the first refinement is only completed when it is verified; the second refinement should not begin until the first refinement is complete. Therefore, it is desirable if the leap from specification to target language can be completed in one refinement. With larger modules, this becomes much less likely.

There is also an art of creating good code, at least in the sense that one should strive to keep the code as simple, readable and maintainable as possible. As a simple example, take the need to convert marks into grades. This could be coded as follows:

```
if mark >= 70 then grade := "A"
else if mark >= 60 then grade := "B"
        else if mark >= 50 then grade := "C"
                else grade := "F"
                endif
        endif
endif
```

The above solution uses a 'nested-if' approach. Clearly, a case construct such as the following would have been more appropriate:

```
case mark of
        70 ... 100 : grade := "A"
        60 ...  69 : grade := "B"
        50 ...  59 : grade := "C"
         0 ...  49 : grade := "F"
        else            write out of range message
case end
```

As well as being simpler, more readable and maintainable, the identification of the correct construct can alert the programmer to at least the possibility of some error condition, in this case an out of range condition.

So, it is of paramount importance in coding to strive to keep the target statements as simple as possible yet ones which accurately reflect the problem on hand. A 'keep-it-simple' philosophy is the best approach to take. This implies that 'clever footwork' in programming is not to be admired or respected. Straightforward simple code is the goal for all software engineers.

7.1.4 Verification

In this section we will deal with verification of module code. Verification is the process of confirming that something is correct. In this chapter, it refers to confirming that module code is equivalent to its specification. Verification can be informal or formal. Informal verification involves a simple check that code and specification match, perhaps with some tests on range and parameter compatibility. Formal verification, by contrast, involves the use of mathematics to prove the assertion that the code and specification are equivalent.

```
IDENTIFICATION DIVISION.
PROGRAM-ID INVCUST.
ENVIRONMENT DIVISION.
DATA DIVISION.
LINKAGE SECTION.
01 INVCODE PIC XXXX.

WORKING-STORAGE SECTION.

01    STRING.
      03    FIRST-PART PIC X(16) INIT 'CUSTOMER NUMBER '.
      03    CODE PIC XXXX.
      03    SECOND-PART PIC X(12) INIT ' IS INVALID'.
PROCEDURE DIVISION.
MOVE-FIELD.
      MOVE INVCODE TO CODE.
      STOP RUN.
```

Table 7.2. Sample COBOL Module.

In order to use formal verification rigorously, a significant foundation in mathematics is required and techniques, notably VDM[2], exist which permit their use in a systematic way. Though such discussion goes beyond the scope of this book, an attempt is made shortly to cover some issues in formal verification.

(1) Informal verification
Informal verification is appropriate only where the module code is a trivial implementation of the specification. Consider figure 6.24, which is a structure chart for the 'display customer details' transaction. An example of a trivial module would be modules which format error messages, so let's consider the 'FORMAT INVALID CUSTOMER-NO MESSAGE' module.

The data dictionary would contain an entry for the full text of the error message. Assume it is 'CUSTOMER NUMBER XXXX IS INVALID'. So the module involves embedding the customer-no parameter, which is in some way invalid, into the error message string. Table 7.2 shows the module implemented in COBOL. Now it is still important to perform an informal verification here, even though it seems such a trivial module. For example, typical que   s might be as follows:

- Are the number of characters in the parameter the same as those allocated in the string?
- Is the type of the parameter consistent with the type in the string?
- Is the type of the parameter and string field appropriate for its purpose? (For example, when validating for a numeric field, it might be necessary to

receive it into a character field for validation purposes. Only when it is known to be correct should it be converted to a numeric field.)

(2) Formal verification

The first thing to be said about verifying modules is that there is a wide variety of module to consider. Sometimes modules may contain only straightforward sequences of instructions; in some there will be selection constructs; in others there will be iterations.

Most modules will contain combination of these. On top of these differences some modules will contain only elementary data items such as integer or real, whereas others will contain composite data structures such as records or entity occurrences. A number of examples will be covered to illustrate some of the different problem areas to be encountered, but first it is necessary to provide some theoretical background.

Any program or module can be considered as a mathematical function. In mathematics, a function is defined as a 'set of ordered pairs in which the first element is unique'. In fact, there is a lot more to this definition than meets the eye. Consider the following simple module:

```
var  i : integer;
begin
    i := i + 1;
end.
```

Now , the 'set of ordered pairs' in the definition refers to the inputs and outputs of the module, so if the number 1 is input, the number 2 is output. This is an ordered pair and is written (1,2). Since i can be any integer, there are an infinite number of ordered pairs for this function. The set of ordered pairs would be written:

$$\{\ldots, (1,2), (2,3), (3,4), (4,5) \ldots\}$$

where the braces represent 'the set of' and the '...' represent a continuation of the same pattern or sequence.

Some functions may have a finite number of ordered pairs, in which case it would be possible to write down every ordered pair (or member) of the set. However, it can become unwieldy, so shorthand forms are permitted such as:

$$\{(i, i + 1)).(i \; \varepsilon \; Z)\}$$

This is the way a mathematician might write down the function. The new symbols are:

'.' which can be translated to 'such that'.

'ε' which stands for 'is a member of'.

'Z' is 'the set of integer numbers' (sets are always described with capitals).

So the whole expression can be read as 'the set of ordered pairs where the second element is one more than the first such that the first element is a member of the set of integer numbers'. (Observe that since the set of integer numbers is infinite, the second element of the ordered pairs is also always a member of the set of integer numbers.)

It should now be clear why mathematicians prefer the shorthand – it is far more concise and precise. It is also a bit clumsy to keep referring to the first or second elements, so names are given to the set of each of these. The domain is the set of first elements in an ordered pair of a function; the range is the set of second elements in an ordered pair of a function.

Sometimes programs or modules use more than one variable, so the next question is how to describe functions with, say, two variables. The notation is extended as follows:

$$\{((i,j), (i+1, j+2)).(i,j \ \varepsilon \ Z)\}$$

A module which would mimic this function would be:

```
variable i, j : integer;
begin
    i := i+1;
    j := j+2;
end.
```

7.2 DATA SPACE VERIFICATION

The data space is the set of all instantiations of defined variables, i.e. the set of all possible valid combinations of values that the variables can assume. So for the first module discussed, since there is only one variable, the data space is the set Z. However, the second module has two variables i and j. So the data space is $\{(i,j).(i,j \ \varepsilon \ Z)\}$.

Note that the concept of data space is not the same thing as a function – in fact it is a totally different concept altogether. A data space defines all potential combinations of input or output values that a program may take. A data state is one instance (or one member) of the data space. So, for the second module, an input data state could be (−100, −1000). For that matter an output data state could also be (−100, −1000).

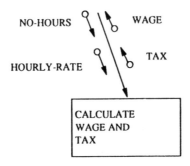

Fig. 7.3. Sample calculation module.

However, in practice not all potential combinations are valid combinations in terms of what a program or module has to do. This is because the domain can be a proper subset (i.e. contains some but not all of the members) of the data space. In fact, this is frequently seen in computer programs, e.g. variables may be defined as real or integer, yet the domain for a particular function may be restricted to the set of natural numbers N, i.e. {0,1,2,3,...}. It is vitally important therefore when specifying a module to take care over the exact limits of a variable's domain. This would be included in the design documentation.

We are now ready to apply this background theory to module verification. Consider the module in figure 7.3. The data dictionary provides the following information:

no-hours is an integer $>=0$
hourly-rate is a real number >0
wage is a real number $>=0$
tax is a real number $>=0$
wage is defined as (no-hours * hourly-rate * 3)/4
tax is defined as (no-hours * hourly-rate)/4

The module might be coded as follows:

```
var : nohours : integer;
     hrate, wage, tax : real;
begin
     wage := hrate * nohours;
     tax := wage/4;
     wage := wage – tax;
end.
```

By scanning the code in the module, we can examine the implications for the data space:

(1) Input data space combinations
From the data dictionary it is known that no-hours is greater than or equal to zero and hourly-rate is greater than zero. This means that the data space for wage is any real number greater than or equal to zero. So the first question is whether a wage equal to zero might cause problems later on in the code. In fact, it does not in this case. Tax also has a data space of any real number greater than or equal to zero, but from the second line tax $<=$ wage (if wage is zero, so is tax.) So, the final output data space for wage is consistent with the specification.

(2) Overflow considerations
Computers are finite machines. Although the maximum number, whether it be integer or real, can sometimes be very large, there is still a limit to the magnitude of a number that can be held on a computer. A problem may arise in any calculation in which addition, multiplication, exponentation, subtraction (by a negative number) or division (by a number less than one) takes place. Although some languages such as Ada have built-in exception handling procedures for this, unfortunately other languages do not.

One way of ensuring integrity is to define the limit of the domains in the specification. So, no-hours could be defined as $\{0,1,2,\ldots,168\}$ say, and hourly-rate as $\{x \varepsilon R.(0<x<=100)\}$. As long as the upper limits of the calculated variables are within the known upper limits for their types, then the program will work as it ought to.

Lastly, remember that very large negative numbers cause overflow just as easily as very large positive numbers.

(3) Artificially restricted ranges
It often makes sense to restrict the range of a variable, because values outside the restricted range have no meaning in the context of the problem. This is why ranges in particular are often limited to non-negative numbers – for example, a negative age has no real meaning. Again, it is important to look at the data space for each output variable and confirm it matches the specified range. Suppose the specification of the module were changed so that a standard tax deduction of, say, 10 units was made instead of 25 per cent of range. This could cause a range violation, because it would be possible for the variable tax to take on a value in range $\{(-10<=tax<0).(tax \varepsilon R)\}$. Either the range for tax was wrongly specified or, more likely, the specification for

calculating tax was wrongly defined. Either way, this kind of verification can highlight problems earlier, thereby reducing the cost of correction.

Range violations can be pervasive in their effect and are not always as straightforward as the above suggests. For example, a variable may be used as the index of an array. If the value goes outside the declared bounds of the array, then clearly something is happening which was not intended. Most languages do not provide any in-built checks for this. This makes the verification process all the more necessary.

(4) Zero divide

Another way in which the integrity of the data space may be jeopardised is by the zero divide condition, which occurs, of course, when the denominator in a division is equal to zero. (This is really a special case of overflow.) The problem can be avoided by inserting a test for the zero condition immediately prior to the division.

(5) Mixed mode arithmetic

Mixed mode arithmetic occurs where variables of different types are used in the same expression, e.g. reals and integers. Output data spaces can be affected by mixed mode arithmetic, particularly where truncation occurs. Also different compilers and machines will respond differently in terms of the accuracy of such calculations. All computations should be examined to identify whether mixed mode arithmetic is taking place and if its effect may be significant. For example, if the variable on the left hand side of an assignment statement is an integer and reals appear on the right hand side, truncation is likely. This may not be intended as far as the specification is concerned.

Another problem area arises in comparing two variables where one is real and the other integer, as in 'if a = i'. Because of the way real numbers are held, the test may be inaccurate and hence the program will not perform as specified.

(6) Selection constructs

The presence of selection constructs complicate data space verification somewhat. Each option in a selection construct must be examined for data space integrity since each is a possible execution path. The impact of selection constructs on this kind of verification is that it increases the amount of analysis required.

Sometimes with selection constructs, a variable's domain may not be completely covered. Consider the following code:

```
begin
    wage := hrate * nohours;
    if wage >=25 then
        tax := wage/5;
    if wage >=50 then
        tax : = wage/4;
    wage := wage - tax;
end.
```

In the above example, assuming that the hrate and nohours have domains as defined earlier, there is no condition to cover $\{(0<=wage<25).wage \; \varepsilon \; R\}$. Now this may be perfectly reasonable from the point of view that employees earning less than a certain amount do not pay tax at all. Equally, it may be an oversight. The point is that verifying variables which are used in selection constructs in this manner is worthwhile since it may identify part of a domain which has been overlooked. There is another related problem in the above example which is to do with the output data space of tax. If wage is indeed less than 25 then the output data space for tax is not defined! (Consider last line of code.) So both input data spaces and output data spaces have to be examined.

(7) Iteration constructs

Like selection constructs, iteration constructs complicate the verification process. However, they are a necessary construct. The best way to consider iterations is as mathematical functions in their own right with input variables and output variables. Consider the following code:

```
begin
    total := 0;
    while (no <> -1) do
    begin
        readln (no);
        total := total + no;
    end;
end.
```

The problem with the above program is a variation of the overflow problem considered earlier. If enough positive numbers are input, then an overflow will occur in performing the addition. Here no amount of domain restriction on the input variable will stop this occurring.

7.3 LOGIC VERIFICATION

Considering modules as if they are mathematical functions gives some insight into the likely correctness of the module, since we can explore the relationship between the input data space and output space. But, it does not go far enough. Just because data spaces are compatible does not prove that the logic inside the module is correct. For example, c := a + b and c := a * b may have the same output data space, but they clearly are two different calculations.

To understand more properly what logic verification is, it is necessary to recognise a major difference between a mathematical function and a module. Consider the function:

$$\{((a,b),(a+b,a-b).(a,b \,\varepsilon\, Z))\}$$

In mathematics, the symbols a and b are invariant in meaning within the function. So if the input data state is a=1 and b=2 then the output data state is a=3 and b=-1. This is called referential transparency. It would be quite wrong to implement the above in a program in the following way:

```
begin
        a := a+b;
        b := a-b;
end
```

This is because the original value in 'a' is overwritten with a new value, so the second statement does not use the original value of 'a'. This problem is referred to as interference and is basically due to the sequential manner in which most programming languages work. Although it cuts across a lot of mathematics, the way round this, for the purpose of an introduction here, is to consider a mathematical function as a 'simultaneous' mapping between the input variables and the output variables. This then allows us to simulate a mathematical function in a computer program or module.

7.3.1 Verification of sequential constructs

If variables are non-interfering, then the order in which the calculations are performed inside a program does not matter. In this case, all that is required is to check that each statement matches its counterpart in the specification (assuming the programming language used contains the requisite instructions). However, if the variables are interfering then some way has to be found to distinguish between one version of a variable and another. A commonly

WAGE		**TAX**
LINE 1	$WAGE_1 = HRATE_0 * NOHOURS_0$	$TAX_1 = TAX_0$
LINE 2	$WAGE_2 = WAGE_1$	$TAX_2 = WAGE_1/4$
LINE 3	$WAGE_3 = WAGE_2 - TAX_2$	$TAX_3 = TAX_2$

Table 7.3. Notation applied to calculation module.

used notation is to subscript each variable by a number to indicate which line in the program or module it refers to. Table 7.3 contains this notation applied to the wage and tax module introduced earlier. (It is only necessary to track variables which appear on the left hand side of assignment statements.) To 'prove' that the module is logically correct, the final version of the variables must be consistent with the specification in the data dictionary.

(1) Express wage in terms of original variables
This is done by a backward substitution process:

$$\begin{aligned} wage_3 &= wage_2 - tax_2 \\ &= wage_1 - wage_1/4 \\ &= 3*wage_1/4 \\ &= 3*hrate_0*nohours_0/4 \end{aligned}$$

This matches exactly the specification in the data dictionary for wage.

(2) Express tax in terms of original variables

$$\begin{aligned} tax_3 &= tax_2 \\ &= wage_1/4 \\ &= hrate_0 * nohours_0 / 4 \end{aligned}$$

This matches the specification for tax.

7.3.2 Verification of selection constructs

There are three basic kinds of selection construct. These are the IF-THEN, the IF-THEN-ELSE and the CASE construct. They can all be defined using the same general format. The format is:

$$[c1 \rightarrow s1 \mid c2 \rightarrow s2 \mid \ldots cn \rightarrow sn]$$

where $c1, c2 \ldots cn$ are conditions and $s1, s2 \ldots sn$ are sequences of statements. The square brackets are used to denote that it is a specification. Specifications by convention usually appear at the beginning of a piece of code.

Because all of the domain of a variable has to be considered, a method is required in the notation which caters for those parts of the domain that have not been explicitly covered. For instance, the implication in an IF-THEN construct is that if the test is false then nothing (i.e. no assignment) takes place. Consider the following specification:

[wage > 50 → tax := wage/4 | ELSE → IDENTITY]

The phrase 'ELSE → IDENTITY' is given to mean that where previous conditions have not been met then the mapping is the identity function, i.e. any variables retain their original values. The IF-THEN construct is the most straightforward implementation of this kind of pattern, because the non-existence of an ELSE clause ensures that variables do not change their value.

Similarly, consider the following specification:

[wage > 50 → tax := wage/4 | wage <=50 → tax:=wage/5]

or

[wage > 50 → tax := wage/4 | ELSE → tax := wage/5]

The IF-THEN-ELSE construct is a straightforward implementation of this pattern.

In many ways the CASE construct is just an extended IF-THEN-ELSE construct. There are two important points to remember about a CASE construct. The first is that the conditions are tested from left to right until a condition which is true is reached. At this point the defined sequence of statements corresponding to that condition is processed and then control returns to the next statement after the CASE construct. This is true even if subsequent conditions are also true. The second point is that, as far as we are concerned, the CASE construct always has a catch-all clause at the end to deal with those parts of the domain not explicitly tested.

So, the CASE construct used earlier would be specified:

[(mark) 70...100 → (grade :=) "A" | 60...69 → "B"
| 50..59 → "C" | 0...49 → "F"
| ELSE → OUT OF RANGE MESSAGE]

(1) Verification of IF-THEN and IF-THEN-ELSE constructs
These two constructs are dealt with together because of their similarity of specification. The basic approach is to consider each condition separately, and prove that it is correct for the part of the domain that it represents. If all

conditions are correct for their respective domain partitions then the selection construct meets its specification. Consider the following:

    [wage > 50 → tax := wage/4 | ELSE → IDENTITY]
        if wage > 50 then
           tax := wage/4;
        endif.

To prove this correct, we need to prove each partition correct.

(a) partition 1.   wage > 50 → tax := wage/4
     This is trivially true.
(b) partition 2.   ELSE → IDENTITY

If WAGE <= 50 then no assignments take place, so variables retain their original value.

   In this example, it is to be hoped that tax was initialised to zero before the selection construct began, otherwise the value of tax would be undefined for this partition.

   Consider the following:

    [wage > 50 → tax := wage/4 | ELSE → tax := wage/5]
    If wage > 50 then
        tax := wage/4;
    else
        tax := wage/5;
    endif.

Again, each partition is considered separately.

(a) partition 1 is identical to the previous example
(b) partition 2 is ELSE → tax := wage/5

If the result of the test is false then this path is executed, which trivially matches the specification.

   Sometimes it will not be so obvious that a particular clause matches its counterpart in the specification, especially so when sequences of statements apply instead of single statements. In such case the rules for verifying sequences have to be followed.

(2) Verification of the CASE construct
Sometimes, as in the example converting marks to grades, the proof is just an extension of the approach used to verify an IF-THEN-ELSE construct. This

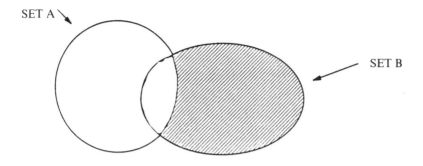

SET A: SET OF CUSTOMERS WHOSE STATUS = "A"
SET B: SET OF ORDERS WHOSE VALUE > 1000

Fig. 7.4. Implication of use of case statement.

is because all the partitions are discrete, i.e. given that each partition is a set, the sets do not intersect and can be called a simple CASE construct. However, there are occasions when partitions do overlap (complex CASE construct) and these have to be dealt with slightly differently. Consider the following specification:

[customer-status = "A" → priority := 1
| order-value > 1000 → priority := 2
| ELSE → priority :=3]

Remember the way that CASE works. It tests from left to right until it finds a partition condition that is true, then it stops. This means that if it gets to the second condition, the first condition must have been false. Figure 7.4 illustrates the circumstance.

Expressed more mathematically, if we get to the second condition and it evaluates to true, we say:

$\neg c1 \wedge c2$

i.e. c1 is false and condition 2 is true. Similarly, for the third condition, we have $\neg c1 \wedge \neg c2 \wedge c3$ and so on.

So for the example above there are three partitions to be proved:

partition 1 : customer-status = 'A'
partition 2 : customer-status $\neg$ = 'A' AND order-value > 1000

partition 3 : customer-status $\neg$ = 'A' AND order-value $<=$ 1000

If the programming language used has a CASE construct which requires that all partitions are discrete, then a complex CASE construct has to be converted to a simple CASE construct. Nevertheless, the implications of the complex CASE construct have to be well understood, both when identifying constructs as well as verifying them.

7.3.3 Verification of iteration constructs

The verification of iteration constructs is the most difficult kind of verification to perform. Iteration constructs are a necessary tool in the toolbox of structured programming. We cannot live without them, so we have to learn to use them properly and therefore verify them as far as we reasonably can.

The easiest kind of iteration construct to verify is the fixed iteration construct. In this construct the number of iterations is known, when the iteration construct is executed. Consider the following module to compute the sum of values of elements in an array:

$$[s = \sum_{i=1}^{n} Ar\,(i)]$$

var n, s, i : integer (n $>$ 0)
       Ar : array (1..n) of integer;

begin
    s := 0;
    for i := 1 to n do
        s := s + Ar (i);
    endfor;
end.

The proof for fixed iteration constructs is a bit like that for sequence constructs because they can be written out as a sequence, i.e.:

$s_0 := 0;$
$s_1 := s_0 + Ar\,(1);$
$s_2 := s_1 + Ar\,(2);$
$s_3 := s_2 + Ar\,(3);$
$s_n := s_{n-1} + Ar\,(n);$

Since **s** = 0, this reduces to:

$$s_n = Ar(1) + Ar(2) + Ar(3) \ldots Ar(n);$$
$$= \sum_{i=1}^{n} Ar(i);$$

= specification.

Notice that the FOR construct and the prior assignment to the variable s were really all part of the same proof. In fact, it is quite usual to include any initialisation assignments with proofs for iterative constructs as well, as we shall see shortly.

Since the fixed iteration construct is easy to use and prove, it should always be chosen in preference to the more complex variable iteration constructs, WHILE-DO and REPEAT-UNTIL.

It would have been possible to have implemented a program using a WHILE-DO construct to meet the above specification. It would look like this:

$$[s = \sum_{i=1}^{n} Ar(i)]$$

```
var n, s, i : integer (n > 0)
    Ar : array [1..n] of integer;
begin
    i := 0;
    s := 0;
    while i ¬ = n do
        i := i + 1;
        s := s + Ar (i);
    endwhile;
end.
```

Apart from taking up more lines, it is a lot more work to prove correct. The stages of the proof are:

- Check that the loop will terminate.
- Identify an invariant condition.
- Check that the invariant is correct when the loop is begun.
- Check that the invariant is correct when the loop ends.
- Check that the invariant is correct during each execution of the loop.

(1) Check that the loop will terminate
This is demonstrated by the following argument. Variables i and n are both integers. Initially, variable i is set to zero and variable n is greater than zero. Each iteration of the loop adds 1 to the variable **i**. So, there must come a point when variable **i** equals variable **n**. At that point, the loop terminates.

(2) Identify an invariant condition
The concept of an invariant is, for some people, an elusive one. The use of invariants is only required in variable iteration constructs, so at least they are not required elsewhere. An invariant condition is a truth which is valid no matter what stage of the iteration is being considered, hence the reason why the checking is done at the beginning, during, and at the end of the loop. But what is the nature of the truth? What expression would be true for all stages of the above loop? Well, if we think about what the loop is trying to do and how it is doing it, one valid statement might be 'the invariant is the sum of the elements of array so far'. The 'so far' phrase is vital, because it reflects the fact that as variable i is incremented from 0 to n, the value contained in variable s holds the sum up to that position in the array. Clearly only when it reaches n, will the value in variable s equal the sum of the whole array.

Expressed more mathematically, the invariant is

$$s = \sum_{j=0}^{i} Ar(j)$$

Note the variable j can take on the value zero in the above expression, which takes account of s_0. For our purposes, we can assume that $Ar(0)$, which is outside the bounds for the array Ar, is equal to zero. So the snapshot taken at the beginning of the loop is also catered for, i.e. $s_0 = 0$.

(3) Check that the invariant is correct when the loop is begun
This has just been discussed informally. More formally, recall the invariant is:

$$s = \sum_{j=0}^{i} Ar(j)$$

At initialisation, $i = 0$

$$s = \sum_{j=0}^{0} Ar(j) = Ar(0) = 0$$

But in the program at initialisation, $s_0 = 0$. So this is also correct.

(4) Check that the invariant is correct when the loop ends
At termination $i = n$. So the invariant becomes

$$s = \sum_{j=0}^{n} Ar(j)$$

$$= Ar(0) + \sum_{j=1}^{n} Ar(j)$$

$$= 0 + \text{specification}$$
$$= \text{specification}$$

(5) Check that the invariant is correct during each execution of the loop
This check uses mathematical induction as the basis for proving correctness. As software engineers we do not need to know the proof for mathematical induction or indeed understand it as such. It is sufficient that we are able to follow the steps outlined.

The induction theorem says that if we assume that the invariant condition is true for the ith iteration and can deduce that the (ith + 1) iteration is of the same general format, then it follows that the invariant is true for all iterations of the loop.

Before applying this to the example, a little more notation is required. Because the variable i will hold a different value depending on the iteration, it is necessary to be able to distinguish the value in i from one iteration to the next. This is similar to the problem in sequence constructs. So, for example, the variable i′ is given to mean the value in variable i, one iteration later; i.e. i′ is equivalent to i + 1 in the example.

So the proof runs as follows:

1 The invariant is assumed i.e. $s = \sum_{j=0}^{i} Ar(j)$.

2 The desired conclusion is identified i.e. $s' = \sum_{j=0}^{i'} Ar(j)$.

3 By executing the program for one more iteration, we get:

$i' := i + 1;$

$s' = s + Ar(i');$

$$= \sum_{j=0}^{i} Ar(j) + Ar(i + 1);$$

$$= \sum_{j=0}^{i+1} Ar(j);$$

$$= \sum_{j=0}^{i'} Ar(j);$$

= desired conclusion.

Identifying an invariant after the code for a loop has been written can be more difficult than identifying it when the loop is being written. Indeed, many people feel that formal verification methods generally are not worth the effort. That argument has some validity if the proof is done after the module has been constructed rather than while it is being constructed. But if formal verification is seen as part of the construction process then the additional time spent is rewarded in increased quality. Let's work through an example in which formal verification is part of the construction process. Figure 7.5 shows a module which checks whether a code is a member of a set of valid codes, which is a common validation problem.

From the data dictionary it is established that code is a positive integer (> 0) and array is an integer array. This is a realistic problem even if implemented in languages like Pascal, which through the use of TYPE allows

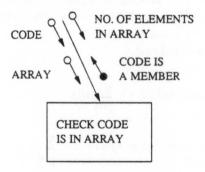

Fig. 7.5. Array membership problem.

members of sets to be defined. This is because in a commercial situation the members of the set may be volatile, i.e. change constantly, and clearly constant recompilation would be undesirable. This is why the array and number of elements are also parameters in the module call.

The specification for this function could be written in mathematical terms as [found := code ϵ array $(1 \ldots n)$] where found is Boolean.

Step 1 – visualisation

Here we simply think about how the module will operate. It is clear that we need to go through the array element by element, testing as we go along until we find a match, at which point we need go no further. But the code may not be in the array, in which case we would continue checking until the end of the array is reached.

Step 2 – identification of construct

Going through each element of the array indicates that an iteration construct is required. Because the exact number of iterations to be performed is not known at the start of the loop, a variable iteration construct is required, i.e. either WHILE or REPEAT-UNTIL. Given that there is at least one element in the array, there will be at least one iteration of the loop so either construct could be chosen. We will choose REPEAT-UNTIL, since WHILE has already been discussed.

Step 3 – codification/verification

As stated earlier, we will interleave parts of the formal verification process with the codification process. The broad format of the REPEAT-UNTIL construct is:

INITIALISATION
REPEAT
    LOOP BODY
UNTIL END-CONDITION.

Step 3.1 – consider termination criteria

Somewhere inside the loop progress has to be made through each element of the array. This suggests a statement such as $i := i + 1$. In addition, to fulfil the needs of the verification it must be suitably initialised and have a check for termination. So, the module code becomes:

    $<$any other initialisations$>$
    i := 0;
    repeat

        i := i + 1;
        <rest of loop body>
    until i = n.

This allows us to meet the verification argument.

Step 3.2 – identify invariant
The invariant condition must be true at the beginning, the end, and during the loop execution. However, note in the REPEAT-UNTIL construct, that the test is made after the execution of each iteration. This need not change the invariant (since an invariant must be true at all points in the loop), but it will change the place at which the test for repeating the loop is made.

   The invariant in the last example, represented the 'sum so far'. A similar approach may be taken here, by suggesting that the invariant is 'no match so far'. However, unlike the last example, there is a specific problem with the current element. Here the current element may yield a match. So a better description of the invariant is to say 'no match before current element'. Specifying this more mathematically:

A match would be : (code = Ar(j))
A match before current element (i): $(\exists j.1 <= j < i)$(code = Ar(j))
No match before current element (i): $\neg (\exists j.1 <= j < i)$(code = Ar(j))
('$\exists$' means 'there exists')

In fact, this particular structure of invariant occurs regularly.

Step 3.3 – consider initial loop criteria
We have to show that the invariant is correct when the loop is begun. For a REPEAT-UNTIL construct the test is made after the first iteration, so variable i = 1. The invariant becomes:

$$\neg (\exists j. 1 <= j < 1)(code = A(j))$$

Since there cannot be a j such that $j >= 1$ and $j < 1$, the invariant is certainly true.

Step 3.4 – consider end loop criteria
We have to show that the invariant is correct when the loop ends. Now there is still one inconsistency between the visualisation narrative and the module code as it is defined so far and that is that when a match is found, no further iterations need take place. So the termination criteria needs to be modified to read 'UNTIL FOUND OR i = n'. (Note that this still meets the criteria in step

3.1). Since there are two exclusive components to the test, these need to be dealt with separately with respect to checking the invariant.

(a) found = true
This is to cover the situation where a match is found, i.e. when a match is found then the variable found is set to true. This suggests that the statement might be:

```
if (code = Ar(i)) then
    found := true;
endif.
```

This would be substituted for the rest of the loop body. This allows us to deduce that the invariant is correct as follows:
    If found is true then (code = Ar (i)) must be true. If a match is found on the current element it follows that there could not have been a match up till now. Therefore the invariant condition holds.

The module code now looks like:

```
<any other initialisations>
i = 0;
repeat
    i := i + 1;
    if (code = Ar(i)) then
        found := true;
    endif;
until found or i = n.
```

(b) i = n
Actually, i = n is not the correct expression here. In fact, it is 'FOUND = FALSE AND i = n', because the clause after UNTIL is a standard selection construct.

found = false implies that code $\neg$ = Ar(n) and the invariant tells us that since i = n

$$\neg (\exists j. \; 1 <= j < n - 1)(code = Ar(j))$$

Therefore, combining these facts, we have

$$\neg (\exists j. \; 1 <= j < n)(code = Ar(j))$$

which is consistent with the invariant.
    If not already recognised it is necessary that either found is initalised to

false, or an IF-THEN-ELSE construct is used in the loop body. This implies the module code as follows:

```
found := false;
i := 0;
repeat
    i := i + 1;
    if (code = Ar(i)) then
        found := true;
    endif;
until found or i = n.
```

Step 3.5 – check invariant is correct during loop
This is now the last remaining step in the verification process. Recall that what is required is to check that the invariant is preserved from one iteration to the next. This particular example will highlight a common misunderstanding with invariants and therefore is an opportunity to clear it up.

The REPEAT-UNTIL termination tests are made at the end of each iteration. Figure 7.6 illustrates this.

To confirm invariant preservation, one full iteration has to be executed, starting from the test point in one iteration and ending at the test point at the next. The problem arises because during that execution cycle, it is possible to exit from the construct, which seems at odds with the concept of an invariant

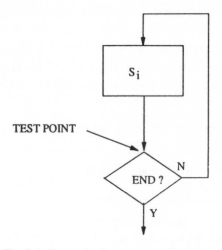

Fig. 7.6. Test point for repeat-until construct.

condition. As far as this kind of verification is concerned it is only necessary to consider those sets of circumstances which permit another full iteration of the loop to be executed. In other words, there are four verification tasks, one checks termination, another checks invariant preservation and so on. Each on their own only does part of the task; together they cover the whole iteration.

1 The invariant is $\neg (\exists j. 1 <= j < i)(\text{code} = \text{Ar}(j))$
2 The desired conclusion is $\neg (\exists j. 1 <= j < i')(\text{code} = \text{Ar}(j))$
3 A number of factors are known:
   (a) the invariant gives us 'no match before i'
   (b) found = false
   (c) $i \neg = n$
   (d) $i' = i + 1$

Point (b) is useful. If found is false, that means that $(\text{code} \neg = \text{Ar}(i + 1))$. Combining that with point (a), we can say that there is 'no match before i + 1' i.e. $\neg (\exists j. 1 <= j < i + 1)(\text{code} = \text{Ar}(j))$. But $i' = i + 1$, so we have the desired conclusion.

7.4 SUMMARY

It has to be accepted that this may have been a difficult chapter for some readers to absorb and identify with. So let's put it in perspective. Even if all software engineering students left their courses armed with skills in formal mathematical methods, they would soon find that a large proportion of the software industry today is not practising mathematical ideas or indeed is even aware of most of them. Yet, there should be little doubt that these techniques can improve the quality of the code produced, though the price is increased time and the ability to overcome some mathematical notation. Again, we find ourselves in a costs versus benefits situation. Do the costs outweigh the benefits? At the end of the last chapter it was observed that the deployment of reusable modules could reduce the number of modules to be written in a system by around 50%. Some modules will be reused over and over again. So, what price quality? Having said that, it is also true that some modules are relatively trivial and therefore it is less certain if additional benefits will obtain from the use of mathematical methods ðn these. Perhaps a realistic approach is to survey each structure chart and identify the type of verification (i.e. formal or informal) that is appropriate for each module based on complexity and scope for reusability and then proceed accordingly.

In this chapter, the following concepts have been introduced:

- The idea of stepwise refinement was presented as the means by which module code can be constructed. Though stepwise refinement has four distinct tasks (i.e. visualisation, identification of construct, codification and verification), it was shown by example that it is desirable to perform codification and verification as a single activity.
- A cause-effect graph was proposed as a means of identifying essential sequences in a task.
- Some mathematical concepts were introduced which included basic set notation and the idea of functions and data spaces. Perhaps the hardest concept was the idea of an invariant which is of use in a variable iteration construct. An invariant is a statement which is true regardless of where you are within the construct.
- Data space verification explored a number of tests which can be used to check the integrity of the input and output data spaces.
- Logic verification was concerned about whether the program code was consistent with its specification. Because code comprises sequential, selection and iterative constructs, each construct was examined in turn and examples provided to illustrate typical information system situations.

7.5 FURTHER READING

1 Myers, G. (1979) *The Art of Software Testing*, John Wiley, New York, discusses the cause-effect graph. Though Myers presents the graph as a technique for aiding testing, he does make the point that the graph is a good way of identifying ambiguities and incompleteness in specifications.
2 Jones, C. (1986) *Systematic Software Development using VDM*, Prentice-Hall, Englewood Cliffs, New Jersey, is recommended for those interested in exploring a formal notation.
Gries, D. (1981) *The Science of Programming*, Springer-Verlag, New York, is a good introduction to the problem domain.

7.6 EXERCISES

1   Figure 6.25 shows a structure chart for 'INSERT CUSTOMER DETAILS'. Scan each module identifying those which are candidates for formal verification and those for informal verification.

2 Formally verify the 'VALIDATE CUSTOMER-BALANCE' module in figure 6.25 against both data space and logic criteria. Make any appropriate assumptions about the size of data items, etc.

3 Using stepwise refinement, develop and verify the code for the 'GET VALID CUSTOMER DATA' module in figure 6.25. Note that there needs to be a variable iteration construct to allow return to the screen to collect re-entered data. Use any target language you wish.

Chapter 8
Testing and Debugging

8.1 INTRODUCTION

In this chapter the topics of testing and debugging will be considered. Because the method described in this book partitions programs into relatively small modules, many problems that confront other approaches are avoided when it comes to testing and debugging. This is because large programs are very difficult to test in a comprehensive way whereas small modules though not at all trivial are at least easier to test. Of course an additional burden is integration testing which confirms that modules work together to form a program, but on balance it is still considered worthwhile to create small modules.

First of all, let's review the basic idea of testing.

(1) What is testing?
Testing is the act of confirming that some piece of executable code exactly meets its objectives. The obvious interpretation is that a program or module must do everything required of it, i.e. it should not do less than required. Equally, it should not do more. For example, if a matrix is passed to a module so that some totalling can be performed, that matrix should not be corrupted in doing so. Although this is unlikely with the techniques described earlier, it illustrates the point and brings us to the second issue.

(2) Testing should be error-seeking
The attitude that one adopts while testing is important. One has to be careful of the self-fulfilling prophecy, i.e. a programmer wants the module to be right, so the test data invented will tend to confirm rather than deny that desire. There is little point to this kind of testing. No, somehow the programmer has to be more critical of the work done and logically seek ways in which the program can be broken. Only by doing so can one begin to have confidence that one's program will stand up to the rigours of real-world use. One approach which can work well is to get programmers to create test data for someone else's modules.

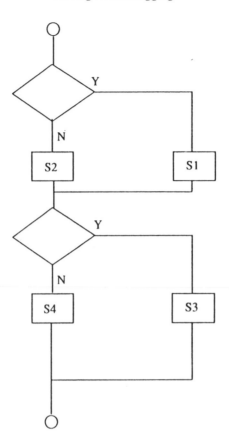

Fig. 8.1. Two consecutive selection constructs.

(3) Exhaustive testing is just not practical

Exhaustive testing is the name given to a kind of testing that checks every conceivable path in a program. The problem is a combinatorial one. Consider figure 8.1. Here two selection constructs occur one after the other. Assuming it is semantically feasible (as sometimes it is not) there are four possible paths. Iteration is worse. Consider the WHILE loop in figure 8.2. Depending on the value of the variable upon input to the WHILE loop, there may be up to a very large number of iterations, i.e. different paths traversed. Exhaustive testing would have to test each one of these cases i.e. case 1 = 0 iterations, case 2 = 1 iteration ... case n+1 = n iterations. But the real problem arises when constructs are combined with each other. Suppose the two selection constructs in figure 8.1 were embedded in the while construct in figure 8.2.

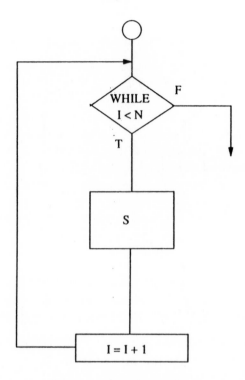

Fig. 8.2. A WHILE construct.

Then each iteration has four possible paths. Simple combinatorial logic tells that there are four to the power n possible paths in an iterative construct with n iterations. So even for relatively simple modules, it can be seen that exhaustive testing is really not a practical approach.

(4) Seek cost-effective testing
As in most issues in software engineering the secret lies in weighing up the costs and the benefits. What is required is to identify a set of test cases which is likely to find a high proportion of errors yet not be uneconomic in terms of the programmer's time or indeed the machine resources used.

There are two kinds of testing. These are black-box testing and white-box testing. Since a black-box is something that you cannot see inside of, black-box testing is testing which does not involve knowledge of the internals of a module, i.e. only the specification is used to generate test cases. White-box testing, sometimes called glass-box testing, by contrast, does rely on the detailed logic or code inside a module to help generate test cases.

8.2 WHITE-BOX TESTING

There are no algorithms for generating white-box test data, partly because of the cost-effective aspect mentioned above and partly for other reasons.

Described here is a method for generating white-box test cases by reviewing a checklist of key questions about the module. As each question is addressed, the programmer may add test cases to his list or refine it to give more power to the testing. However, this process is non-trivial and demands careful thought at each stage. As test data is added, the refined list becomes a more comprehensive set of data which is better able to detect errors in the module. In such manner is a hopefully small, yet powerful set of test cases built. Myers[1] formalises these questions in a way as to, in effect, classify each as a separate type of white-box testing:

Has every line of code been executed at least once by the test data? It is a trivial matter to derive test data to ensure the above criterion. Clearly, on its own, it is not particularly useful. One point to watch is in languages like ADA which have exception-handling routines. The programmer should ensure these are invoked too.

Have all default paths been traversed at least once? A default path can occur on a selection or iteration. For a selection, a default path occurs when there is no ELSE clause. For an iteration, a default path occurs only when the type of iteration construct permits zero iterations such as in a while loop. Figures 8.3(a) and 8.3(b) show examples of default paths.

Have all significant combinations of multiple conditions been identified? Multiple conditions can occur on selection and iteration constructs. They complicate matters because they generate permutations of circumstances which have to be verified. Further, there may be redundant combinations. Consider the AND condition in a selection statement such as IF A AND B THEN S.

Clearly there are four permutations:

1 A is true, B is true
2 A is true, B is false
3 A is false, B is true
4 A is false, B is false

One of these combinations is redundant in the sense that it will make no contribution to the testing of the module. This is best illustrated by drawing

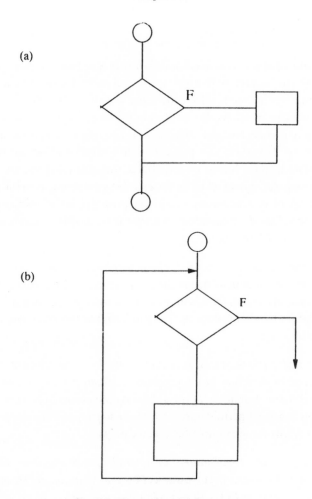

(a)

(b)

Fig. 8.3. Examples of default paths.

the control-flow graph for the AND condition as in figure 8.4. As can be seen there are only three different paths. This is because once A is evaluated to false, it makes no difference what the value of B is. Note that if the sequence in the statement had been IF B AND A THEN S, then if B is false, it does not matter what A is.

A similar conclusion obtains with the OR condition, although here when the first condition is true it does not matter what the second is. A control-flow graph for the OR condition is shown in figure 8.5. Although, out of vogue now, the control-flow graph, often referred to as the flowchart, is a useful

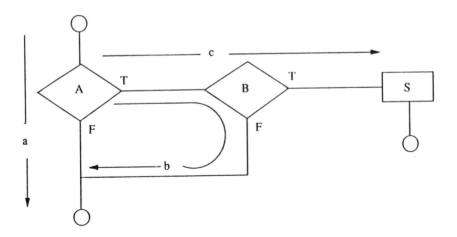

Fig. 8.4. Paths generated by AND condition.

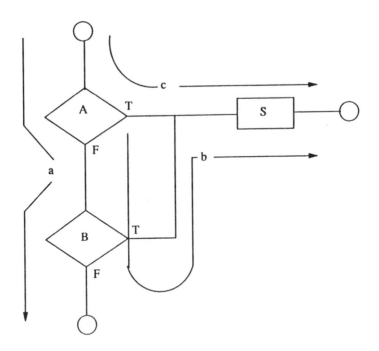

Fig. 8.5. Paths generated by OR condition.

vehicle for identifying significant combinations, particularly so when there are three or more conditions in the multiple condition. In fact, a simple formula can be used to provide the upper limit for the number of independent paths in a control-flow graph. This is known as McCabe's formula for cyclomatic complexity. The formula is:

$$V(G) = P + 1$$

where $V(G)$ is the upper limit of paths in the graph and P is the number of simple conditions.

Observe that this formula is consistent with the conclusions reached above concerning the AND and OR conditions. The reason why the formula only

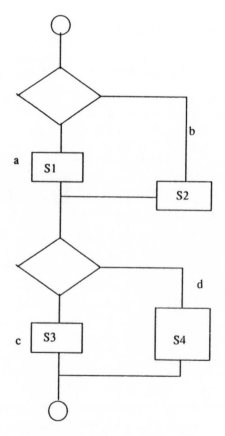

Fig. 8.6. Example of separate tests.

provides an upper limit is because the actual number of independent paths depends on the way in which conditions are combined. Consider figure 8.6. In terms of the number of test cases that need to be generated, we note that there are only two independent paths, i.e. either ac and bd or ad and bc, whereas figure 8.5 had three independent paths a, b and c. In figure 8.5 the testing was nested, whereas in figure 8.6, there only are two separate tests required.

It is suggested that by using the control-flow graph in conjunction with the checklist outlined earlier, a practical way is provided for identifying independent paths and keeping the number of tests to a minimum.

8.3 BLACK-BOX TESTING

One might imagine that a comprehensive list of test cases has been built up using white-box techniques. However, one area of weakness lies in the fact that the test data has been solely generated by consideration of the module code only. There has been no effort placed in determining to what extent the code meets the specification.

The following black-box techniques can usefully supplement the list generated by the white-box approach.

8.3.1 Equivalence partitioning

Equivalence partitioning uses the idea of equivalence classes. An equivalence class is a set of data which as far as the specification is concerned will be treated identically (equivalently). So the object in equivalence partitioning is to identify those classes of data which will cause the module to respond in a different manner from other classes. This is done by reading the specification and creating a list of all characteristics of the program, e.g. field must be numeric, two integers are input. A key concept in the identification of classes is 'negation' i.e. if a characteristic is identified as an equivalence class, then one should immediately negate the characteristic in order to find examples of classes which should cause the module to do something different such as create an error message. Characteristics identified in the specification are valid equivalence classes. Negated characteristics produce invalid equivalence classes. Note that sometimes negated characteristics may produce more than one invalid equivalence class e.g. if a number n must be in a range between say 100 and 500 inclusive, then two invalid equivalence classes are required, one

characteristic	valid equivalence class	invalid equivalent class
first character must be alphabetic	letter	non-letter
next three numeric	all numeric	one character not numeric
range 100-500	in range	above range below range

Table 8.1. Equivalence class table for customer-account-no.

to check n < 100 and the other to check n > 500. Here one invalid equivalent class is insufficient.

Table 8.1 shows an equivalence class table for a customer-account-no. The rule is that the first character must be alphabetic, the next three must be numeric with a range between 100 to 500 inclusive.

So, here three valid equivalence classes and four invalid equivalence classes are generated. Only five test cases are required however because in this example one test case can be used to check all three valid equivalence classes. Invalid equivalent class test cases should never be combined since it is important to check out each error situation individually. The list of test cases identified should be checked against the existing list (produced by the white box technique) to see if there are any new test cases. As stated earlier, equivalence partitioning can identify scenarios not spotted in the white-box approach. This is often because some assumption has been made when writing the code which is not justified. For example, suppose a program expected two numbers but only one was input. How would the program react? If this situation had been overlooked when coding the module, the white-box approach would not have identified a test case for it.

As another example, suppose the programmer tried to test the range of the number and that characters 2, 3 and 4 are numeric by coding the following:

IF NUMBER > '100' AND NUMBER < '500' ...

Using the white-box approach, the programmer would simply assume the correctness of what had been coded and identify appropriate test data for default paths, multiple conditions and so on. Using equivalence partitioning there is a good chance the programmer would see that something was wrong, because there is an invalid equivalence class for testing each individual digit. The act of having to generate test data to test the invalid equivalent class may well be enough to alert the programmer that a mistake had been made. By going back to the specification and using it to generate test cases, equivalence partitioning can identify important new cases not discovered using the white-box approach.

8.3.2 Boundary-value analysis

Intuition tells us to test cases close to boundary conditions in a module. In other words, it is surely more exacting to create test cases for NUMBER = 99, 100, 500, 501 rather than NUMBER = 50, 250, 900 in the example above. Clearly, these do not have to be separate test cases; they could be existing test cases which are modified to test on or near a particular condition. Having said that, it is important not to overwork test cases. It might sometimes be better to have a slightly larger list of cases, where it is clearer exactly what the purpose of each case is. Indeed, when creating the test data list, it is a good idea to include a column with a brief description of the test case.

Two further points remain about boundary-value analysis. The first is that there are other issues implied by boundary-values. For example, if a module uses a file of records, how will the program react if there are no records on the file? If a transaction file is updating a masterfile, have all permutations of end-file conditions been considered? If a module is passed an array, what if it contains zero elements? Has it been tested when it contains its maximum number of elements? And so on. These kinds of limits are also important boundary conditions which demand faithful testing. However, unlike the boundary conditions in a selection construct, it is difficult to be prescriptive about such factors since they are dependent on what is being done in the module. The second point is to observe that boundary-value analysis applies to output conditions as well as input. This is derived from the fact that it is a black-box technique. Again, by analysing the specification, boundary conditions and limits can be identified for output and test cases constructed to test these. Can the module output a file containing no records? Will the module display a mark of 100 or are only two display digits allowed?

Boundary-value analysis is not so mechanistic as some of the other techniques, because it demands creative thinking concerning possibilities at the extremes of the module. It does, however, make a clear contribution to the quality of test cases used, thus increasing the probability of finding errors.

TEST DATA ITEMS	EXPECTED RESULT	DRY RESULT	ACTUAL RESULT	CORRECT
income = -2000	not in range	not in range	not in range	✓
income = 10000	270	270	300	X

Table 8.2. Test Data Results Table.

8.4 DEBUGGING

Debugging is not the same thing as testing. Testing is the attempt to identify errors in a program or module; debugging is the task of identifying the causes of errors. In most circumstances it is better to totally separate the two activities. In other words, prepare a set of test cases as previously described and then run that set of test data against the program or module. (Table 8.2 shows the Test Data Results Table in which results can be formally documented.) Only once this has been done should debugging begin. This is for two reasons. The first is that further test runs may shed some light on the nature of the problem. Secondly, there is an inherent danger in fixing bugs on the fly – you might create more errors. So it is normally much safer, wiser and more cost-effective to debug away from the screen.

Discussion of debugging is considered at the module level. If errors arise at the program level or higher, the first task is to locate the delinquent module. If not obvious, then the technique for doing this is similar to identifying a bug inside a module.

There are three techniques for debugging:

- cause analysis
- the 'binary chop'
- hypothesis testing

(1) Cause analysis
The simplest and often the quickest way of identifying a bug is to look at the code and try to find a reason or combination of reasons why the error occurred. Clearly it is dependent on the situation. Perhaps the wrong variable was used or the logic is wrong. Maybe a variable was not initialised. Because modules should be relatively small, the logic of the whole module and its nuances are often able to be absorbed by the programmer, which makes it easier to debug. With programs of say 50 lines or more this becomes more difficult. At over 200 lines it is effectively impossible.

(2) The binary chop

If cause analysis is not fruitful then one has to look for clues to the cause. Print or display statements can be inserted at points in the program to provide the current values of key variables which may help in finding the error. But where should the statements be inserted? If there is no clue then the binary chop technique may be used to locate the error. Each iteration of the binary chop approximately halves the number of statements to be searched. It works as follows:

1 Identify a point in the module, where everything was known to be correct. This may be the beginning of the module.
2 Identify the point where you have detected something was wrong. This may be the test result or error message.
3 Identify a point roughly mid-way between points 1 and 2, where it is appropriate to insert display statements for the affected variables.
4 If the display statements reveal that the affected variables are correct at this point, then the error must have occurred later in the module. If they are incorrect then it occurred earlier.
5 Repeat the process using the revised information until the error line is located.

(3) Hypothesis testing

Hypothesis testing as used here is not to be confused with hypothesis testing in statistics. But it is concerned with formulating some hypothesis about the cause of an error and then finding a way of confirming the correctness of the hypothesis. Hypothesis testing can be used when some facility or calculation in the program does not appear to be working the way the programmer thinks it should. To confirm this, the programmer writes the smallest possible program to simulate the problem. If the problem still remains, his hypothesis is probably correct. If it does not then he must look for other causes. It is important that a separate program is written to test the hypothesis, rather than, say, deleting lines out of the existing program, because there may be unseen errors in the existing code. Writing from scratch reduces the possibility but does not eliminate it.

8.5 SUMMARY

Testing is a discipline which has never been properly exploited across the industry, probably because the use of monolithic programs mitigates against

Chapter 8

comprehensive testing and therefore the benefits to be gained from testing are somewhat lost. This chapter has attempted to show that testing at the module level is practical and worthwhile and that simple techniques exist which are effective in creating comprehensive test data thereby increasing the likelihood of trapping errors. Debugging as a technique for identifying the causes of problems was also discussed and simple strategies for debugging proposed. The following techniques were discussed:

- White-box testing was proposed as a means of creating a set of test data which covers the significant paths taken within a module.
- The use of the control-flow graph (or flowcharts) was recommended as a way of viewing the problem graphically.
- Equivalence partitioning was introduced as a black-box technique for supplementing the list obtained by white-box means. Black-box techniques concentrate on the inputs and outputs as a way of generating test cases.
- Boundary-value analysis was another black-box technique discussed which improves the quality of the list of test cases by examining the limits of tests made.
- Three strategies for debugging were proposed. These are cause analysis, the binary chop and hypothesis testing.

8.6 FURTHER READING

Myers, G. (1979) *The Art of Software Testing*, John Wiley, New York, is recommended reading for those interested in serious testing.

8.7 EXERCISES

Create lists of test cases for the 'VALIDATE CUSTOMER-BALANCE' module in figure 6.25 and the 'GET VALID CUSTOMER DATA' module also in figure 6.25.

Part B
A Method of System Development

Chapter 9
System Investigation

In this chapter we will explore the first questions the systems analyst asks about the system he has to develop. Because they are the first questions, they reflect for the most part the need to gather information about the system and its problems. The questions asked are:

- What does the current system do?
- What are its problems and what improvements are desired?
- What data does the current system need to store in order to operate?
- Is what has been established so far about the current system correct?

9.1 WHAT DOES THE CURRENT SYSTEM DO?

The purpose of investigating the current system is to learn and document how the system as it currently operates actually works. This is important for two reasons. Firstly, often the systems analyst knows little about the system never mind its problems or indeed the improvements that could be made. So the system investigation is a vehicle for the analyst to learn about the system. Secondly, by documenting the current system using techniques such as the DFD and the data model, the diagrammatic foundation for highlighting problems and specifying improvements is thereby established.

Most of the time there will be an existing system, although not in every case. One unfortunate example of this in recent times has been the need for larger companies, who have had to shed significant sections of their workforce, to set up a redundancy advisory system under which candidates for redundancy can obtain advice on the terms of compensation and other alternatives open to them. Often there is no previous system in operation and therefore no experience amongst staff. In such cases DFDs could be drawn in anticipation of how such systems would operate, although there can be some difficulties with this, since staff may find it difficult to visualise.

But for the most part there is an existing system which is currently manual, computerised or a combination of both. If the existing system was developed using the same method, then provided the documentation is up-to-date, a lot of the effort in this phase is avoided. Otherwise, detailed analysis of existing documentation from departmental procedures manuals, user and operations manuals where they exist is required. However, in either circumstance, it is necessary to interview users to establish their perspective on the system, especially in the area of problems experienced with the current system and improvements they feel could be made.

The particular circumstances of a system with respect to whether there is an existing system or whether it is computerised or not, will determine the way in which this task will proceed.

9.1.1 Create a current physical DFD set using the net-flow technique

Physical DFDs of the current system are prepared by first drawing a context diagram followed by lower-level DFDs. It is to be expected that as some details of the system become apparent, higher-level diagrams may need to be altered. For example, suppose while drawing a level 1 diagram, a copy of a form sent to another department is overlooked. This may only become apparent when drawing a level 2 diagram and is likely to require modification of the level 1 diagram. The process of creating current physical DFDs is therefore an iterative one and the opportunity to use software tools to save time in making such modifications should not be overlooked or underestimated.

Another tactical issue is the way in which the decomposition from level to level is achieved. For example, one reasonable approach to decomposition would be on the basis of departments within system, sections within department and so on, i.e. there would be a context diagram for the system at level 0, level 1 DFDs would show departments, level 2 would show sections and so on. Since the physical DFD set is used as a communication vehicle with users, this approach to partitioning makes for ease of understanding on their part. That partitioning by 'organisation chart' may not make sense from a systems perspective is something which can be addressed later.

The net-flow approach is used at this point because the essential task is one of capture rather than analysis. The analyst at a later stage will review what he has captured to determine its correctness. Also, users seem to relate more easily to diagrams which use the net-flow concept since it equates more to how they see the problem.

9.1.2 Document all current, leaf processes

Leaf processes are processes which are not exploded any further in a DFD set, so they will appear at the lowest levels of the hierarchy. Non-leaf processes in one sense are redundant because they add nothing new, i.e. they are simply the 'sum' of their lower level processes. When it comes to documenting processes, it makes sense therefore only to attempt to record leaf processes. Having said that, for clarification purposes the analyst may sometimes feel it desirable to 'sketch' non-leaf processes, especially where they are complex or are at the boundary of the system.

9.1.3 Document all dataflows and datastores

Examples of these can be obtained during the user interviews. They should be documented using data dictionary techniques.

9.2 WHAT ARE THE CURRENT SYSTEM'S PROBLEMS AND WHAT IMPROVEMENTS ARE DESIRED?

9.2.1 Initiate a problem/requirement list

During the investigation a number of factors become known to the analyst which make sense to record so that their progress can more formally be monitored. These factors include:

- General system requirements (probably identified during the feasibility study).
- System constraints e.g. the need to use existing hardware.
- Audit/security/control requirements as they become apparent.
- Problems with the existing system.

If possible, these should be documented in a way which does not limit creativity in searching for a solution. The easiest way to do this is to create and maintain a list of problems and requirements which are specified as logically and precisely as possible, e.g. instead of recording 'Jones needs a PC', record 'the orders clerk needs assistance in calculating the value of an order'.

9.3 WHAT DATA DOES THE CURRENT SYSTEM NEED TO STORE IN ORDER TO OPERATE?

The material to address this question has probably already been collected during the user interviews and involves viewing this information from the standpoint of the data analyst. There are two main tasks in this step. The first task is to produce a refined first-cut data model. The second task is to record descriptions for each entity, attribute and relationship identified.

9.3.1 Create a refined first-cut data model

A data model may well be in existence. This will be the case where a data analysis function has been set up to maintain a corporate database approach. Here, the task is one of confirmation, i.e. that the existing data model meets the requirements of the system. Where there is no data model, however, the steps outlined in chapter 3 have to be followed to create the data model.

9.3.2 Document entity, attribute and relationship descriptions

Just as processes on the DFD are complemented by process descriptions, so a data model needs supporting documentation in terms of recording information about each entity, each attribute of an entity and each relationship between entities. Such information would typically be stored in a data dictionary. Incomplete information in a data dictionary can act as a source of questions for the analyst to pursue during the course of investigation.

9.4 IS WHAT HAS BEEN ESTABLISHED SO FAR ABOUT THE CURRENT SYSTEM CORRECT?

It is important to recognise that a significant amount of time and effort has gone in to accomplishing the preceding tasks. This work represents an investment which, if it is to be of value to subsequent activities, should be as correct as possible. This makes it cost-effective to take this opportunity to confirm its correctness. Simple techniques are applied to establish this. Some use the fact that there are now two models of the system. One is the DFD set and the other is the data model.

If mistakes or omissions are identified, then steps are retraced to ensure the correctness and consistency of all existing documentation before proceeding further.

9.4.1 Construct a semi-logical DFD

In a later stage of the method, a fully logical DFD will be drawn. Only tasks that make this stage of analysis easier are incorporated into the creation of the semi-logical DFD.

It is important to see the distinction between a diagram designed for users and one for analysts. The DFD hierarchy is best suited for working with users since the partitioning permits users to see only a small part of the system, i.e. the part of the system they are concerned with. This means that a highly-complex system can appear to be relatively straightforward to individual users. The analyst however needs a diagram that shows the whole system, its relationships and therefore in one way its complexity. The semi-logical DFD is the best diagram for the analyst at this point because it provides the complexity needed from a fully logical DFD but it does not require further logicalisation which may be redundant and unnecessary if mistakes are found and work has to be re-done. There are two tasks involved in creating the semi-logical DFD:

(1) Convert the net-flow, hierarchical DFD set to a single-level R-I-M-D DFD containing only leaf processes

This is created by ignoring all non-leaf processes and creating one complete diagram of only leaf processes. A difficulty can arise through the size of the single-level DFD produced. Where it is clear it will become excessively large it should be partitioned into two or more diagrams so that the interfaces between diagrams are minimised, i.e. so that their overall coupling is low.

The act of reviewing each net-flow access and converting it to its counterpart in an R-I-M-D diagram tests the analyst's understanding of the nature of the access and may cause him to return to the user for guidance. As an example of a diagram which shows R-I-M-D accesses, see figure 10.1.

(2) Make each access atomic

By atomic is meant that each datastore access within a process is unambiguous. In the majority of situations this will already be so. However, sometimes this is not the case. Two examples are provided. The first example is where each record in a stock file is read to determine if the stock item needs to be re-ordered. If it does, then a field in the record has to be modified to denote that stock is currently being ordered. In terms of the analysis being performed, there are two atomic accesses here. These are an 'R' and an 'M'. Secondly, imagine an attribute of an entity contains a value and that this value is reduced each time a modify transaction acts on the entity occurrence. However, when the value of the attribute reaches zero the entity occurrence is to be deleted from the entity. So the access may either be an 'M' or a 'D'. This is avoided by creating two accesses out of the one in the original DFD, so that each access is unique.

9.4.2 Confirm feasibility of each leaf process in the semi-logical DFD

Feasibility was discussed in chapter 2. Its importance here lies in that it can detect inconsistencies early and with relatively little penalty. The inputs are checked against outputs. If the inputs cannot generate the outputs then the reason why has to be established. It may be, for example, that a faulty dataflow description was recorded in the data dictionary or it may highlight the existence of a datastore not previously identified.

9.4.3 Create datastore/entity cross-references

Since the DFD and the data model were created independently of one another, a degree of useful comparison between the two models of the system can take place. In particular, datastores from the semi-logical DFD which

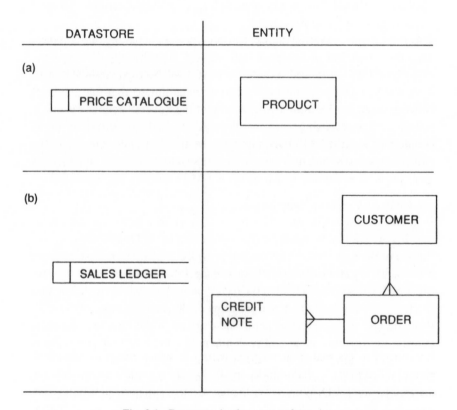

Fig. 9.1. Datastore/entity cross-referencing.

store the information used by the current physical system can be compared with the entities in the data model which are the result of a more idealised and logical analysis of the system's data requirements. Figure 9.1 provides two examples of cross-referencing. In figure 9.1(a), we have a fairly straightorward situation where the PRICE CATALOGUE datastore is broadly equivalent to the PRODUCT entity. In figure 9.1(b), the contents of the SALES LEDGER have attributes in three different entities. In both cases, the data dictionary is consulted to identify the contents of datastores and entities, so that proper matching can take place.

At this stage the purpose of the comparison is not to ensure that every item in every datastore has been identified within an entity. Indeed, there is little point in verifying this at this stage, because so many decisions which will affect the existence or non-existence of data items have still to be taken. This can be especially significant where the user is invited to consider the options available. What is important, however, is that the analyst has some degree of confidence that there is no significant gap in the analysis so far.

When datastores are cross-referenced with entities two possibilities occur:

(1) Entity does not exist for which there are data items in a datastore
This means that either the data modelling step has failed to consider a valid part of the system's data requirement or that the data items held in the datastore are redundant and not necessary for the purposes of serving the system. The analyst will have to decide what is correct and take the appropriate action. In doing so, it must be remembered that it is likely that data items will exist in datastores which have not yet been identified as attributes in entities (although the entity itself has been identified). This is acceptable at this stage and is not cause for concern. More valuable is the case where an entity or entities have been overlooked.

(2) Datastore does not exist for which there are attributes in an entity
It may be either that the data analysis had identified attributes which are not required by this particular system, or that some part of the current system's processing has been overlooked in the analysis.

9.4.4 Create an entity/process matrix

An entity/process matrix is simply a matrix in which the rows consist of entities taken from the data model and the columns are leaf processes from the semi-logical DFD. Where a DFD process accesses a particular entity then the access type (i.e. an 'R', 'I', 'M' or 'D') or access types if the process is

	REJECT ORDER	ACCEPT ORDER	BACK ORDER	HOUSE-KEEPING
CUSTOMER	-	M	M	D
ORDER	-	I	M	D
ORDER LINE	-	I	R/M	D
STOCK	R	M	M	-

Fig. 9.2. Entity/process matrix.

complex, are inserted at the appropriate intersection in the matrix. See figure 9.2. Each row in the matrix contains all the accesses to that entity that are shown on the DFD.

This provides an opportunity to look for mistakes or omissions. For example, every entity occurrence has to be at least inserted and deleted. If either of these does not appear somewhere on each row then either that transaction is outside the scope of the current system or it should have been identified as part of the essential processing. Often the latter will be the case because when discussing procedures with users, the setting up or deleting of say a customer account or a stock item is often assumed or forgotten. Another aspect that warrants investigation is where there are no read accesses in a row. It rather defeats the purpose of storing information in a data structure if it is never to be read. This phenomenon is sometimes seen in manual systems which store complex documents, only parts of which are ever used later.

Sometimes two separate processes in a DFD might achieve the same end, e.g. there may be two ways of setting up a customer entity occurrence. This means that there will be two insert accesses in that row in the matrix.

By reviewing each row in turn the entity/process matrix allows a check for the general sensibility of accesses against each entity to be made. At this stage the object of the check is to identify fairly obvious errors. Such errors fall into three categories:

1 The analyst misunderstood what the current system actually does and so one or other of the models would be incorrect.

2 Processes were simply omitted from the DFD set.

3 The current system specification is unworkable. This can happen again in manual systems where, because of its original poor specification, the human participants in some way work round the problem.

9.4.5 Review investigation with users

Once the internal checking has been done, it is then appropriate to review the investigation with the key members of the user community involved in the project. The review has two main objectives. Firstly, the system boundary has to be reconfirmed with users and management as the analysis may have uncovered issues which could influence the scope of the system. Secondly, in reviewing the analysis, users are afforded the opportunity to make corrections to or clarifications upon any of the detail in the data model, DFD set or problem/requirements list. The review represents the first major milestone in the project, when sufficient examination of the system has been undertaken to enable the analyst to knowledgeably discuss the system details with the user community. It is important that users have confidence in the analyst's knowledge of the current system, otherwise they would be unwise to authorise further development. From the analyst's point of view, it is an opportunity to obtain formal confirmation about the scope and nature of the system with some degree of reassurance from the user community.

The review should be carried out in a relatively formal way to underline the importance that this activity represents. The following recommendations support this:

- Documentation along with an agenda should be distributed in advance of the meeting to all affected parties.
- High-quality and well-prepared presentation materials (e.g. slides, flip charts) are necessary to convince the audience that the discussion is also high-quality and well-prepared.
- Adequate rehearsal and background preparation is required of all active participants.
- Formal minuting of all comments made should be taken.

Lastly, the object of this review is to gain agreement and commitment to further development. The analyst must not allow the meeting to diverge from its primary task, for instance in trying to resolve points of detail or of political issue.

9.5 SUMMARY

The first three questions in this chapter relate to the information gathering activity, while the last question is there to confirm as far as possible that what has been established is correct. Information gathering is a time-consuming activity. Much of it is unstructured in the sense that it is obtained through user interviews, documents of all sorts, the terms of reference and so on. This is why it is important to use the structured techniques of data modelling and dataflow diagramming to begin to put some degree of rigour on the system. It is also why there is an early need to perform verification and validation. The verification is achieved by cross-referencing the two models of the system that have been obtained; the validation involves going back to the users with what has been gathered. Validation is done after the verification since it is important that discussions with users are on the basis of the best possible intelligence.

Cross-referencing at such an early stage in development means that corrective action if necessary is comparatively inexpensive to do and it increases the analyst's confidence that the work accomplished is on the right lines. In addition, there is another benefit in terms of gaining an appreciation of how much duplication of data and of effort exists in the current system. For example, most manually operated systems contain datastores holding similar information stored independently in different departments. Using a database creates the opportunity to reduce the effort required to maintain this information by storing only once in the database. Soon, the analyst will need to quantify the costs and benefits of any proposed system and so a knowledge gained from surveying the existing system and quantifying any redundancy is useful ammunition.

The steps in system investigation are:

1 What does the current system do?
   - Create a current physical DFD set using the net-flow technique.
   - Document all current, leaf processes.
   - Document all dataflows and datastores.
2 What are the current system's problems and what improvements are desired?
   - Initiate a problem/requirement list.
3 What does the current system need to store in order to operate?
   - Create a refined, first-cut data model.
   - Document entity, attribute and relationship descriptions.

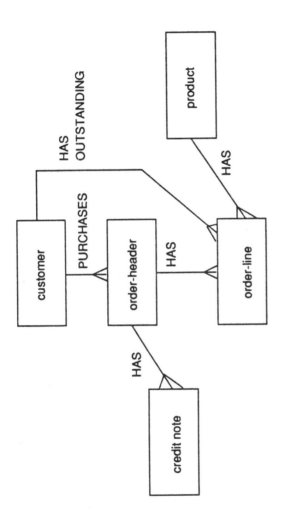

CUSTOMER: CUST-NO,CUSTNAME,ADDRESS,CREDIT-LIMIT,BALANCE
ORDER-HEADER: ORDER-NO,ORDER-DATE,INVOICE-NO,INVOICE-DATE
ORDER-LINE: PROD-CODE,QUANTITY
PRODUCT: PROD-CODE,DESCRIPTION,UNIT-COST,STOCK-QTY,UNIT-OF-MEASURE
CREDIT-NOTE: CREDIT-NOTE-NO,AMOUNT

Fig. 9.3. Data model and associated attributes.

4 Is what has been established so far about the current system correct?
   - Construct a semi-logical DFD.
   - Confirm feasibility of each leaf process.
   - Create datastore/entity cross-references.
   - Create an entity/process matrix.
   - Review investigation with users.

9.6 EXERCISES

Using the case study, proceed through the stages of system investigation. Much of the work has already been done in previous exercises. Generate the problem/requirement list by examining the case study and identifying obvious problems. (Figure 9.3 shows a solution for the refined first-cut data model.)

Chapter 10
Requirements Analysis

This chapter is devoted to arriving at a statement of what is required of the proposed system. This is sometimes incorrectly described as a business specification; strictly speaking, a business specification involves describing enough of the required system such that the business requirements are specified and no more than that. Because it is solely concerned with the business end, a business specification need not describe, for example, whether a transaction is on-line or batch as long as the basic requirements of the business is met. The business specification is therefore fairly abstract in nature and tends in its purest form not to be well received by users since it can be difficult to visualise. A more practical specification for user review purposes and therefore feedback is one which makes it easier for people to visualise, i.e. one which identifies the kind of transaction to be used, whether the output is on screen or report and so on. This we will refer to as the requirements specification. In a nutshell, it is the business specification plus enough of the new physical system to permit a decision to proceed with more detailed analysis. Perhaps a better way of looking at the requirements specification is to say that it describes the external or user view of the new system, i.e. what the users see. Because of its appropriateness for user reviews it is the requirements specification and not the business specification that is the natural end-point for this phase of the analysis.

The basic questions the analyst asks are:

- What does the new system require?
- How can these requirements be met?
- Is what has been specified correct?

10.1 WHAT DOES THE NEW SYSTEM REQUIRE?

To answer this question the analyst has to identify ways of resolving existing problems and meeting new requirements. This is not an easy task and demands creative ability. Another difficulty is that there is no objective way of evaluating different solutions to establish which is better.

10.1.1 Logicalise the DFD

The semi-logical DFD is used as the input to the logicalisation process. This diagram is well on its way to becoming a logical DFD. The logical DFD is the vehicle used by the analyst to describe the essential system and should not contain elements which distract that analysis. The refinements made are designed to make analysis easier and therefore improve the quality of solution identified:

(1) Remove physical references
Physical DFDs reflect how the current system is actually processed. They are physical in that there may be references to the actual (i.e. physical) documents, e.g. blue material requisition card. Clearly, in order for the system to perform, the card does not have to be blue; indeed neither does it have to be a card. The same applies to processes which are 'physically' dependent on the machinery used like typewriters, decollators, key-to-disk devices, etc. The role of logical DFDs is to assist in the analysis of the system. It is therefore important that extraneous physical details of the kind discussed above are removed, so that the analyst is free to concentrate on the underlying system.

(2) Remove non-essential processes, datastores and associated dataflows
The next level of logicalisation is concerned with removing processes, datastores and associated dataflows which exist in the physical system for non-essential reasons, i.e. for reasons to do with how the current system just happens to have implemented its procedures. For example, invoices may be stored in a temporary datastore such as an out-tray until such time as there is sufficient quantity to send along to the warehouse. As long as there is no business or logistical reason for this kind of procedure, all associated processes, datastores and dataflows should be removed from the DFD.

(3) Replace datastores with corresponding entities
The new system will be based on the data model identified, so it is helpful here to declare entities on the diagram which will be used to search for solutions to the systems problems. A slight drawback to this is that the number of 'entity datastores' on the logical DFD is bound to be more than the number of original datastores, so it makes the diagram clumsier. It is possible to declare and use 'composite' entities, which are composites in the same sense as composite data can be decomposed into elementary data items, but its use is recommended only in extreme circumstances. However, on balance, using entities brings advantages to the analysis process which outweigh any disadvantages as described here. Figure 10.1 shows part of a logical DFD.

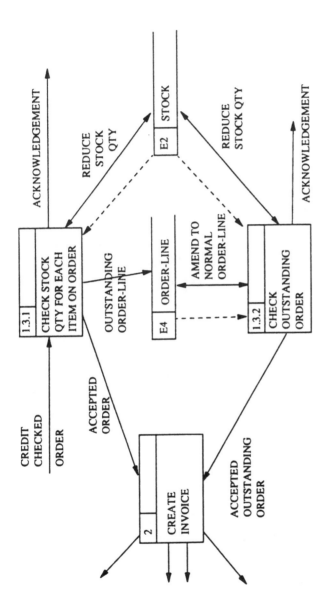

The logical DFD uses the R-I-M-D technique. Here, STOCK is checked (ie. read) to see if it contains enough stock for that item. If true for all items on the order, then the order is accepted and the necessary modifications made to STOCK. If insufficient stock exists, outstanding order-lines are created.

Fig. 10.1. Part of a logical DFD.

10.1.2 Add support requirements to the problem/requirement list

Support requirements are those requirements that any computer system has to provide. They relate to procedures for recovery should the system crash, ensuring unauthorised access does not happen and so on. These requirements are considered mandatory in a new computer system. The categories of support requirement can be summarised as follows:

(1) Fall-back policy
If the computer building should be burnt down or the system suffer from an irretrievable crash, what arrangements and what procedures are there for alternative processing?

(2) Recovery
A statement is also required concerning the mechanisms and timescales for recovering from so-called 'retrievable' system crashes. This is not a technical statement, it merely documents which data needs to be recovered and how quickly. Depending on the database software used, much or all of what is required may be available with the software. Alternatively, it can lead to the identification of recovery programs which require to be specified, designed, coded, etc.

(3) Privacy
Privacy concerns the access and availability of data to unauthorised personnel. Clearly, it is unacceptable for individual salary data, for example, to be made available to all or for unauthorised personnel to be able to modify a customer's credit limit. A privacy statement at this stage identifies the necessary constraints required for legal access to the system. Typically, this will be implemented by password control but in some instances could require data encryption for example.

(4) System controls
System controls are those key statistics which allow some degree of checking that the system is operating as it is intended. They can include statistics on the number of documents accepted and rejected, the total value in stock at a particular point in time and so on. These controls may well form part of a wider set of procedures operated by a user department and could link in with the auditing cycle.

(5) Auditing
Many commercial systems such as payrolls, stock control and ledger systems

must meet minimum legal requirements regarding what information should be kept and for how long it should be kept. Auditors from time to time inspect these systems to confirm that the information produced by these systems represents a 'true and fair' view of the company's operations. This can impose additional data and processing requirements on the computer system.

(6) Data retention
Outside of auditing retention requirements, there is sometimes a need to retain data for extended periods either in file form or through other means such as archiving. Again this should be defined at this stage.

10.1.3 Prioritise problems and requirements

It is valuable to establish a priority system so that the relative importance of each problem/requirement can be compared against the others. In order to do this, quantitative data about the problem/requirement is gathered and recorded into the problems/requirements list, so that its magnitude and therefore significance can be assessed. For example, suppose that there is currently an unacceptable delay in processing documents. This should be quantified as well as a statement of what the acceptable timescales are. Even where the problem's repercussions are somewhat vague, e.g. in lack of goodwill, some attempt should be made, presumably by user management, to quantify this in terms of lost business.

10.1.4 Identify candidate solutions to problems/requirements

Once quantified, potential solutions can be sought. If there are obvious computer-based solutions then these can be quickly specified as a precursor to discussions with users. Care should be taken to ensure that the analyst does not pre-empt decisions by overlooking other possibilities, so the candidate solution should initially be described as generically as possible to avoid this. Also if there are alternative solution strategies each should be documented with a brief statement of their relative strengths and weaknesses. The real task, however, is to get the users involved in identifying their own solutions. A later chapter discusses 'socio-technical analysis' which explores this area in greater detail. Note also that every solution may not be computer-based and some may have organisational implications which require follow-up with user management.

Chapter 10

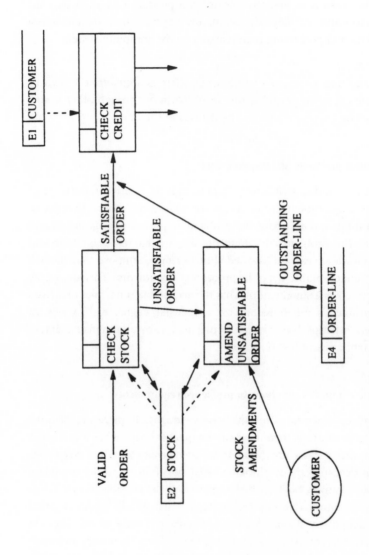

This part of an RSO shows stock being checked before credit. If the order is unsatisfiable (because of stock inadequacies), the customer supplies amendments (possibly a reduced number of items or alternative items). If satisfactory it is sent on to be checked for credit, otherwise it becomes an outstanding order-line and is stored as such in ORDER-LINE.

Fig. 10.2. Part of an RSO.

10.2 HOW CAN THESE REQUIREMENTS BE MET?

The deliverable from this phase is the requirements specification. From a list of candidate solutions the preferred solution has to be obtained. Unfortunately, it is not really practical to present the users with a list of candidate solutions and it falls on the analyst to help the users in visualising the eventual system. This is done by developing a small number of Required System Options (RSOs) which are presented to the users as alternative system solutions and through this a selection is made.

10.2.1 Identify Required System Options (RSOs)

Required System Options are new logical DFDs which show enough of the physical processing to demonstrate how that particular option would be implemented. Essentially the current logical DFD is modified to reflect the changes implicit in the individual solutions to problems and requirements. Physical location references are added and any key physical processing which distinguishes that option from the others. Figure 10.2 shows a sample RSO.

10.2.2 Submit RSOs to users for selection

Ideally about three RSOs are identified and these are submitted to the users for final selection. In discussing the RSOs it is important that the nature of the solution is covered with an indication of the likely costs and benefits, not forgetting any organisational implications as mentioned earlier. Since each problem/requirement has its own cost/benefit statement, it will be possible through discussion to arrive at a hybrid solution which takes preferred individual solutions from parts of the different RSOs.

Identifying about three different RSOs is useful because it provides the opportunity to visualise and contrast different solution approaches and inevitably leads to animated discussion and sometimes disagreement amongst users. With more than three RSOs the range of choice can confuse; with less than three there is perhaps too little choice.

Note that it may be desirable to convert the R-I-M-D accesses in an RSO to net-flow accesses, if this is likely to cause confusion amongst users.

Lastly, note that the particular RSO finally chosen may have implications for the data model too, in terms of the specific attributes required.

10.2.3 Update the problem/requirement list

The decisions made in selecting an RSO, will impact what is stated in the problem/requirements list. Some will have been accepted, some ignored and some modified. Also, physical solutions to some may have been indicated during discussion. The problem/requirements list should now be updated, since it acts as a source of policy in later stages of the method.

10.2.4 Fully specify the chosen option

So far the RSO has only been specified in sufficient detail to enable an informed decision to be made about which option to choose. Once the authorisation to proceed has been given, it is then necessary to complete the specification of the chosen option. This involves the following:

(1) Complete the new physical DFD set
The RSO DFD is a single level DFD. This needs to be expanded to a full, hierarchical, physical DFD set which contains details of all relevant processes, dataflows, etc. It is recommended that unless there are good reasons otherwise, the partitioning should be on a functional i.e. departmental basis. This will make subsequent walkthroughs with user personnel more straightforward.

(2) Create an enquiry and update transactions catalogue
Having captured the new system in terms of a DFD set, the next step is to catalogue i.e. create a list of all enquiry and update transactions. Note that reports are one type of enquiry transaction. Enquiry and update transactions therefore represent all the events that operate on entities. This catalogue is used in a later step when the system logic is investigated.

(3) Create screen and report layouts
Clearly these are an important part of the specification of the system. It may well be the case that some of these layouts have been developed when the RSOs were defined, perhaps by using prototyping (which will be discussed in a later chapter). However, the main purpose of this step is to ensure that the inputs and outputs of each transaction are specified. This is because at this stage we are still more concerned with the feasibilty of each transaction rather than how it could be implemented. The design process will concern itself with the internal screens, if any, within a single transaction.

(4) Specify logic for all new and modified transactions
Because of the changes that have just been incorporated there is a need to update the data dictionary with details of any associated processing logic.

10.3 IS WHAT HAS BEEN SPECIFIED CORRECT?

It is important to get feedback from users quickly about the requirements of the system and before any unnecessary further analysis work is undertaken. This checkpoint is the first real opportunity to do so.

10.3.1 Review requirements specification with users

In section 10.2.2, the users were asked to decide on their preferred system. The work done since then has been to complete the picture in as much detail as possible of what the eventual system will look like, based on the outline provided. By now, the users will have had some time to be sure about their requirements and any misunderstandings can be ironed out before further work takes place. It also gives the analyst some time to work through the implications of what was agreed and to confirm any concerns before proceeding.

10.4 SUMMARY

Some important software engineering principles have been illustrated in this chapter. The first one is the use of the logical DFD as the analytic vehicle for identifying solutions to problems. Since solutions are typically visualised in terms of the processing they require, the DFD is the natural choice for this. Because it is a logical DFD, all unnecessary detail has been removed, thereby allowing the analyst as much scope as possible for thinking creatively.

The identification of candidate solutions to problems or requirements is a most important task and one that demands careful attention and effort. Ideally, the analyst should try to work as much as possible with users and draw on their knowledge. But one cannot build in tasks to a method to guarantee that the best creative solutions will be found! That is more likely to come from a good working relationship between analyst and user. So people-oriented skills are very important for the software engineer.

The use of RSOs and submitting only a limited number of these back to users is a practical way of assisting users in deciding on their system. Ideally, all individual candidate solutions should be reflected in one of the RSOs, so that the variety of solution need not be jeopardised. Yet, because solutions are packaged into RSOs, the profusion of solutions is not overwhelming to the user.

Lastly, the requirements specification represents an important milestone in the development of the system. Because of the final user review, it defines what the users want from the system and enough of the external interface for the analyst to further develop the system using the requirements specification as a guide. It defines what the system has to do, but not more than that because that could be wasted effort given that the next stage involves considerable checking of the logic of the system.

It can be seen that the requirements analysis activity requires a special blend of skill and imagination. This would include solid analytic skills, people-orientated skills and creative faculties.

The tasks in requirements specification are:

1 What does the new system require?
   - Logicalise the DFD.
   - Add support requirements to the problem/requirement list.
   - Prioritise problems and requirements.
   - Identify candidate solutions to problems/requirements.
2 How can these requirements be met?
   - Identify required system options.
   - Submit RSOs to users for selection.
   - Update the problem/requirement list.
   - Fully specify chosen option.
3 Is what has been specified correct?
   - Review requirements specification with users.

10.5 EXERCISES

1   Logicalise the DFD produced in the exercise at the end of the last chapter.

2   Identify and draw two RSOs which resolve some of the major problems in the problems/requirements list.

Chapter 11
Systems Analysis

The object of this phase of the method is to confirm that the requirements specification is feasible in terms of being implementable. There is no guarantee that the requirements specification as it stands is feasible because no sustained rigorous analysis of it has been undertaken, and certainly it is important before proceeding further with the development of the system to establish as far as possible just how feasible the requirements specification is. This is essentially a verification task and a time-consuming one at that, hence the reason for the user validation of the requirement specification immediately prior to this phase. Firstly, we must produce a data model which can meet all of the new system's requirements. This is vitally important; if this is incomplete then the system cannot possibly work. Secondly, we must work through the underlying logic of the new system to confirm its correctness and feasibility. Often, additional transactions are identified in this analysis which are critical to the successful operation of the system.

The major deliverable here is known as the information systems specification which is, in effect, a complete and correct requirements specification. In order to ensure correctness and completeness, a lot of critical evaluation, using analytic tools, has to be undertaken. This is called systems analysis and is the name given to describe the overall activity in this chapter.

The main tasks in producing an information systems specification are to:

- Create a data model that can support the requirements specification.
- Confirm the correctness and completeness of the information system specification.

11. CREATE A DATA MODEL THAT CAN SUPPORT THE REQUIREMENTS SPECIFICATION

11.1.1 Create first-cut required data model

The refined first-cut data model (or current data model) created some time earlier is used as the input to this step. The first-cut required data model contains any modifications arising out of the particular option chosen and can be affected in two ways. Firstly, new attributes may be required as a result of decisions taken. For example, perhaps it is required that customers may have permanent or provisional status depending on their payment record, whereas previously this was not required. This will generate an attribute in the CUSTOMER entity. Secondly, some requirement options may result in the creation of new entities and associated relationships. For example, it may be decided that where insufficient stock exists to meet an order item, then it is possible to provide alternative stock items. This will result in an ALTERNATIVE STOCK entity with a relationship to PRODUCT entity.

11.1.2 Perform normalisation

An earlier chapter covered the rules for performing normalisation. It is performed on a set of documents from the requirements specification which span all the attributes in the data model. As discussed earlier, the purpose of normalisation is to confirm the correctness of the (required) data model.

11.1.3 Obtain the 3NF data model

With a little work on the normalised 3NF relations, these can be converted into a data model which is referred to as a 3NF data model. Though a description of creating a data model from 3NF relations appeared in chapter 5, the discussion that follows is a more detailed one. The 3NF model is built from the optimised 3NF relations as follows:

(1) 3NF relations become entities
Quite simply, every relation in 3NF will be an entity in the data model.

(2) Composite keys may generate foreign keys
Because of the special nature of composite keys they are treated differently from the more usual compound keys. It is possible, though not essential, that a composite key contains domains which are unique identifiers, e.g. 'order-no + order-line-no' contains a unique identifier in order-no and a non-unique component in order-line-no. If unique identifiers exist in a composite key they should be marked as foreign keys and dealt with in step (5). Non-unique components are ignored for the purposes of establishing links with other entities.

(3) Link domains of compound keys with their masters
Compound keys contain domains all of which are unique identifiers. Each

domain of a compound key therefore ought to have a master for it, i.e. an entity whose key is solely that domain.

Sometimes hierarchies of relations occur. For example, suppose three relations exist, call them relations 1, 2 and 3, whose keys are respectively, 'a+b+c', 'a+b' and 'a'. In this case relation 3 is the master of 2 and relation 2 the master of 1.

(4) Create operational masters for domains of compound keys without masters
If no suitable master exists as another entity (formerly a 3NF relation), then one is created. It is called an operational master because there is no data for it; it consists solely of the key domain. Because a new entity has been created, it should be related to other entities which contain the key as an element of its key. Also there may be potential relationships with non-key domains in other entities. So, in this case, these non-key domains are identified as foreign keys.

One important exception to this is where the domain in question is a date field. It may not be sensible to indicate dates as foreign keys and therefore this needs careful consideration. This is the only place where an otherwise mechanistic approach is bypassed.

(5) Link foreign keys with their masters
Since, by definition, foreign keys have links to existing entities, this is now formalised by drawing the relationship between the two entities.

The construction of the 3NF data model is, for the most part, a mechanistic process. The model produced contains every logical link with other entities and also hierarchies of entities because of the way it seeks master entities. The relationships generated have no names as such, which is a weakness of the process.

11.1.4 Create a Composite Logical Data Design (CLDD)

We now have two data models, one of which was derived during the analysis phase, which we will now call the top-down data model after the fashion in which it was created. The other is the 3NF data model. The top-down model was constructed relatively early in the life cycle, at a time when the analyst was forming ideas about the system and then subsequently modified in the light of the requirements specification. Consequently, the model produced tends to have incomplete lists of attributes for each entity and perhaps a simple structure in terms of relationships between entities. The 3NF model on the other hand is more likely to contain a complete list of domains in each relation since it attempts to gather and group all known data items within the scope of the system. However, because of the rigours of the normalisation process, the relationships identified tend to be more complex than those in the top-down model.

Given that differences manifest themselves between the two models, and in practice they do, the question is which is the better interpretation. Behind the simplicity of the top-down model, there could be straightforward omissions which have been overlooked in earlier analysis. Equally, the 3NF model could be providing a level of complexity that is not necessary to meet the processing requirements.

If the top-down data model has been constructed properly, it can be considered a 'minimum' data model for system, since it will contain only those entities, relationships and attributes which are absolutely necessary to meet the needs of the system. The 3NF data model on the other hand is descended from an analysis of all the known attributes in the system and effectively contains all conceivable links between entities. It may contain relationships which are not explicitly required by the system and even entities which again serve no useful purpose in the system as currently specified. However, given the demand for non-prespecified computing as exemplified by the growth of Information Centres, in which users are able to quickly access databases to obtain high-value information at short notice, there is a strong argument for the analyst giving thorough consideration to the provision of additional access paths. Clearly, though, this has to be tempered by efficiency factors.

The major intellectual task, therefore, in the creation of the CLDD is to achieve the best compromise between the minimum data model and the rich one in the light of the need to produce a stable data model which will meet the organisation's foreseeable requirements. Equally important in practice, since the consequences are significant, is the opportunity to confirm the correctness of the data requirement afforded by the comparison of the two data models.

Once the entities and relationships of the CLDD are decided, the attributes within each entity need to be confirmed. So a check is performed against the original set of attributes used in the normalisation process to ensure that no attribute has been overlooked. In addition, a state indicator is added to each entity in preparation for building ELHs and the SDD. It is possible to infer states by other means, e.g. by the existence of a non-null attribute, but since states are so critical to further analysis of the system it is much better to identify them explicitly as a separate attribute.

There are a number of issues that the software engineer must address as the CLDD is created and these are now discussed:

(1) Selection of operational masters

Operational masters from the top-down model may often be of a different type to those from the 3NF model. The 3NF operational masters are generated from key domains in compound keys. If not directly required by the specification to service the system, they may be of use as 'doors' into the system in query-handling or for other anticipatable future requirements.

Operational masters shown on the top-down model are likely to reflect the basis by which the user tends to deal with the detail entity behind the operational master. This may be by date or some sort of classification such as a status or category, e.g. PRODUCT CATEGORY could be an operational master of the PRODUCT entity.

Usually the CLDD will contain the operational masters from the top-down model plus some from the 3NF which are considered strategic. The letter 'o' is drawn in the top right-hand corner of the rectangle representing the entity to indicate that it is an operational master. Occasionally operational masters may be promoted to full entities after consideration of the wider long-term aims of the organisation, i.e. attributes are added.

(2) Selection of additional entities

This decision is made on whether it is desirable to carry the extra burden of additional entities in a database. The question is basically one of assessing the likelihood that data will be required in additional entities at some future date. (Note that this issue is not the same as the problem in normalisation where computed data such as total and subtotal fields are removed from the list of data to be normalised. Here the final decision on whether to include such data rests on the trade-off between computer processing time, space and so on incurred in alternative implementations. This is decided in design and not here.)

(3) Selection of relationships (access paths)

Having decided on the number and type of entities, the relationships can now be addressed. The top-down model identifies relationships by examining the meaning of the association between two entities; the 3NF model generates relationships on the basis of common domains. Again, the question boils down to the difference between current and future requirements.

Common relationships

Where both the top-down and 3NF models have common relationships these must be examined to confirm that they do in fact represent the same relationship. There is no guarantee. If they are different relationships, then they fall into each of the categories below.

Relationships on the 3NF model but not on the top-down model
This is likely to arise since the 3NF model identifies all possible links. The real question is which relationships are worth retaining, the answer again lying in the realm of likely future requirements. It may be worth bringing into the decision recognition whether a particular relationship is born out of a straightforward foreign key or as an element in a compound key, since this may reveal an understanding of the purpose the relationship serves.

Relationships on the top-down model but not on the 3NF model
Relationships like these might quite sensibly arise because associations between entities are not always straightforward. This situation is like that shown in figure 3.8 when it was debated whether the IS FATHER OF relationship was redundant. Such relationships may well add to the data model in ways which cannot be simulated by the 3NF approach. Equally, the top-down model may not be correct and so an opportunity for confirmation is afforded.

11.1.5 Document all entities and relationships

By now, considerable data has been accumulated (and perhaps just modified) about each entity and relationship in the CLDD. In particular, volumetric data should be added as this aids decision-making in design, i.e. data about the number of entity occurrences, frequency of add, modify and delete transactions and so on.

11.1.6 Document all attributes

The requirements specification contains details of all attributes input to and output by the system. Earlier when the data model was first created, only obvious attributes were documented. It is now time to ensure that all details relating to attributes are formally captured in the data dictionary. Derived attributes are also recorded, including details of how they are calculated.

11.2 CONFIRM THE CORRECTNESS AND COMPLETENESS OF THE INFORMATION SYSTEM SPECIFICATION

11.2.1 Create a where-used matrix

In the system investigation, an entity/process matrix was created as an early

CLDD \ TRANSACTION	ENTITY : PRODUCT						RELATIONSHIP	ENTITY : ORDER-LINE				RELATIONSHIP
	ACC-ESS	TRANS TYPE	PROD CODE	DESC	UNIT COST	STK QTY	CUSTOMER HAS ORDER-LINE	ACC-ESS	TRANS TYPE	PROD CODE	QTY	ORDER-HEADER HAS ORDER-LINE
CHECK STOCK QTY FOR EACH ITEM ON ORDER	D	M	-	-	-	R/M	*	>	I	I	I	-
CHECK OUTSTANDING ORDER	D	M	-	-	-	R/M	*	>	M	-	-	*

Fig. 11.1. A where-used matrix (incomplete).

check as to whether the system processing captured so far was complete. Here, a more detailed check is done since it is crucial that each transaction can do what is required of it and that no omissions still remain. It is called a 'where-used' matrix because the cross-references establish which transaction utilises which entity, attribute or relationship. See figure 11.1.

Each row of the matrix represents one transaction. It is better to list update transactions first since they are more likely to highlight errors. This is followed by enquiry transactions (both on-line and reports). The column details are a little more complicated than seen previously. There are columns for entites, attributes and relationships. For the entities two pieces of information are entered. Firstly, the required access mode for that entity is entered; this is either a 'D' for direct access or a 'V' for access via a relationship. The second piece of information that is added is what the global transaction type is, i.e. it can be 'R', 'I', 'M' or 'D'. It is called global because it is not necessary for every attribute within an entity to be affected by a particular transaction, e.g. a modification transaction may change the values of some attributes in an entity but not others. Because of this phenomenon, it is necessary to confirm the accesses for each individual attribute; again access types are entered against those attributes affected by that transaction. For the relationship columns an asterisk indicates that a transaction uses that relationship.

11.2.2 Analyse the where-used matrix

The where-used matrix will be used in a more thorough analysis later on, but there are two basic checks that can be done here:

(1) Confirm the integrity of the CLDD with respect to the requirements specification

This basically means that the CLDD is checked to see if it can support the transactions as specified. Firtly, each transaction is 'walked through' to check it is feasible. This is called a horizontal check and confirms that the access mode for each entity is correct and double-checks that the appropriate attributes and relationships are used. By looking down the columns of the matrix (i.e. a vertical check) the following is confirmed:

- Each global transaction type column contains at least one 'R', 'I' and 'D'.
- Each attribute column contains at least one 'R', 'I' and 'D'.
- Each relationship column contains at least one asterisk.

(2) Confirm the feasibilty of producing the derived attributes

The derived attributes are added to the right-hand side of the matrix as additional columns. Remember these attributes are not owned by any entity as such. The data dictionary contains details of those basic attributes used in the calculation of the derived attributes. If it is feasible for the derived attribute to be calculated from the other attributes that are at its disposal then an 'F' (for feasible) is entered in the row of the matrix whose transaction derives the attribute.

11.2.3 Construct normal and abnormal ELHs for each entity in the CLDD

By now the analyst has built up a considerable body of knowledge about the system and each entity in particular. This knowledge in conjunction with the where-used matrix is used to create ELHs for each entity in the CLDD. The normal ELHs are used shortly in the construction of the SDD; the abnormal ELHs are used in a later analysis step along with the SDD.

11.2.4 Create the State Dependency Diagram (SDD)

Using the guidelines in Part A, create an SDD from the normal ELHs. The act of building the SDD will highlight many aspects about the system and its dependences which the analyst may not, as yet, have considered. This may necessitate return to the user for clarification on what should happen in a particular set of circumstances.

11.2.5 Document triggers and constraints

Each transaction in the system is examined to identify triggers and constraints which are then entered into the data dictionary in the transaction catalogue. Triggers and constraints were described in Part A. Each transaction in the system will have one or more triggers which cause it to be initiated. (Different triggers can cause the same transaction to be initiated.) Similarly, each transaction may have constraints associated with it, though not necessarily. For example, on-line transactions will typically require data to be input, and clearly correctly validated data is a prerequisite and therefore a constraint. Equally, it may be that some report programs can be run at any time and require no input parameters. Here there are effectively no constraints on running the program. Note, however, that validation criteria are not usually recorded as constraints since they are documented elsewhere.

The purpose of this step is to focus the analyst's attention on the operation of the new system. Some triggers and constraints will have been present in the original system. If so, the task is one of confirming that they still apply in the new system or, if not, of identifying what the new rules are. Equally, most new systems will contain new processing and it is desirable to clarify this in terms of triggers and constraints. The transaction catalogue is a useful supplement to the SDD and where-used list as it completes the documentation for each transaction and therefore for the analysis which is to follow.

11.2.6 Perform attribute amendment analysis

This task needs a little explanation. What has been developed so far is an 'ideal world' specification in the sense that it assumes certain kinds of mistakes will not happen, particularly so in respect of mistakes of human error creeping into the system. For example, what if the human operator types in an incorrect address in the CUSTOMER entity? What if the operator types in a quantity of 100 instead of 10 on an order item line? Sometimes such mistakes are not discovered until much later. At that point other events may have already taken place, e.g. the order has been sent out with 90 items more than it should.

The purpose of attribute amendment analysis is to address this problem by assuming 'what can go wrong will go wrong'.

Firstly, the where-used matrix is examined. For each attribute (column) in the matrix the same questions are asked:

(1) Can this attribute be altered?
There may be situations, for example a key, where it is not desirable to alter an attribute anyway. Also, sometimes attributes such as dates are generated by the system. So, it may be that the attribute should not be tampered with anyway. If the answer to this question is 'no', the analyst moves on to the next attribute.

(2) What if this attribute has been incorrectly entered?
The SDD is consulted. It holds the key to identifying the implications, if any, on the rest of the system. Let's look at the examples quoted earlier.

An incorrect customer address does not seem to affect anything else in the system. Obviously it has to be changed as quickly as possible, but changing the address will not have any knock-on effects within the system itself. The where-used matrix is now scanned to see if it contains a modification access against that attribute. If it does and if it can be used for this purpose, then no further action needs to be taken. In other words, there is already a transaction defined in the system which can deal with this situation. Note that it is not just as simple as checking whether a modification access exists in the appropriate column in the where-used matrix. It may be that the particular transaction in question is not suitable for this task. For example, take the customer balance attribute. Customer balance is the amount of money owed by the customer to the company. When a customer pays an invoice, the amount paid is decremented from the customer balance. Now the transaction for this would contain a modification access against customer balance, but clearly it would not be able to do the task required of it for our purposes.

The second example is more complex and from examination of the SDD clearly does have a knock-on effect on the system. First of all, it has to be recognised that an incorrect order item quantity may be more or less than what should have been entered. Now, it may be that there are different solution strategies depending on whether the value entered is higher or lower, so each option must be analysed separately. For this discussion we will stick to the case in the example where the value entered is higher than what should have been. Examination of the SDD reveals that there are basically three scenarios. The first is that it is discovered before the invoice has been raised, so since no damage has been done a check is carried out to see if there is a suitable transaction already defined which can be used to perform the modification. The second situation is where the invoice has been sent out and the customer queries the matter. Let's assume that the solution strategy is to re-issue the customer with a corrected invoice. Here we will need to make the necessary corrections to the database, for example in ensuring that customer balance is correctly amended as well as deleting occurrences from the ORDER-HEADER and ORDER-LINE entities. Again, the where-used matrix is used to determine if transactions already exist to do the jobs required. The last scenario is where the problem is only discovered after the invoice has been paid. Suppose the solution strategy is for the customer to return the excess items and for a credit-note to be generated. Once again a similar search pattern is adopted.

If it is decided to use existing transactions to meet any of these new needs, the appropriate triggers should be updated in the data dictionary.

The where-used matrix is therefore the starting point for identifying whether other usable transactions exist in the system already. Where they do not exist, the analyst has identified additional transactions which are necessary for the smooth functioning of the system. The value of the SDD here in highlighting the implications of events such as these should not be underestimated.

11.2.7 Analyse abnormal ELHs

The analysis of abnormal ELHs is important because it offers, in a structured way, an opportunity to identify abnormal or non-standard situations which may occur during the running of the system. These situations require some solution or response in the same way that entity attribute analysis resulted in identifying solution strategies.

Each abnormal ELH is reviewed in conjunction with the SDD in order that each abnormal event can be explored in the context of the overall system. Depending on the decision taken it may be that additional transactions are identified to respond to this situation. Whether new or existing transactions are used the system documentation has to be likewise updated.

11.2.8 Perform structured walkthrough on the CLDD, SDD and changes identified

The systems analysis work done in this chapter is critical to the successful operation of the required system, so much so that it is highly desirable that it be verified by colleagues by means of a 'structured walkthrough', i.e. a presentation of the major deliverables created and a discussion of the important decisions made. The details of how to conduct a structured walkthrough are covered in the chapter on project management. In addition to verifying the work, structured walkthroughs are a good vehicle for communicating and are a good starting point for designers and programmers, who are to be involved in the project shortly.

11.2.9 Review information system specification with users

If the work done in this phase has been fruitful, there will be a number of new transactions identified which were not in the requirements specification and these will be a necessary part of the operation of the system, though some may be considered part of the general 'house-keeping' of the system. In addition, the analyst may have observed some aspects of the system, perhaps limitations or constraints, which it is felt should be discussed or even reviewed with the user community. This review provides the opportunity to clear up these points before moving on to the design phase.

11.3 SUMMARY

The transition from requirements specification to information system specification has achieved three major things.

Firstly, the required logical data model (CLDD) is produced. In producing the CLDD two alternative models are used. These are the top-down data model whose roots lie in the data modelling done early in the analysis of the system and the 3NF data model which is produced mechanistically via the normalisation process. These two views of the data requirement are blended into a composite view which tries to consider future as well as current needs. Considerable time and effort is spent on getting the CLDD right and it is significant that this is the first task carried out after establishing the requirements.

The second major achievement is that of producing a logic model of the system called the State Dependency Diagram. The SDD is constructed by analysing the states of individual entities within ELHs. Where sequential dependencies between one entity state and another exist (not necessarily in the same entity), these are shown on the SDD. The value of the SDD is twofold. In the first instance, the construction of the SDD itself is a useful exercise for the analyst since it forces questions to be confronted about the system which may not yet have been asked or even considered. Once it is constructed it can be used as a tool for identifying the implications of events in the system. This is an important perspective on the system.

Lastly, a more 'complete and correct' specification is achieved in the sense that further transactions may be identified which will ensure the smooth running of the system and without which the system would be seen as inflexible and probably unworkable. This, in the author's view, is the true essence of systems analysis, i.e. it is that activity which verifies the correctness and completeness of a system. The work done here ensures that the transactions identified in the requirement specification are workable and further that previously unforeseen circumstances are also able to be handled. This may require the use of existing transactions; alternatively, new transactions may need to be defined. Although this is described as a verification activity, it is expected that the analyst will be in frequent touch with users and involve them as much as possible throughout.

Because of the additional effort and analytic tools used, the integrity of the information systems specification ought to be much better than the requirements specification which stems from a statement of what users want or at least think they want.

The tasks in producing the information systems specification are:

1 Create a data model that can support the requirements specification:
- create first-cut required data model
- perform normalisation
- obtain the 3NF data model
- create a Composite Logical Data Design (CLDD)
- document all entities and relationships
- document all attributes

2 Confirm the correctness and completeness of the information system specification:
- create a where-used matrix
- analyse the where-used matrix
- construct normal and abnormal ELHs for each entity in the CLDD
- create the state dependency diagram
- document triggers and constraints
- perform attribute amendment analysis
- analyse abnormal ELHs
- perform structured walkthrough on the CLDD, SDD and changes identified
- review information system specification with users

11.4 EXERCISES

1   Go through the stages of creating a CLDD for the case study.

2   Create and then analyse a where-used matrix. Make a list of additional transactions found.

Chapter 12
System Design

In one important sense the information system specification is a 'black-box' specification in that it only defines the inputs and outputs for each transaction. In addition, the previous stages of analysis have taken us to a point where the requirements of the system have been thoroughly examined to a level where some confidence exists about its correctness.

This chapter is about how the system will actually be implemented. In other words it is about design. There are really two major activities in design. The first one is to make decisions about what file access method or database is to be used. Once this is decided the CLDD is converted to the appropriate notation. This is called physical data design. The second activity is to complete the documentation of the processing side of the system in order for it to be programmed. Here, the first essential task is to convert transactions into programs, since it sometimes makes sense to combine transactions within a single program. In addition, for on-line transactions it is necessary to decide upon a menu hierarchy and about the detail for on-line transactions. For batch programs, it has to be determined how they interrelate with each other and how they can be combined into a batch runchart which shows all batch programs in the system and the sequence in which they are run. This is called physical process design.

The major tasks in system design are:

- Produce a physical data model for the required system.
- Complete the physical processing documentation for the required system.
- Confirm the correctness of the design.

12.1 PHYSICAL DATA DESIGN

12.1.1 Decide on access method

The decision to convert the CLDD into a particular access method can often be a trivial one because the company or department may have a policy on which access method is to be used when developing systems. In such situations there is no real decision for the analyst to make. The company may have purchased, say, specific database software, existing systems may already have been implemented with that software and clearly future systems which need to link to current systems would naturally use the same database software so that integration is facilitated.

However, this is not always the case. There may be no such policy; the company may have a variety of different access methods available; the application may be stand-alone running on a different computer from the rest of the company's systems and so on. In such situations the analyst (because there is presumably no-one else) is expected to choose an appropriate access method. But how is this done? What, if any, criteria are used to make the selection between what is probably a large number of available software products, each of which will no doubt be regularly updated and improved? Should the analyst base his decision on the current or future system requirements? Clearly, this is not a simple decision, nor is it one that is likely to be verified in the way that a DFD can be shown to conform to the rules for drawing DFDs. Indeed it is likely to be, to a significant extent, a subjective decision which takes account of factors like the reputation of the supplier of the access methods, how good this support is supposed to be and so on. We will leave fuller discussion of this issue until the chapter on quantification where we will explore ways in which we can attempt to compare different software products. For the moment we will assume that a specific access method has been chosen and that its speed of performance is suitable for our purposes.

Now, it is not possible to detail all the access methods that are available across all kinds of computer. Instead, we will describe four classes of access method and look at two examples of how the CLDD is converted into these. First, however, some background.

File-based access methods have been around for a long time. Files can be accessed in two main ways, i.e. either serially or directly. Serial access implies that records in a file are accessed one after the other starting from the first record on the file until the required record is found. This is a suitable access method for some classes of problem but not for others. For example, it would be suitable for producing a detailed report where the order of the records on the file was the same as that required on the report, but it would be unlikely to be appropriate for an on-line transaction accessing one record from a file of many thousands, since the response time would be unacceptable unless the record happened to be at the very beginning of the file. Direct access methods permit a single record to be accessed, as the name suggests, 'directly' without having to search through every prior record. There is a number of techniques which can facilitate this. They involve using the key of the record to establish, sometimes only approximately, where the record is located. This cuts down access time and makes the response time reasonable in a wide range of circumstances. Some access methods allow a record to be accessed directly and then the file to be accessed serially from that point in the file, which has the effect of increasing the number of useful applications that can be served.

In order for the relationships on the data model to be implemented with files, the key of a member file must be stored in the owner file so that the link can be established. This is known as the access path.

File-based access methods tend to be considered traditional and perhaps out-of-date, yet they remain in wide use and some of the direct access methods are very efficient indeed.

However, database methods have advantages in the way that the data definitions can be separated from the programming instructions. This is particularly useful in the maintenance of systems. There are three main classes of database software. These are hierarchical, network and relational.

(1) Hierarchical databases
Hierarchical databases are based on a tree structure in which each node of the tree represents an entity. A node at one level is related to a node at a lower level, in the same way as a relationship links two entities on a data model. As a hierarchy of nodes, the hierarchical database is restricted in the way it can map itself onto a data model, since a data model is a network rather than a

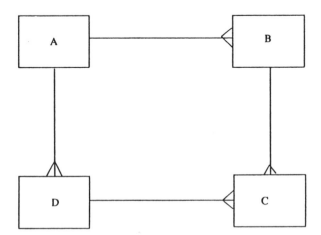

Fig. 12.1. A network of entities.

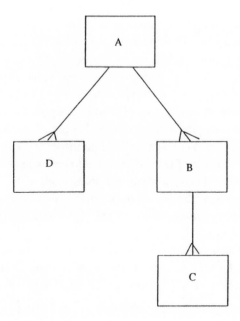

Fig. 12.2. A hierarchy of entities.

hierarchy. In other words, it is not always possible to transfer directly all relationships on the data model to a hierarchical database model. However, in recognition of this problem, hierarchical databases employ mechanisms which allow this to be resolved. Consider figures 12.1 and 12.2.

Figure 12.1 is a network whereas figure 12.2 is a hierarchy. They both permit the same access of information, except figure 12.2 cannot support the one-to-many relationship between entity D and C. In the terminology of hierarchical databases (such as IMS/VS), entity C is said to be the physical child of entity B and indeed the physical storage organisation is based upon this. The mechanism used to overcome this is referred to as the 'logical child/parent approach' in which through pointers a relationship is set up between D and C. The logical parent in D is linked with a group of records in C via a pointer system and therefore a network organisation is simulated. See figure 12.3.

(2) Network databases
Network databases, as the name implies, permit the modelling of networks directly. The nodes of the network represent entities and the links between one entity and another represent the relationship on the data model. Not

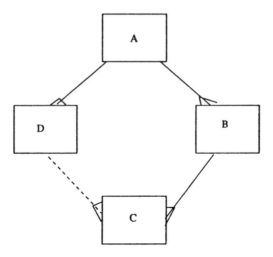

Fig. 12.3. A hierarchy of entities with a logical relationship.

surprisingly, it is a straightforward task to transfer the data model to a network database.

(3) Relational databases

Relational databases differ from network databases in that they are literally sets of tables, i.e. there is no built-in mechanism as such for relating one entity with another. In this respect they are similar to files, although clearly there is more to them than that. CLDDs are readily converted into most relational databases.

Tables 12.1 and 12.2 contain rules for converting the CLDD into VSAM and IDMS respectively. These rules have been simplified a little to aid understanding of the principles of the conversion process.

VSAM permits both serial and direct access and also direct followed by serial. Some of the terms used below are peculiar to VSAM but the idea should be easy to grasp.

The rules are as follows:

1. Each entity with a simple key becomes a file.

2. If the files identified in step 1 have masters in the data model, then the keys of the master entities become alternate indexes for the files.

3. Entities with compound or composite keys also become files where each component of this is an index of the file so that access to respective masters is retained.

4. The files which were operational masters in the data model are deleted since their keys have become alternate indexes on the detail files.

Table 12.1. Converting the CLDD into a file-based method (VSAM).

IDMS is a well-known CODASYL database. CODASYL databases are network databases which conform to certain rules laid down by the CODASYL group. Again, some of the terminology is peculiar to this type of software.

1.   Make operational masters into indexes.

2.   All other entities become CALC, except those with compound keys which have a master. (CALC mode is identical in concept of direct access.)

3.   All remaining become VIA. (VIA mode records can only be accessed as one of a set of records starting from a record in a master entity. It has some similarity with serial access after direct access.)

4.   If CALC entities are the details of masters then that relationship is effected by creating a new set in which the master is the owner and the detail is the member.

5.   CALC entities with corresponding VIA entities are allocated to their own area.

Table 12.2. Converting the CLDD into a network database (IDMS).

To complete the documentation, any database or file definition required should now be finalised.

12.2 PERFORM PHYSICAL PROCESS DESIGN FOR BATCH TRANSACTIONS

An essentially different approach is taken to the design of on-line transactions and batch programs. The reason for this is to do with the unit of work in a system. When users work at a terminal on-line to a system they have typically a specific task to perform; it may be to modify an order-line or delete a customer. These are, if you like, atomic units of work performed upon the system in the sense that it is not meaningful to split the task into smaller units. Note, however, that a single on-line task may access more than one entity and sometimes several entities, so they are not always trivial in terms of the data access they require. Batch programs are usually transparent to the user, i.e. they are performed in background mode. Even though users may initiate the running of a batch program, the user is not concerned with how it goes about its task. Even with today's technology and speed of computation, it is still important to ensure that batch programs run relatively efficiently within a system. Because batch programs often process many records, the efficiency savings when made can sometimes be significant. One approach which can assist efficiency is to pool together in a single batch program those transactions which act against the same entity or entities. For example, if it was required to maintain customer details in batch mode, transactions to delete, insert and modify customers could all be performed within a single program. If the volume of transactions were large enough, this could mean that it would be more efficient to read a file serially rather than directly. In database systems, there are likely to be similar advantages. Also, the administrative convenience of dealing with all customer transactions as a single unit is often an attraction. Batch programs can be run at times when the overall utilisation of the computer is lower, such as overnight, so better average use is made of the investment in the computer.

Batch programs can perform a number of functions including:

(1) Validation
The main purpose is to check input transactions against validation rules.

(2) Simple update
This type of program usually follows immediately after a validation program. Its job is to update the database or masterfile with basic transactions (i.e. insert, modify, delete).

(3) Complex update
Sometimes more is required than just simple updating. In the case study, there is a process which on a weekly basis checks all outstanding order-lines to see if there is now sufficient stock to meet the customer's needs. If there is, a new order is created. Sometimes the problem can be more complex. Suppose it was required to make the best possible use of the stock available. Say a particular item had a stock quantity of 60 and three order lines for three different customers existed of 50, 40 and 20 respectively. If the algorithm worked on a first-come first-served basis then the order-line with 50 may be chosen. However, in terms of using up the stock available and also obtaining more profit, satisfying the other two order-lines would be more acceptable. A program which attempted this would be a complex update program. Sometimes such programs use sophisticated linear programming techniques; in other cases rules of thumb are used.

(4) Reporting
Report programs may be detailed reports or summary reports. In addition, update and validation programs will produce error reports.

(5) Extract
Here data from a file or database is extracted and stored separately for some future purpose.

12.2.1 Identify batch programs

In the information systems specification, a set of batch transactions will have been identified to meet the needs of the system and these were recorded in the transactions catalogue. Batch transactions can be combined into batch programs provided that it makes sense to do so. The procedure for identifying batch programs requires detailed analysis of the candidate transactions. The parameters which are significant in making the decision are:

- temporally cohesive processes (e.g. daily, weekly, ad-hoc)
- access of similar entities (or files)
- if reports, equivalent sort order or sort order unimportant

As an example, consider the SBM case study. The month-end candidate transactions for combining into a single batch program are:

- statement of account
- sales report
- aged debt analysis report
- 'delete occurrences from database' transactions

All are temporally cohesive in that they are all processes which take place at month-end. The first task is to perform delay analysis to establish the impact, if any, of one transaction on the other. Since reports do not affect the SDD as such the only additional constraint identified is that the delete program must take place after the reports have been produced. The SDD also provides the preferred sequence for deletion of entity occurrences.

The Sales Report lists each stock item in ascending order of sales made this month.

$$\text{SALES-REPORT} = \{\text{PROD-CODE} + \text{DESCRIPTION} + \text{SALES-THIS-MONTH}\}$$

The entities accessed are product, order-line and order (order contains order-date which is necessary to limit the report to data for current month only).

The Aged Debt Analysis is a summary report.

$$\text{AGED-DEBT-ANALYSIS} = \text{OVERDUE3+} + \text{OVERDUE2-3} + \text{OVERDUE1-2} + \text{OVERDUE-1}$$

where the OVERDUE items refer to the debt which is overdue based on a particular period of time, i.e. debt over three months old, debt between two and three months, debt between one and two months and debt less than month. Entities accessed are order, order-line, and credit-note.

The sequence of the Sales Report is such that it will require a separate program. However, there is an argument for combining the Statement of

Account program with the Aged Debt Analysis, since they use similar entities and because in the Aged Debt Analysis report, the order in which individual entity occurrences are accessed is not important. The delete program could also be combined with the other two programs since they have common entities, but it is suggested that unless there is a severe efficiency problem, such delete programs should be run only after all other programs have run and any final checks made. This is typical of the kind of design trade-off frequently faced. That is, program efficiency versus program flexibility/reusability.

12.2.2 Create batch runcharts

Having identified the batch programs it is now necessary to document them in a way that describes the frequency and sequence of program execution. Such a document is of use to the programmer and operations staff and is referred to as a batch runchart. A separate batch runchart is produced for

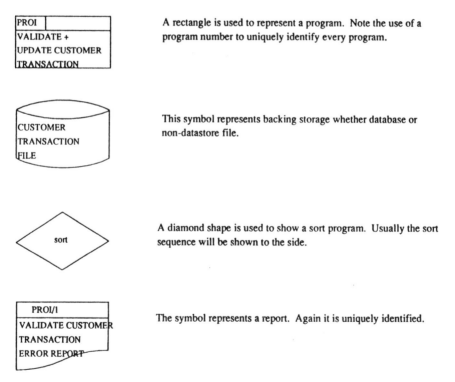

A rectangle is used to represent a program. Note the use of a program number to uniquely identify every program.

This symbol represents backing storage whether database or non-datastore file.

A diamond shape is used to show a sort program. Usually the sort sequence will be shown to the side.

The symbol represents a report. Again it is uniquely identified.

Fig. 12.4. Notation for a batch runchart.

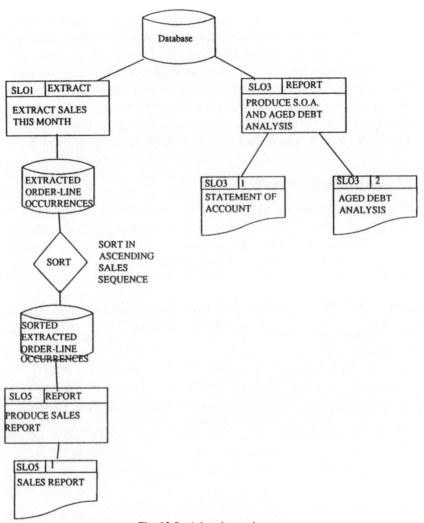

Fig. 12.5. A batch runchart.

each period of frequency, i.e. daily, weekly, etc. The notation used in a batch runchart is explained in figure 12.4 and the monthly runchart for the example discussed above appears in figure 12.5.

12.2.3 Construct a structure chart for each batch program

Chapter 6 described in detail how to go about creating structure charts. The designer will need access to the data dictionary, where-used matrix and batch runchart in order to find the information needed to complete the design.

12.3 PERFORM PHYSICAL PROCESS DESIGN FOR THE ON-LINE TRANSACTIONS

The on-line part of the system involves the user directly interacting with a terminal. The total interaction is called a dialogue, so clearly within a dialogue a user may accomplish many individual tasks such as deleting a customer entity occurrence and so on. A dialogue consists of a series of exchanges. An exchange is defined as either:

- The display of information on a terminal along with its associated processing.
- The entering of data at a terminal along with its associated processing.

It should be clear from the above definition that exchanges exist as components of on-line transactions because, in information systems, it is almost always necessary to enter data which will be used to read from or write to the appropriate datastore(s). In fact, some on-line transactions can be quite complex involving many exchanges. They may also have 'control input' which determines what happens next in the dialogue. Because there are typically many on-line transactions in a system, it is necessary to organise the dialogue in such a way that it is easy for each user to access those transactions of interest. (Indeed for security reasons it is important that the users are not permitted to use unauthorised transactions.) So, before the individual transaction is initiated there is likely to be a series of exchanges which bring the user to the point of executing that transaction. In information systems, this is usually achieved through a hierarchy of menu screens.

Figure 12.6 shows the main symbols used to describe dialogues. The symbols for selection, iteration and grouping are identical to those used in Entity Life Histories. The controlling conditions for selections and iterations are recorded as comments against the control flow.

12.3.1 Identify on-line programs

On-line programs are not the same thing as on-line transactions, though in many cases they will be. On-line programs can be composed of transactions. Two examples are cited here.

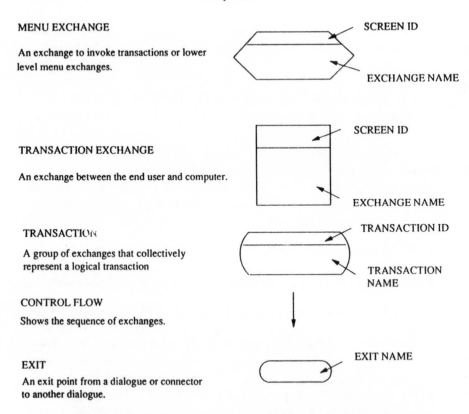

MENU EXCHANGE

An exchange to invoke transactions or lower
level menu exchanges.

SCREEN ID

EXCHANGE NAME

TRANSACTION EXCHANGE

An exchange between the end user and computer.

SCREEN ID

EXCHANGE NAME

TRANSACTION

A group of exchanges that collectively
represent a logical transaction

TRANSACTION ID

TRANSACTION
NAME

CONTROL FLOW

Shows the sequence of exchanges.

EXIT

An exit point from a dialogue or connector
to another dialogue.

EXIT NAME

Fig. 12.6. Notation for menu hierarchies and on-line diaolgues.

In an information system, before say deleting an entity occurrence it is
sound practice to display the contents of the occurrence on screen to confirm
that the correct occurrence is to be deleted. Now, the first part of the dialogue
here could be designed identically to a display transaction which will probably
be required anyway. This would reduce the design and programming
overhead involved. So, on-line programs are identified in a way which
capitalises on the opportunity to reduce the workload and simplify the user
interface.

A second example is where more complex tasks are performed. For
instance, it would be sensible for a user to want to add a complete order as one
activity. This would involve adding one order header followed by many order
item lines. Sometimes complex activities involve many entities and therefore
many individual transactions. When identifying on-line programs of this
type, the SDD should be consulted and delay analysis performed. This will

tell the designer if it is feasible to run different transactions within a single on-line program.

12.3.2 Define menu hierarchy

The tasks involved in creating a menu hierarchy are:

- list on-line programs identified
- define the lowest level menu exchanges
- define higher level menu exchanges
- define help facilities
- define control flow
- review with user

(1) List the on-line programs identified
This is a trivial step which simply lists the on-line programs just identified. These will have to be partitioned in a way appropriate to user needs.

(2) Define the lowest level menu exchanges
In this step on-line programs are grouped for the purpose of being defined on the same menu. In other words, consideration of the user working environment is required to identify groups of programs which are likely to be required by one individual during the same session.

It is important that there is some logic to the partitioning of these programs, as this will make the menu hierarchy more understandable to the

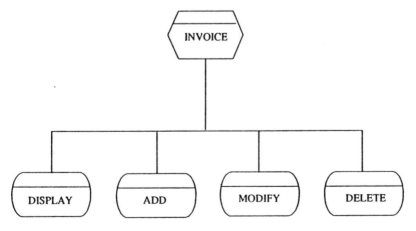

Fig. 12.7. Lowest-level menu exchange for invoice.

user. For example, the programs could be grouped by the data upon which they operate. Figure 12.7 shows the lowest level menu exchange for a set of programs which deals with invoices operating on a sales ledger. Since it is likely that display, add, modify and delete invoice programs will be required during the same session, this will make sense to the user.

Occasionally, perhaps for reasons of confidentiality or authorisation, it may be necessary to restrict the view of programs available, for example where certain staff are not authorised to delete information but are permitted to add information. So the exchanges are then reviewed and modified if necessary in accordance with this need.

Lastly, it may be found useful to add other programs to the menu where a commonly occurring requirement would otherwise mean that the user has to navigate up and down the menu hierarchy to obtain information. For example, it might make sense to add display customer information to the invoice menu exchange.

(3) Define higher level menu exchanges
This applies to situations in which there are lots of programs where it is

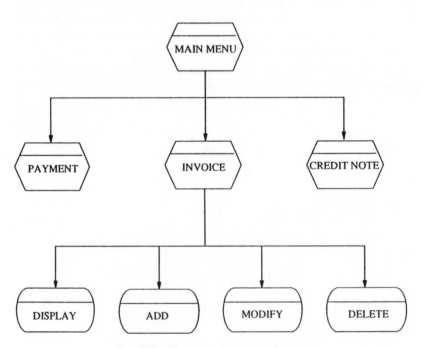

Fig. 12.8. Higher-level menu exchanges.

necessary to have intermediate levels within the hierarchy. Again the overriding consideration is to obtain groupings which minimise navigation and make sense to the user. See figure 12.8.

(4) Define help facilities
Help facilities come in three kinds:

Common help facility. Here a help sub-system can be called from anywhere in the on-line system. Such facilities allow the user effectively to jump out of the current dialogue and explore the help subsystem for help, with the option to return to the dialogue. It is best to document this help facility separately.

Context-sensitive help. This kind of help facility allows users to be given detailed assistance on a particular point within an exchange. For example, a user may be attempting to enter a date but may have forgotten the agreed format for dates. Executing a context-sensitive help option at this point would display a screen which would provide the detailed information required. Context-sensitive help is best recorded within the transaction documentation itself.

Help option. Perhaps the simplest implementation of a help facility occurs through a menu option which calls up help screens. Where this is implemented it should be recorded on the menu hierarchy.

The decision about which kind of help facility to choose is dependent on whether there is an installation standard, sophistication of the users and the trade-off on the work involved in providing such facilities, since particularly context-sensitive help can consume a lot of extra effort.

(5) Define the control flow
Control flow shows the permitted options for the movement from one screen to the next. A useful additional piece of information can be added at this stage and that is the actual value of the control input required to initiate that option. This is shown as CI (for control input) plus the digit or character. So 'CI4' indicates that to execute this option the digit 4 is to be depressed.

Sometimes installations have standards for on-line systems which have a bearing on this task. These standards typically apply to all on-line systems in the company, and therefore need to be reflected here. For example CI9 might always mean 'return to main menu', CI8 might mean 'help' and so on. See figure 12.9.

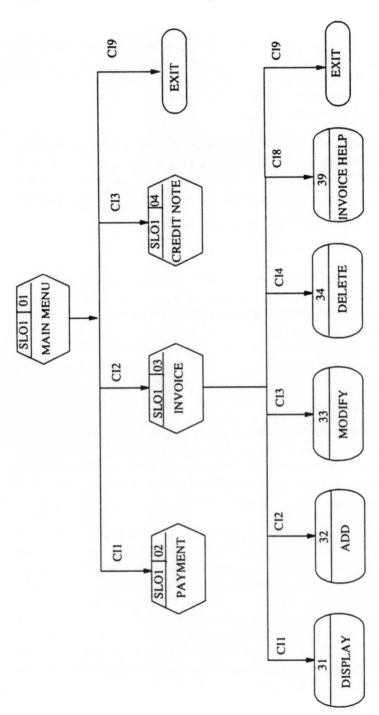

Fig. 12.9. Menu exchange with help and control flow added.

(6) Review with user

The menu hierarchy can now be reviewed with the user in conjunction with screen layouts. This will enable him to visualise the menu hierarchy more clearly.

The analyst should try to obtain the following from the review:

- That all necessary programs have been identified.
- That the groupings of programs are meaningful and helpful to the user.
- That all exit and return options have been identified.
- That help facilities are useful and relevant.

12.3.3 Define the on-line program dialogues

The following is carried out for each on-line program:

- List the exchanges in the program.
- Define the sequence of exchanges.
- Define controlling conditions for selections and iterations.
- Define the data passed between exchanges.
- Review with user.

The program dialogue is built up in a similar bottom-up manner to the menu hierarchy, starting by simply listing the components and progressively adding detail until it is complete.

(1) List the exchanges in the program

This stage involves identifying the components of a program by listing each situation where either data is input or information is displayed. For instance, to add invoice data to a sales ledger, firstly data would be entered. If any fields were invalid then an error message would be displayed; otherwise a success message would be displayed asking the user if adding another invoice is required.

If an identical series of exchanges has already been identified under another program, then it need not be repeated here and the connector symbol is used to establish the link.

(2) Define the sequence of exchanges

This task involves drawing the program dialogue using the notation introduced earlier. Note that good program dialogues are characterised by validation iterations in which the dialogue cannot proceed to the next stage until all validation criteria have been met, as in figure 12.10.

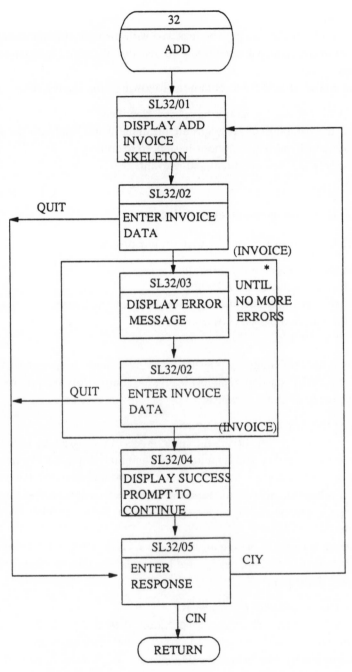

Fig. 12.10. On-line dialogue for add invoice transaction.

(3) Define controlling conditions for selections and iterations

Control inputs for selections are entered on the relevant control flow and the controlling condition for iterations is normally recorded beside the iteration symbol.

Sometimes, however, the nature of the dialogue can be more complicated. For instance, the next stage in the dialogue may be dictated by the content of the data entered, e.g. where a part is either purchased from an outside supplier or manufactured internally. If purchased, one type of screen showing purchasing details is displayed, if manufactured a different screen is displayed. In such circumstances the controlling conditions would be denoted 'CI/PURCHASED' and 'CI/MANUFACTURED'.

(4) Define the data passed between exchanges

Any data entered or data retrieved from datastores which is then passed on to the next exchange is formally recorded on the dialogue. To distinguish this data from control input, brackets are placed round such data.

(5) User review

A user review is now necessary to confirm that the internal screens and method of operation are both practical and user-friendly.

12.3.4 Construct a structure chart for each on-line program identified

On-line program structure charts often contain reusable components, so in constructing the charts, the designer should seek out opportunities for reusability. Access to the data dictionary, where-used matrix and on-line program dialogues is required.

12.4 CONFIRM THE CORRECTNESS OF THE DESIGN

Some of the steps above are ones which go back to the user to show and confirm the work done. Clearly this is useful for areas of work where users can sensibly provide feedback. Equally there are other parts of the design where it is not possible to involve users directly, e.g. with the physical data model and the structure charts. Here the problem is that of verification rather than validation.

12.4.1 Identify key deliverables for verification

In an ideal world all deliverables would be verified. However, where time does not permit, those deliverables which are 'more important than others' should at least be verified. This would include deliverables at the heart of the design such as the physical data model and high volume, high frequency or complex programs. A list is generated of those deliverables in preparation for their verification.

12.4.2 Conduct walkthroughs of key deliverables

Structured walkthroughs are now performed on these deliverables taking care to involve experts such as the database administrator where appropriate.

12.5 SUMMARY

The system design process has been described as a process which develops and extends the deliverables created in earlier phases. However, the emphasis of that work has for the most part been concentrated on how the system can achieve its goals rather than what the goals are. This is seen in the kinds of activity undertaken.

Physical data design is essentially a task of deciding on the specific software product (where necessary) and converting the CLDD into the notation for that product. Ideally, the software engineer should liaise with an expert in that particular product as there may well be refinements which can improve the overall efficiency of the system. Indeed, in large computer departments nowadays, it is unusual not to have a resident database administrator who either provides advice or carries out the physical data design. Organisations without access to such expertise run serious risks.

Likewise physical process design is also a question of deciding how the system can achieve its goals. Much of it is to do with packaging. For example, batch transactions are packaged into batch programs, on-line programs are packaged into a menu hierarchy and so on. This does not change the system objectives, it merely facilitates its implementation. The other part of physical process design is to do with deciding on the components of a program, i.e. producing structure charts. Again, this is very much a business of deciding how a program is to be implemented rather than what it has to do.

The distinction between analysis and design is one over which many people debate. The issue is where exactly to draw the line. The interpretation proposed in this book is just one of many possible. What is important, however, is that design is not delegated to some back-room activity which does not involve contact with users. As demonstrated in this chapter, there is a clear need to confirm the work done with users and involve them in the design process and it is important that the opportunity to do so is taken.

The tasks in system design are:

1 Produce a physical data model for the required system:
   - decide on access method
2 Complete the physical processing documentation for the required system:
   - identify batch programs
   - create batch runcharts
   - construct a structure chart for each batch program identified
   - identify on-line programs
   - define menu hierarchy
   - define on-line program dialogues
   - construct a structure chart for each on-line program identified
3 Confirm correctness of design:
   - identify key deliverables for verification
   - conduct walkthroughs of key deliverables

12.6 EXERCISES

1   Create a batch runchart for the program which 'deletes occurrences from the database'.

2   Draw on-line program dialogues for the display, delete and modify invoice programs.

Chapter 13
System Construction

This chapter will discuss the system construction process. Most people connect the programming task with this and of course the programming of modules is an important part of the system construction activity. However, it would be very wrong to assume that programming is the only activity in system construction or indeed the most important one. In software engineering all activities are important. System construction as discussed here is an assembly task in which modules once programmed are assembled into programs and programs are then assembled into the system. At each stage, necessary planning and testing is carried out to ensure that the assembly process is being implemented properly.

System construction is a phase in which many people are working on the system. Programmers are coding, data centre staff are assisting in the plans for implementation, analysts are perhaps training users in addition to checking out test results and planning for the final events in the construction process. At the same time, there is a considerable amount of documentation being produced. There are four major activities associated with construction. These are:

- Construct and test individual modules on the structure charts.
- Develop and implement plans for the testing of each program.
- Develop and implement plans for the system to be put into a live environment.
- Complete all outstanding documentation.

13.1 CONSTRUCT AND TEST INDIVIDUAL MODULES ON THE STRUCTURE CHARTS

13.1.1 Construct module code for each structure chart

The technique for achieving this was discussed in chapter 7. An important design goal is that reusable modules will have been identified and that therefore the work load here is as small as possible.

13.1.2 Create test data results table

This table was described in chapter 8. To create it, one has to enter all test cases identified, dry running results and expected results. Dry running results are obtained by manually working through the module code using the test cases in the table. These tables form part of the system documentation since they can be used in maintenance. They tell the programmer what was tested originally. The programmer can then modify this to take account of the amendments being made to the module.

13.1.3 Confirm correctness of module

The module is compiled and any compilation errors are corrected. Each module is then run against each of the test cases by using driver modules. A driver is a small dummy program which enables the programmer to simply call up and test a module. It may contain logic which allows the module to be called up many times, thereby allowing a number of scenarios to be tested. The results are entered into the test data results table. Where there is a variance between expected and actual results this is investigated and resolved using the debugging techniques discussed in chapter 8.

13.2 DEVELOP AND IMPLEMENT PLANS FOR THE TESTING OF EACH PROGRAM

13.2.1 Create an integration test plan for each program

Once an individual module has been tested, it should be integrated with its counterparts so that the program itself can be verified as working properly. Of critical importance here is the interface between modules; just because individual modules work on their own is no guarantee that they will work correctly when combined together. The number, sequence and type of parameters passed from one module to another is clearly crucial.

There are two different approaches to integration testing. The first, which is not recommended, is called the 'big-bang' approach. Here, all modules are tested separately and then in a 'one-off' attempt are integrated and the whole program is run. The big-bang approach has implications for how the modules are to be tested. Because individual modules are tested separately first, this means that both driver and stub modules will be required. (A stub module is a dummy module which mimics the effect of a real module. It is useful when

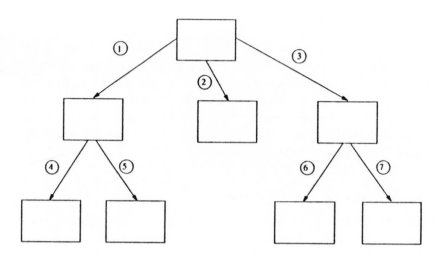

Fig. 13.1. Breadth-first testing.

testing a module which calls up a lower level module.) With the big-bang approach one driver and one stub are required for each arrow (arc) on the structure chart. In addition, interface errors are not able to be identified until after individual module testing is complete. Also, debugging is made more difficult because the location of an error could be anywhere.

The alternative to 'big-bang' is an 'incremental' approach in which modules are brought together level by level. There are two ways of doing this, either top-down or bottom-up.

(1) Top-down testing

Testing begins at the top of the structure chart and works its way downward either using a breadth-first strategy (see figure 13.1) or depth-first strategy (see figure 13.2). Top-down testing implies that stub modules are required but no drivers. An advantage of this approach is that any interface problems occurring towards the top of the structure chart are identified earlier. Observe that higher-level modules are likely to contain more complex logic than lower level modules and therefore are more susceptible to error.

(2) Bottom-up testing

Testing begins at the bottom of the structure chart, so that only drivers are required. Testing is easier to perform with bottom-up because the driver can call up the module many times to test many cases. Top-down is harder because the stubs may have to be changed to simulate different effects.

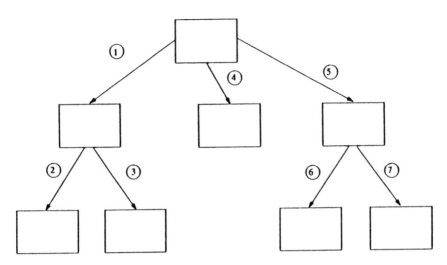

Fig. 13.2. Depth-first testing.

Because input and output takes place at the lowest levels, it is useful to have this tested early so that new data can be input.

Each approach has its own merits. Some software engineers adopt a compromise approach, called 'sandwich' testing in which both top-down and bottom-up is done.

The approach recommended here is generally bottom-up. Only where top modules are particularly complex or for other reasons such as to demonstrate the user interface early, should a departure from this philosophy take place. One last point to note is that families of low-level modules can be identified quite early in the life cycle. This can often be done even before structure charts are specified. For example, given appropriate departmental standards, if it is known that a new attribute will need to be input on-line, then a family of modules which validates the attribute and creates error messages for it can be written, tested in advance and be waiting to be used in integration testing.

13.2.2 Confirm correctness of structure charts and menu hierarchy

The test plan created in the earlier section is implemented. Any error found causes the programmer to return to an earlier stage of development to effect a correction. The menu hierarchy, which in large systems can be quite extensive, has to be developed and tested like any other part of the system. In fact, the easiest way to deal with the menu hierarchy is to consider it as a program in its own right.

13.2.3 Conduct inspections on selected programs

The chapter on project management describes inspections in detail. Basically, they are part of the quality assurance system and are particularly useful for evaluating the quality of programs. It is worthwhile identifying critical programs for inspection and this should be scheduled into the plan so that there is no temptation to avoid inspections because of time pressure.

13.3 DEVELOP AND IMPLEMENT PLANS FOR THE SYSTEM TO BE PUT INTO A LIVE ENVIRONMENT

13.3.1 Create and implement a system test plan

The aim in system testing is to ensure that the system meets the original objectives laid down for it. Sometimes the objectives are technical, e.g. speed of response, size of memory, volumes to be processed. These can be relatively easily confirmed by creating appropriate test cases and should be done, as far as possible, in as realistic an environment as possible. For example, speed of response and overall ability to process agreed volumes should be checked at periods in the day which are low, average and peak in terms of computer usage. Sometimes objectives are implicit such as those to do with overall acceptability of the system to the user. Here, the user manual, which is discussed shortly, is an indispensable tool as it can be used to generate a range of scenarios which are representative of use of the system by users. Since the system test actually runs the system, it is an opportunity to confirm the user interface with the users and that the package of documentation (i.e. the user manual, any training materials and so on) is acceptable.

13.3.2 Create and implement an installation test plan

The system test proves that the system meets its objectives; but it still needs to be embedded in its production environment and run using operational procedures. The installation test is designed to confirm that this has been done correctly. Mature data centres have their own staff who are responsible for a wide range of tasks connected with making sure a newly developed system is passed over properly and embedded into the production environment. Such tasks include writing their own 'production' job control language, allocating partitions in the operating system (if necessary), writing recovery procedures, setting up user passwords and ensuring availability of networking facilities. Part of the documentation produced by the development team is the operations manual, which sets out the information required by the data centre. Again, in conjunction with the objectives for the system, a set of test scenarios is constructed which form the basis of an installation test.

13.3.3 Create and implement a changeover plan

There has already been some discussion on system testing and installation testing. Once these are successfully completed, the system may begin live running, i.e. the new system is run in 'production' instead of the old one. The question of how to go about this is referred to as changeover. Changeover is concerned with the transition from the old system to the new one. There nearly always is an old system, even if it is only a manual system. More frequently nowadays, the transition is from an existing computer system, albeit a batch or file-based system, to an on-line database system. In changeover it is necessary to identify and put in place the initial database (or files) so that the new system can start from an up-to-date basis. Secondly, it involves identifying how and when to cut across from the old system to the new one.

(1) Identify data changeover strategy
If data exists in the old system in, say, files, a utility program may be required to load it into the new system. Often this is complicated by the fact that in the new system the data is formatted differently. Worse still, there may be additional data required which was not in the original system's files. So a data changeover strategy has to be devised to address this problem. It is important that the timing of this is right so that all data transferred is current. Often on-line transactions or batch programs already identified for the new system can assist this activity.

(2) Identify procedure changeover strategy
Here we need to address the questions of when and how the new system will take over from the old one. There are four basic ways:

- direct changeover
- parallel run

- retrospective pilot run
- staged pilot run

Direct changeover.   In direct changeover the new system simply replaces the old one. See figure 13.3(a). It is the easiest of the four ways and also involves least effort and cost. However, it is the riskiest since if the new system is disastrous, it may not be easy or possible to return to the old one.

Parallel running.   Parallel running involves running both the new and old systems simultaneously. See figure 13.3(b). As far as is feasible, the results from the new system are checked against the results from the old. This is an expensive method because it requires running two systems at once with all the

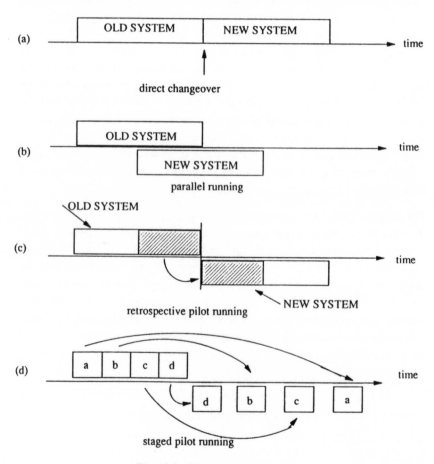

Fig. 13.3. Changeover strategies.

time, cost and effort that entails. However, it does have the advantage that if the new system is materially wrong, the old system can still be used. It is useful where a new computerised system is close to an old one.

Retrospective pilot running. See figure 13.3(c). This is the same as parallel running except that it uses data from a previous period rather than the current period. The advantage is that the cross-checking in effect can be spread over two time periods, i.e. the first period can be used to prepare the data for cross-checking, the second to actually do the checking. However, its disadvantage lies in that the new system is one period behind and further arrangements are required to make it current.

Staged pilot running. In staged pilot running the system is implemented in parts. This means that during this implementation, parts of the new system are working alongside parts of the old. See figure 13.3(d). This is a particularly useful approach with large complicated systems, as it allows a gradual move from the old to the new and importantly allows the users to proceed at their own pace. However, the logistics of the transition are often non-trivial requiring a detailed transition plan.

13.4 COMPLETE ALL OUTSTANDING DOCUMENTATION

13.4.1 Package program documentation

The various components of program documentation already exist, but for ease of access should be packaged into a single document so that information can be quickly retrieved.

13.4.2 Create a user manual

The user manual is the users' guide to the system. It therefore has to contain everything they need to know about the system (including who to contact if there are queries or problems). Although called a 'manual' it may have other components such as computer-based training (CBT) sessions to aid user familiarisation with the system. It ought to contain the following:

- Brief narrative of the system including scope and boundary.
- Details of facilities provided.
- Illustrations of screens and reports, including explanations and references to the CBT sessions.

- Instructions on how to complete any batch input documents.
- Details and instructions on any manual procedures in the system.

13.4.2 Contribute to operations manual

The operations manual is the data centre's guide to running the system. As such it should be written by data centre staff, though clearly development staff will contribute heavily in terms of providing much of the source material for it. The data dictionary can supply much of the information required. It should contain the following:

- All program, menu hierarchy and runchart details.
- Database details.
- Recovery, fall-back and retention procedures.
- Links with other systems, planned and existing.
- Computer utilisation, e.g. partition sizes, space requirements, network utilisation.
- Anticipated growth rates.
- Control checking procedures.
- Privacy statement, i.e. permitted access to data and procedures.
- Sample outputs.

13.5 SUMMARY

This is the last phase of the development of the system save for the maintenance cycle (which in effect is a reiteration of all stages of the life cycle). It brings to a focus all the work that has gone into developing the system. Not surprisingly it is a time of high activity and high criticality. If something seriously goes wrong here it is almost impossible to avoid missing the deadline. So it is an important phase and if the work in earlier phases has been done properly, then this phase should go smoothly. If the system construction phase is chaotic, it is a sign that earlier work is inadequate.

The major tasks in system construction are:

1 Construct and test individual modules on the structure charts:
   - construct module code for each structure chart
   - create test data results table
   - confirm correctness of modules
2 Develop and implement plans for the testing of each program:

- create an integration test plan for each program
- confirm correctness of structure charts and menu hierarchy
- conduct inspections on selected programs

3 Develop and implement plans for the system to be put into a live environment:
- create and implement a system test plan
- create and implement an installation test plan
- create and implement a changeover plan

4 Complete all outstanding documentation:
- package program documentation
- create a user manual
- contribute to an operations manual

13.6 EXERCISES

1   Question 1 in section 8.7 required that lists of test cases be created for two modules. Convert these lists into test data results tables and dry run them.

2   Create an integration test plan for the ADD INVOICE program. Make assumptions about the need to show part of the user interface early, so that some sandwich testing is required.

Part C
The Environment of Software Engineering

Chapter 14
Project Management

14.1 INTRODUCTION TO PROJECT MANAGEMENT

In chapters in this part of the text, it is intended that discussion moves beyond a particular method, so that broader issues can be addressed. Hopefully, in doing so, the reader will obtain deeper insight into the business of software engineering. This chapter deals with project management, i.e. the management of the development of an information system. No matter what particular method is used, it is proposed that projects still need to be managed, because they involve typically thousands of individual tasks performed by many individuals, sometimes in groups, sometimes not, and often involving many thousands of pounds, dollars or whatever. Perhaps the best way to justify project management is to consider what would happen if a project were not managed as such.

For the people working on the project, the most likely consequences would be those arising from a failure to communicate what was happening on the project and from a failure to co-ordinate the work-flow within the project. These kinds of failure manifest themselves in the project team member not knowing what is to be done, when it is to be done and also through work-products not being available at the beginning of the task. Because people are unable to do what they should be doing, the work of the project is not being progressed and delay is inevitable. Clearly, in order to avoid this, a scheme of planning is necessary to ensure that work is given to team members, responsibility for tasks is allocated and that team members know who to talk to.

Suppose now that adequate planning, communicating and co-ordinating had taken place, but no other kind of project management was done. What we have now is a project that could be successful as long as everything goes to plan, i.e. there is no room for mistakes, tasks taking longer than expected and so on. This is clearly unrealistic. As the project progresses it has to be accepted that there will be variations to plan. These variations have to be monitored and the impact on the project assessed, so that corrective action can, if possible, take place to allow the project to meet its deadline. This is called project control and takes place during the life of the project, i.e. while the information system is being developed.

It is clear, therefore, that project management has to address the above if a project is going to be successful. But how do you know if a project has been successful?

There are three factors in considering the success or failure of a project:

- quality
- time
- cost

Quality.   Systems must be implemented to an acceptable level of quality, but acceptable to whom? There are many different people involved, e.g. users, the computer operations department, the programmers, designers and so on. This is why a specification is such an important concept in software engineering. It is a specification's job to define all the criteria for the success of a component of a system. This includes not only correctness but other criteria such as performance constraints and memory constraints.

Time.   Projects have deadlines which have to be met. If a project goes past a deadline:

- Other projects may be delayed.
- The organisation's business could be affected because assumptions were made about the availability of the system.
- The manager's and the computer department's credibility is reduced.

So time is an important factor in projects. But on what basis is the deadline set? One way is to estimate how long each task will take. By combining estimates together taking account of prerequisite tasks and available resources, the total estimated elapsed time can be calculated and a deadline set. But who makes the estimate and upon what basis? Clearly, the accuracy of the estimate is a significant factor in setting realistic deadlines.

Cost.   See figure 14.1. Once-off or non-recurring costs are costs incurred when either developing the system or in facilitating its environment, e.g. providing hardware for users. Development costs include the cost of staff and all consumables used, computer time, etc. Recurring costs are the costs associated with the on-going use of the system once live and include consumables, the cost for operating the system including staff time and so on. Again, the difficulty of estimation arises.

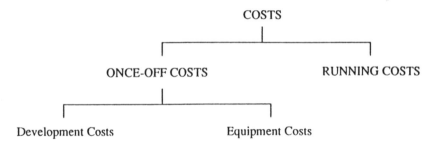

Fig. 14.1. Cost breakdown in a project.

The above seems to raise more questions than it answers, but before moving on let's summarise what has been covered so far. Project managment has been introduced as a necessary part of the development process, vital for the success of the project. The following tasks are therefore part of project management:

- communicating
- coordinating
- organising the work on a project
- determining the resources required
- allocating resources on a time scheduled basis
- allocating responsibility
- integrating the work of all parties involved
- controlling progress by identifying causes of problems and taking appropriate action
- anticipating events and avoiding problems
- estimating time till completion
- handling unexpected events
- budgeting and financial control
- working within time and cost constraints
- ensuring quality objectives are met

The above discussion has also highlighted or at least hinted at a number of other issues about project management, for instance the problem of estimation. These issues form the remainder of the chapter and are introduced below.

(1) Principles of project management
The management style adopted can have a significant impact on the morale of the team and through that whether a 'team spirit' emerges. Current

management thinking is that, given the type of people who work in computing, their education and background, the most effective style for a project leader is that of a facilitator who can remove inhibitors in the environment and let staff get on with the job they are supposed to do. As well as lessons from general management theory, there are also aspects that are specific to computer projects which represent lessons learnt the 'hard way' and which are consistent with the overall management philosophy. Together these present a mature approach to running computer projects.

(2) Project management techniques
The principles of project management just mentioned represent, if you like, the 'people-side' of running projects. Complementary to these principles is the need to employ basic procedures or techniques which will assist the project leader in planning, controlling, communicating and so on. It is the combination of good management style and the use of solid project management techniques which, it is submitted, makes for sound project management.

(3) Estimation
This section takes a critical look at estimation techniques available and discusses why estimation remains a 'thorn in the flesh' of good project management practice.

(4) Project organisation
People work in project teams. In order for groups of people to be effective in achieving overall project aims, it is usual for individuals to be allocated specific tasks and responsibilities. Clearly this can be done in different ways and there are implications for the motivation of team members and for productivity generally in the way that projects are organised.

(5) Quality assurance
The difficulty of ensuring high-quality work products is another important issue in project management. This section looks briefly at what quality assurance is, what mechanisms exist for quality assurance and also the role that quality assurance can play in the provision of a 'quality' environment.

14.2 PRINCIPLES OF PROJECT MANAGEMENT

14.2.1 Adopt a risk-reducing philosophy

A sign of a lack of project management is that the project is in a generally

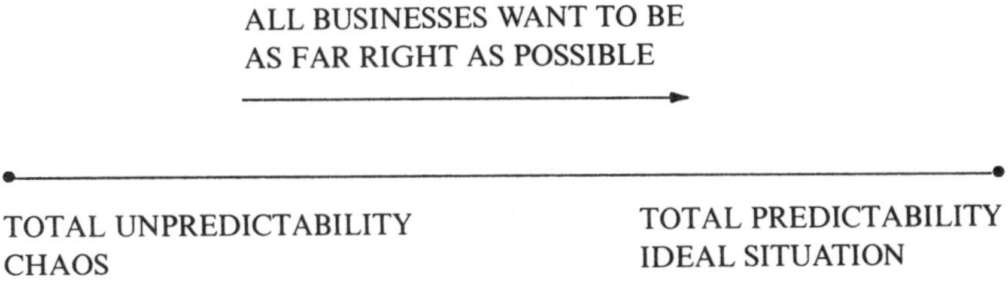

ALL BUSINESSES WANT TO BE
AS FAR RIGHT AS POSSIBLE

TOTAL UNPREDICTABILITY   TOTAL PREDICTABILITY
CHAOS   IDEAL SITUATION

Fig. 14.2. Continuum of predictability/unpredictability.

chaotic state. Such disarray is inconsistent with the desire that all businesses have, which is to be in control of their own destiny by knowing or by being able to anticipate exactly what will happen. See figure 14.2. Though it may not be possible with computer projects to reach an ideal situation of total predictability, a mature management outlook would be one which aimed to reduce the risk of failure as far as possible by sound planning and control of the project. Decisions taken, therefore, would be ones which sought to reduce risk.

14.2.2 Adopt an evolutionary approach to planning projects

In the business world, it is common for the provider of services to commit to charges and timescales before the work has begun. When applied in the computing context, this inevitably means that such commitments are made before detailed analysis has begun. Yet without detailed analysis, there is no way of knowing just what is to be done or how much effort is involved. Consider the method introduced earlier in this book. Having drawn the DFDs, does the analyst know how many programs are required to be written, never mind how much work is involved in them? At later stages, the users themselves may ask for additional facilities or reports. How can this be taken into account when providing a cost estimate at the very beginning?

As mentioned earlier, some way has to be found to make estimates on the basis of 'known' amounts of work. One way is to move away from the idea that the whole project is able to be estimated at the start. This implies that the user community has to be converted to a different viewpoint. Here, detailed estimation is only attempted for the next stage of the project. Although broad estimates would be required for overall project length and cost, it has to be well understood that these are only approximate guides. As each stage is completed, estimates for the next stage can be finalised and agreed with the users and so on until the project is finished. The evolutionary approach is known colloquially as 'creeping commitment' because as the next stage of the project is reached, the overall picture becomes firmer.

14.2.3 Make work units an appropriate size

Work units should be of an appropriate size to provide quick feedback. For the development of information systems, the ideal size of task is probably somewhere between 20 and 40 hours. If less than that, then there will be so many tasks in the project that information overloading will arise. If tasks are too big, then corrective action may be too late.

14.2.4 Apply the principle of contingency

Contingency is an allowance of time which is consumed when unexpected events occur during the life of a project. An allowance of 10 to 15% is typical for most DP projects. It is important that individual project members do not assume that each task (or member) is entitled to its own contingency allowance. Authority for using contingency is the responsibility of the project manager and is only given when justified by, typically, external events, e.g. non-delivery of hardware.

14.2.5 Generate both qualititative and quantitative data about the project

Both qualitative and quantitative data must be available from a project status reporting system. Quantitative data provides the basis for establishing that something may be going wrong. Qualitative data may provide a clue as to the cause of the problem.

14.2.6 Adopt a 'control and monitor' philosophy

Common sense tells us that when changes are made within a project it is necessary to monitor these in terms of the effect that they have. For example, it may be that the action taken has the desired effect; equally it may not – it could have no effect, too much effect or a different effect. So it is important to follow up actions taken to confirm that the desired effect has actually taken place.

A working model for the control of projects is therefore:

• plan next project phase

- compare actual against plan
- take action and adjust plan if necessary
- observe outcome, adjusting again if necessary

14.2.7 Use the concept of estimate to completion

The idea of 'estimate to completion' is an important concept in project management. Suppose a task was originally estimated at 20 hours. After 10 hours have been completed by the project member, if the estimate was accurate, 10 hours remain. However, suppose in the opinion of the team member, 15 hours still remain. What the team member is saying here is that after some experience of working on the task an arguably better estimate can be provided. Now there may be a number of different reasons for the increase in estimated length of estimate, for example, poor estimating, machine problems and so on, but if the cause is one which will repeat itself in other tasks then it is important that it is identified as early as possible so that appropriate action can take place.

14.2.8 Control the work

Work is controlled, not people. In other words a 'witch-hunt mentality' is unlikely to be a productive one. The role of the project leader is to remove excuses for non-delivery of tasks. Once they have been removed, then staff will begin to produce the goods.

14.2.9 Provide feedback to members

Feedback data should go back to the project member who did the work. Here the concept of self-control is important. Where appropriate, rather than imposing corrective action, the project manager can involve the project member in finding solutions. This is a preferred way of handling problems and is more likely to be effective since those most directly affected are involved in the solution.

14.2.10 Always review a project after its completion

One of the major causes of lack of progress in the maturation of the computer industry as a whole is its consistent failure, in a semi-formal way, to learn from its mistakes and try to do better next time. At the end of each project a formal project management review should take place asking questions such as:

- What went wrong and why?
- What went right and why?
- How can we improve our strengths and reduce our weaknesses?

14.3 PROJECT MANAGEMENT TECHNIQUES

A number of techniques are presented here which assist in planning and/or controlling projects. Each technique plays only a part in the overall process. No one technique is capable of solving all problems. The techniques are introduced in roughly the sequence they are likely to be used.

14.3.1 Work breakdown structure (WBS)

The starting point for creating a plan for each stage in a project is the Work Breakdown Structure. When structured methods are used, this is straightforward because individual tasks within a stage are easily identified.

What may not be clear in some instances is the number of times a task may need to be repeated. For example, in investigating the current system, a hierarchy of DFDs is drawn. But, it will not be known in advance just how many level 2 and level 3 DFDs will need to be drawn. Here, the project leader's best guess should be used, which should be based on an understanding of the scope of the project. The Work Breakdown Structure is simply a hierarchy of tasks in a project. It is therefore based on the method used. To illustrate the concept, figure 14.3 shows a simplified WBS for developing a program using a structure chart.

14.3.2 Network analysis

Some of the detailed tasks which were identified in the Work Breakdown Structure, will be dependent on the completion of other tasks. It is important to recognise this because it affects when tasks can be started. It is possible to draw a diagram which records the dependencies between tasks. This diagram is a network of tasks (hence the name network analysis) and enables the project leader to make decisions about the project. The networks are often known as PERT (Program Evaluation and Review Technique) networks or CPA (Critical Path Analysis) networks. These names come from the kind of analysis that is typically done on the network. In PERT, the idea is that the

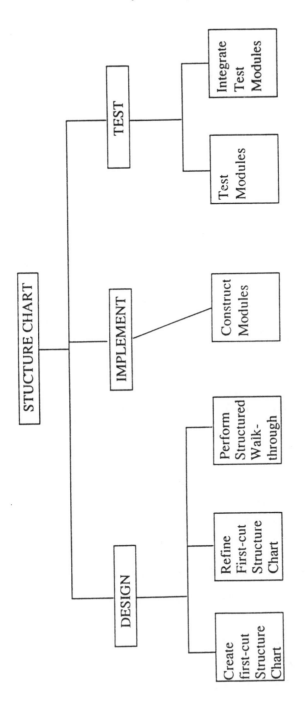

Fig. 14.3. Simplified Work Breakdown Structure for a structure chart.

TASK	DESCRIPTION	TASK	PREREQUISITE TIME (Hrs)
A)	create first-cut structure chart	10	-
B)	refine first-cut structure chart	3	A
C)	perform structured walkthrough	2	B
D)	construct module 1	10	C
E)	construct module 2	5	C
F)	construct module 3	5	C
G)	test module 1	3	D
H)	test module 2	2	E
I)	test module 3	1	F
J)	integrate test structure chart	4	G, H, I

Table 14.1. Prerequisites table for simplified structure chart.

project's progress is updated and assessed on the network. In CPA, the emphasis is on finding the longest path of tasks, i.e. the critical path, which enables management to focus on the more important tasks in terms of deadline. There are two notations for drawing networks. They are called the precedence notation and the arrow (or I-J) notation. The precedence notation is used here because often, with the arrow notation, 'dummy' arrows proliferate which tend to clutter up the diagram.

(1) Drawing the project network

Each task in the project stage is listed. By considering each task in turn, the task number of any prerequisite task is recorded against it, as well as the time estimate for that task. Table 14.1 shows this for the structure chart problem used earlier; for brevity it is assumed there are only three modules. It is then a relatively straightforward matter to draw the network in figure 14.4. Each box represents a task, each arrow a dependency. The estimated duration of the task appears in brackets within the box. Some common terminology is introduced which also illustrates the power of networks:

Serial tasks.   These occur when one task must end before another can start, e.g. tasks A and B are serial tasks.

Parallel tasks.   These are tasks which can occur at the same time, i.e. one task is not dependent on the other. For example, D and E are parallel tasks.

Earliest start (ES).   This is the earliest possible time a task can begin. It is

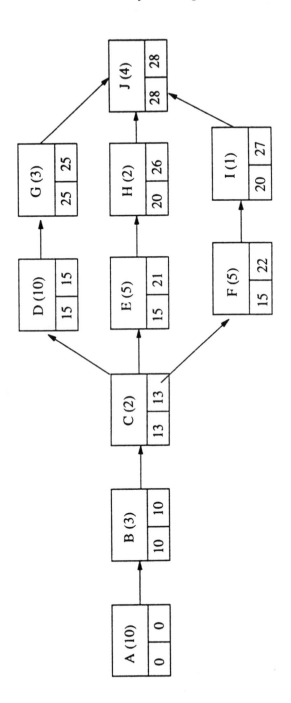

Fig. 14.4. Precedence network for simplified structure chart.

calculated by summing task estimates on the longest path to that task. This is shown in the bottom left-hand side of the box. So, the ES for task E is 15.

Latest start (LS).   This is the latest time a task can begin and still remain on schedule. It is calculated by working backwards from the end of the network. This is shown in the bottom right-hand side of the box. So, the LS for task E is 21.

Total float (TF).   This is the maximum time a task can be delayed without delaying the project completion date. TF = LS – ES. So the TF for task E is 6.

Critical path.   The route with the longest sequence of task times through the network, i.e. the sequence with zero float. (Note that the total project time in figure 14.4 is 32 because task J takes 4 hours.)

(2) Resource scheduling

The network as it stands is very useful. Floats, earliest and latest starts provide data about how flexible a starting date for a particular task is. But it is unrealistic in one important respect. It takes no account of available resources, i.e. how many people are available to work on the various tasks. In fact, it assumes unlimited resources. Now it is possible to create a resource schedule for the project. This involves, firstly, identifying what resources are required for each task, e.g. designer, programmer or whatever. Then a bar-chart is drawn from the network. See figure 14.5. Each task on the network is represented as a bar on a time-based schedule. The dashed lines represent total float. At the bottom of the chart, the different resource types required

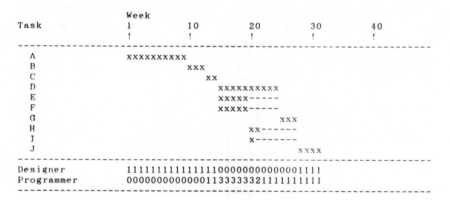

Fig. 14.5. Resource schedule for simplified structure chart.

are shown. By simply accumulating the resources required by resource type, a total for each period of the number of each resource type is established. So, on a period-by-period basis, the number of designers, programmers and so on required for the project is now known. In figure 14.5, because of the float, we can see that only two programmers are sufficient to keep to the original project deadline, i.e. one programmer could perform tasks D and G, and the other programmer tasks E, H, F and I. The process of evening out the overall load in this fashion is called resource smoothing or resource levelling.

14.3.3 Manpower plan

Every development group needs to keep a manpower plan, which details when each member of the department is available to be allocated further work. Manpower plans are often detailed down to day units. By consulting the manpower plan, it can be established if the resources are available when required. See figure 14.6. If they are, then the project can go ahead as it stands and individuals can be allocated specific tasks and this will be updated in the manpower plan. However, it is often the case that the resources are not available either in the numbers required or when they are required. Now it may be possible to find the resources by taking advantage of the available float. What this means is that the starting date of one or more tasks may be delayed within their available float, so that the resources required can be met by the resources available in the department at that time, as happened in the discussion on resource scheduling. If this can be done in all cases then the project completion date originally determined by the network can still be met.

However, it is important that assumptions built into the network are not seen as immutable. Two significant examples are discussed here. Firstly,

```
            !    WEEK 20      !    WEEK 21     !    WEEK 22
--------------------------------------------------------------------
              struc
Designer A    chart     design
              scl       prog xyz
--------------------------------------------------------------------
              struc
Programmer B  chart
              scl
--------------------------------------------------------------------
              struc
Programmer C  chart     prog xyz
              scl
--------------------------------------------------------------------
```

Fig. 14.6. Manpower plan showing allocated tasks.

Fig. 14.7. Extract from a full project schedule.

consider figure 14.7. The assumption here is that all programs need to be specified before programming on any one of them may begin. This is unlikely to be the case. It will normally be possible to start programming as soon as individual structure chart specifications are completed. So, the start of programming may be brought forward.

Secondly, it is feasible that some tasks could be done in less time if more resources are allocated to them. One has to be careful with this notion, however, because it has dangerous implications. The relationship between numbers of resources and time is almost certainly not linear. In other words, doubling the resources may not halve the time. In most tasks it will be necessary for staff to communicate with each other about problems, progress and so on. The more staff, the more time spent on communication. This will eat into the time allocated. Clearly, it depends on the nature of the task, but it is generally accepted that adding numbers to tasks is a cavalier policy. Brook's book[1] contains some classic anecdotes about the folly of such attempts. However, what is recommended is a common-sense approach to resource scheduling. Alternatives such as the ones described above ought to be at least considered. But they should not be allocated so tightly that it is inevitable that something will go wrong.

Even after all alternatives have been considered, it may still be that the resource constraints are such that the completion date just cannot be sensibly met. In such cases the completion date has to be extended. Whatever is decided, ensure that the resourced network plan is reflected in the manpower plan.

14.3.4 A simple project status reporting system

Although project planning is an important activity in project management, it is only one half of the partnership. Project planning is impotent if it only allows for the creation of good plans, i.e. if it does not allow feedback about the plan as the project unfolds. Feedback against the plan is the first stage of project control whose aim is to take early corrective action in order to continue to meet the project objectives and deadline. Project control cannot be achieved unless there is a mechanism for identifying how well the project is going to plan. This is the purpose of the project status reporting system.

A simple project reporting system might contain the following elements:

- weekly timesheet
- weekly project report
- project summary

(1) Weekly timesheet

Each member of staff involved in the project would complete a weekly timesheet. See figure 14.8. The timesheets provide details of progress made

```
                      WEEKLY   TIMESHEET


Name: _____  Emp-no: _____  Week No. ___

----------------------------------------------------------------
Project   Task                   Hours
Code      No.     Description     Carried  S M T W T F S    Total
----------------------------------------------------------------
a)   Project Duties

MS01      15      Design SC1       0        4 7                11
PR05      17      Design XYZ       10       2   6 6 4          18




----------------------------------------------------------------
b) Project Overheads

MS01      01      Weekly Meeting            1                  1
PA05      01      Weekly Meeting            1                  1
MS01      09      Travel                            2          2
                               ---------------------------------
                               Totals  - 8 7 6 6 6 -           33
                               ---------------------------------
                               c) Non project   Sickness
                                                Training       4
                                                Leave
                                                -----------------
                                                Wkly Tote      37
----------------------------------------------------------------
d) Comments




----------------------------------------------------------------
```

Fig. 14.8. Sample weekly timesheet.

WEEKLY REPORT PROJECT

Project: _____ Week No: _____ Week Ending _/_/_

* TASK SUMMARY *

Task No.	Emp.	Description Status	b/f	this week	todate	est. comp	est. total	plan	var.
15	JS	design sc1 comp	0	11	11	-	-	10	-1
12	JS	design sc2 comp	7	3	10	-	-	12	2
16	DM	design sc3 started	2	5	5	5	12	12	-
17	EM	str'd w/thru sched	0	0	0	-	4	4	-
		cum b/f	501	19	520	cum	plan	534	

* PROJECT OVERHEADS *

			b/f	this week	todate			plan	
01		weekly meeting	35	5	40			38	
02		travel	21	4	25			20	
03		support	45	2	47			20	
		o'head subtotal	101	11	112			78	
		project total	602	30	632			612	

Fig. 14.9. Sample weekly project report.

PROJECT SUMMARY

PROJECT _____

Week No.	Week Ending	No. Task Planned	%	No. Task Comp'd	%	Hours Planned	%	Hours Comp'd	%	% Planned To Actual	Planned O/head Ratio	Actual O/head Ratio
27	8/7/89	6	5	5	4	357	14	368	15	97	6	4
28	15/7/89	9	8	8	7	481	19	501	20	96	6	6
29	22/7/89	11	10	10	10	534	21	520	21	103	6	7

Fig. 14.10. Sample project summary.

during the week. Each task worked on during that week is recorded with the number of hours that were spent on it. Also, an estimate of how many hours that still have to be put in is provided. At the bottom of the timesheet, categories for overheads exist, which are not directly charged to the project itself.

(2) Weekly project report

Weekly timesheets are consolidated onto a weekly project report. See figure 14.9. It is here that the project leader or manager starts to review the progress of the project. The approach is straightforward. Comparisons are made between planned and actual figures; estimate to completion figures are provided for incomplete tasks. If the project leader is concerned about a particular delay on a task, reference to the corresponding weekly timesheet supplies qualitative comments on the problem.

(3) Project summary

Each week, the details from the weekly project report are transcribed onto the project summary. See figure 14.10. This report merely summarises the main figures from each week. It is possible to detect trends in the project by comparing one week's figures to the next. (A better way of determining trends is to draw a graph, of course.) By analysing these reports or graphs, the project leader is able to detect trends early. The causes of the trends can then be ascertained and perhaps corrective action taken. It is important, therefore, that the plan is not seen as some static entity, which becomes obsolete as soon as the project begins. As progress is made, it is vital to keep all the planning aids up-to-date. This is particularly true of the network. Changes to the actual times taken to perform tasks may affect the critical path. The critical path could alter and consequently management may need to monitor previously non-critical tasks.

It is possible to produce many other kinds of reports from a project status system. One important type of reporting in wide use is accounting reports, in which costings for tasks and categories for tasks are reported in a time-series manner. This is of use in large projects, particularly where budgets are agreed in advance and monitored as progress is made.

14.3.5 A change control system

Sometimes referred to as a configuration management system, its purpose is to ensure that changes to the system specification are coordinated in such a way as to have minimal impact on the development of the system. A fact of life in most projects is that after the system has been specified, changes are proposed. Sometimes they are unavoidable, e.g. when new legislation makes the current system obsolete. Sometimes they arise because errors or omissions are discovered further downstream in the development cycle. In other cases, it is because the users change their minds about what they want.

Each time a change is proposed, it should be assessed to determine how critical it is and what the impact will be on the development of the system, e.g. does it mean work already completed will have to be re-done? If so, how much? Once the assessment has taken place it may be declared as either a pre- or post-implementation change depending on its criticality and then scheduled accordingly. The scheduling activity naturally involves allocation of tasks to team members and modification of plans, costs and deadlines.

To maintain a change control system the following is found to be desirable:

- Unique numbering of each change.
- Priority system to ensure that more critical changes are implemented faster.
- Communication mechanism (e.g. weekly review meeting) to ensure changes are known and implications understood.
- Reporting mechanism to track status of changes.

14.3.6 A problem management system

Problem management is the name given to the coordination of the resolution of problems occurring in live systems. Like change control it needs certain control mechanisms so that the problems can be effectively monitored, e.g. unique numbering of problems, a system for prioritising problems and a system for communicating and reporting the status of problems. It is of relevance here because if large or important enough, such problems become projects in their own right.

14.3.7 Software support for project management techniques

There is clearly significant labour-intensive activity in the use of the above techniques. Often, the workload such techniques impose acts as a disincentive to actually using them, so software support which reduces the effort involved in maintaining the project plan and controlling its progress is often seen as mandatory. The needs of computer projects are similar enough to other kinds of projects, such as construction projects, that the same software can be used for both. Software is available to do the following:

- Create and maintain critical path networks.
- Produce standard graphs and reports from the network.
- Attempt to automatically resource-smooth the network given resource constraints.
- Manpower planning.
- Computerised status reporting systems.
- Computerised change control systems.

The next chapter will discuss the potential for computerised support of the project management function in more depth.

14.4 ESTIMATION

This section is to do with estimating the length of time it will take to perform a task within a project, major parts of a project or indeed the whole project itself. Before describing the techniques that are available, it is worthwhile to review why such estimates are required and to formalise the earlier discussion on the difficulties of estimation.

It was stated earlier that businesses typically expect the providers of services to be able to tell them in advance when the facility will be available and how much it will cost. From the business's point of view this is a perfectly reasonable request; the fact that it is not a practical request from the computer department's perspective is neither here nor there. In addition to the business wanting to know, clearly the computer department will find it useful as well, so that planning for staff on future projects can be done. However, since there is so little information available at the start of the project about what is required, such 'global' estimation is bound to be approximate at best and possibly wildly inaccurate at worst. By adopting an evolutionary approach to estimation, the scope for inaccuracy probably decreases somewhat but it is not eradicated.

When team members in a project are given tasks to do, it is necessary to provide them with an estimate of how long the task will take, so that their progress can be monitored. Task estimation is a much lower level form of estimation than global estimation, but the basic question posed is essentially similar – how do you know how much work is involved in a particular task? One attempt at answering the question has been to try to work backwards from the deliverables and find relationships. For example, in programming a traditional paradigm has been to use the number of lines of code in the program as a measure (metric) of how difficult the program is and therefore of how long it will take to write. Even supposing this correlation was true, how would it help the estimator? Obviously, the lines of code are not known by the estimator before the program is written. So, instead of estimating the length of the task, the estimator has to estimate the length of the program! But there is no guarantee that the estimated lines of code will be any more accurate and this is the fallacy of techniques which attempt to use lines of code as a predictor of task length. If all that is used to estimate the number of lines of code is guesswork, then we are no further forward.

A way has to be found of using what (little) is known about a task before it is attempted and to use this as a predictor of the length of time it will take. For example, by reviewing the specification of a program can some of its difficulty or straightforwardness be revealed and therefore used as a predictor of its task length? Some approaches take this line and incorporate numbers of inputs, outputs, files and so on as parameters in a calculation. Interestingly, this philosophy can be applied to other areas. For example, the length of time it takes to draw a DFD is probably related to the number of processes, datastores and so on which it contains. The difficulty we unerringly return to is that often that kind of information just is not known until the DFD has been drawn.

Yet at the end of the day, it is wrong to give up on estimation as if it were a bad idea. The need for estimation and its potential for contributing to sound project management remain unaltered by the difficulties of its implementation. It is imperative that the computer industry develops a positive attitude towards estimation. At first, simple techniques should be used, perhaps in conjunction with each other to provide confirmation or extend their range. For the future, it is important to recognise that much of the onus for providing the raw data for estimation lies in the hands of the practitioners themselves. People must be prepared to capture and store their own data, and make it available to researchers.

Five bases for estimation are presented here: .

- professional judgement
- historical databank
- the use of experts and the delphi technique
- standard times
- formulae

14.4.1 Professional judgement

This is (unfortunately) a very popular technique. It relies on the experience, background and maturity of the estimator to guess how long a particular task will take to complete. If the estimator has experience of a particular task then the estimate may not be unreasonable. The estimator is often an analyst or project leader who at one time was a programmer. When new software is brought into an installation, the estimator's experience is not likely to cover it, so inevitably his estimates becomes less valid. The same applies to tasks in system development methods. If an estimator has never had to perform, say, a normalisation, how can he estimate the time it will take someone else to perform it? Because there is no structure to this kind of estimate, there may be factors that have been overlooked. Professional judgement is not recommended as a basis for estimating in a software engineering environment. However, there may be times when no other technique is available and so no alternative exists. It can always be used in conjunction with other techniques as confirmation that the other method is reasonable.

14.4.2 Historical databank

A databank of past project task times can be built up and maintained. Where tasks in the current project are similar to tasks in previous projects, the actual or perhaps modified times can be used as estimates. The assumption is that the previous data will be a reliable estimate, which may or may not be the case. But the real disadvantage with this approach, is that few installations have bothered to store previous project data in a way that can be used later. A related problem is obsolescence. As new techniques and software are employed, the historical data becomes less applicable.

14.4.3 The use of experts and the Delphi technique

Outside experts, such as consultants or suppliers' representatives, can be brought in to provide estimates. Clearly, this can be of value where there is no existing expertise within an installation and is likely to occur when a product or technique is being used for the first time. Outside experts, however, may not be so familiar with in-house practices, turn round times and so on, so these estimates may require some modification.

A sophisticated form of the use of experts is called the Delphi technique and was developed by the Rand Corporation to obtain expert consensus without introducing group pressure. Whenever experts congregate together and are asked to use their expertise it has been found that one expert may be swayed by the reputation, position or experience of another. In order to avoid this, the Delphi technique is designed in such a manner as to allow the pooling of expertise to be done anonymously so that individuals are not pressurised into agreeing with others.

Clearly, calling in a number of experts in this way is liable to be an expensive pursuit and should only be done when the stakes are high.

14.4.4 Standard times

Another approach is to employ the use of standard time factors to assist in estimation. These are factors which have been constructed by analysing many previous project times so that a standard time is obtained. There are two ways in which this can be used.

(1) Proportional task times (PTT)
A model of the relative proportion of the different stages in a project is used. The proportion for each stage is expressed as a percentage of elapsed time of the whole. See figure 14.11. Depending on the method used, different proportional times may be applicable and similarly the software used could also change the relative proportions.

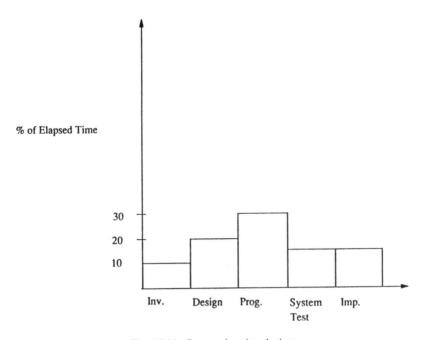

Fig. 14.11. Proportional task time.

Consider, for instance, the difference in programming effort between a third generation language like COBOL or Ada and a fourth generation language. Bigger still, what if an application package is chosen? So, many PTT models are required to meet the variety of software used within most departments. PTTs are of use where an estimate for the whole project exists and it is required to split this up into phases.

(2) Actual task times (ATT)
These are based on the idea that project tasks will require the same effort as similar tasks performed in previous projects and therefore estimates can be based on previous average times for that type of task. The actual task times approach differs from the historical databank approach in that these average times are established (supposedly at any rate) over many similar previous projects and therefore such figures are arguably fairly reliable. Any hiccups peculiar to a particular project are averaged out. This is less likely with the databank approach unless qualitative information is also stored. Having said that, ATTs are not likely to take into account the 'peculiarities' of a particular computer installation such as special tools used, turnround times and so on which might affect standard times. Another drawback with ATTs is that there can be a vast difference in time taken between an experienced and inexperienced programmer for example.

14.4.5 Formulae

The use of formulae in estimation implies that some quantitative basis or model for the formula exists and in that sense, at least, represents a more sophisticated approach to estimation. The question is whether the model is an accurate predictor. Two formulae-based techniques will be reviewed here. The first one is a technique for estimating the length of the whole project; the second is discussed here as an estimator of the length of individual tasks.

(1) COCOMO
The first formula-based technique we will look at is called COCOMO[2]. COCOMO stands for the 'Constructive Cost Model' and was developed by examining data from 63 software projects. It classifies programs into three types and these are called organic, semi-detached and embedded. These types of program approximately correspond to application, utility and system programs respectively, so the interest in this book is in the organic type of system. The COCOMO formula (shown in table 14.2) uses estimated lines of code or KDSI (1000s of delivered source instructions) as the predictor.

The formula for organic systems is:
$$PM = 2.4 * (KDSI)^{1.05} * AJ$$
$$TDEV = 2.5 * (PM)^{0.38}$$
where
KDSI is 1000s of delivered source instructions
PM is the number of person months.
AJ is the adjustment factor
TDEV is the total development time in months.

Table 14.2. COCOMO formula for organic system.

An adjustment factor is calculated by taking the product of a number of multipliers, each of which is in a predefined range around 1 which is the nominal value, i.e. if all the multiplier factors were considered nominal then each multiplier would be 1. This would mean that the adjustment factor would be 1. This in turn means that the adjustment factor would not alter the development time. There are different categories of adjustment factor and these are:

- Product attributes. This category has multipliers for required software reliability, database size and product complexity.
- Computer attributes, i.e. execution time constraints, main storage constraints, virtual machine volatility and computer turnround time.
- Personnel attributes. These are analyst capability, applications experience, programmer capability, virtual machine experience and programming language experience.
- Project attributes, i.e. modern programming practices, use of software tools and required development schedule.

An assessment is made for each multiplier on the basis of the situation within the current project. Each multiplier has an upper and lower limit. For instance, the PRODUCT RELIABILITY multiplier happens to have a lower limit of 0.75 and an upper limit of 1.40. So, for example, if PRODUCT RELIABILITY has to be high, then a multiplier greater than 1, say 1.30, is chosen. What this means is that the contribution this multiplier makes to the final estimate is that it requires better reliability, which will inevitably increase the time for the task.

It is assumed that installations which employ COCOMO are solid software engineering environments, i.e. they are using the principles of software engineering to implement the project. The estimates generated are based on that assumption. The level of estimation is at the system (global) level and not the task level, i.e. number of months to complete the whole system. Clearly, this provides little assistance to the project leader when estimates of tasks within a project are required. Another difficulty is obtaining an accurate estimate for the likely number of lines of code. It is hard enough trying to do this at the stage just before the programming effort begins; it is almost impossible, for example, at the start of the project!

(2) Function points

The original work on function points was described by Albrecht[3] in which function points were used to correlate the overall length of a project with some of its characteristics. So, the function points approach can be used as an alternative to COCOMO. However, we will discuss function points in the context of how they can be applied to estimating specific tasks within a project, with particular reference to programming tasks.

The idea of a function point is that it represents a unit of effort that the software engineer has to perform. In Albrecht's paper, he identified that the number of inputs, outputs, inquiries and master files had a bearing on the amount of effort, i.e. the function points for a whole project. Further, he recognised that each of these characteristics might have a different degree of influence on the function points for a system. For example, most people would probably agree that the number of master files is more significant than the number of inputs to a system. In recognition of this, each characteristic was given a different weighting factor.

The same principle can be applied at the task level where the characteristics are known beforehand. For example, consider module construction. The significant characteristics of a module might be:

- inputs
- outputs
- file/database processing
- complexity

For inputs and outputs, points can be awarded on the basis of their number and how difficult they are. Points for file or database processing can be derived by considering their number and the difficulty of access. For the complexity component, the module may be classified as easy, average or complex – each would have its own set of points. So, a module is reviewed in terms of the functions it performs and points are awarded based on the degree of difficulty. In practice, given that the relative points had already been established, all that is required would be to look up tables to find matches for the program's characteristics.

However, the raw function point score is inadequate in the sense that it takes no account of, for example, the experience of the programmer, the programming language used or the degree of automation in the software environment (e.g. on-line versus batch compilation facilities). With COCOMO we saw a number of significant multipliers used to refine the estimate and clearly this seems a reasonable thing to do with function points also. The effect of these refinements would be to increase or decrease the raw function point score. Lastly, this score is then multiplied by a weighting factor which converts the function points into an estimate of man-hours for that task. Such weighting factors could include allowances for testing and documentation provided they were considered part of the same task.

There are two main difficulties with using function points in practice. The first is that there is not enough agreement about what factors are the major predictors in a particular task and with that how these factors combine in a formula to make the estimate reasonably accurate. There is no short answer to this – it is a question of trial and error and a willingness to publish results (even of failure) so that others can benefit.

The second difficulty is to do with the kind of task that lends itself to a function points approach. Common sense tells us that where hard information is available about a task, it is likely that a function points approach is possible. So, for example, one might postulate that an estimate to perform a normalisation might be a function of the number of documents used and the total number of attributes. Similarly, creating an SDD will be strongly influenced by the total number of ELH stages and so on. The common denominator is that there is fairly quantifiable data available. The problem is that there are many tasks for which there is little or no quantifiable data at the outset, e.g. drawing a physical DFD set or performing data modelling. So, what does one do for such tasks? One solution, and it need not take too long, is to perform an estimation survey before a task is started. This survey would attempt to quantify the significant parameters so that an estimate can then be derived.

14.4.6 Review of estimation techniques

The situation with estimation is far from ideal. The techniques presented here all have limitations, although by using them in combination with each other, some weaknesses may be removed. The following approach to estimation is suggested as one way of getting the best out of the techniques:

1 At the very beginning of a project, use a rough COCOMO and any relevant data from the historical databank about the length of previous similar projects in conjunction with proportional task times. Clearly, at this stage, very little is known about the requirements, not least the constraints within which the project will be implemented. For example, observe how absurd the following question is: 'How many lines of code will a production control system take?' However, by using professional judgement, estimates can be input into COCOMO (taking nominal values for the multipliers where no better figure is available) to provide a very rough estimate. This can be compared against any figures from the historical databank. The point is that these estimates are probably better (although perhaps only a little better) than professional judgement by itself. Proportional task times can then be applied to identify rough times against each major stage within the project. This will provide global estimates for the whole project, i.e. not just the next phase.

2 As discussed earlier, at the beginning of each stage in a project, a more detailed plan is necessary. The point in time just before a stage begins is clearly the best time to make detailed estimates. Function points can be used to estimate, for example, the programming tasks and, ideally, equivalent data will be available for other stages in a project. If not, standard times should be used, or if unavailable, extracts from the project databank. If tasks within a project have never been attempted before, then the use of experts is recommended unless the task is relatively minor.

3 As the project develops, more information becomes available about its nature and constraints. It is worthwhile at, say, major review points, to rework COCOMO and extract data from the historical databank based on the revised circumstances. This provides revised global estimates which may indicate overall trends in the project.

4 After the project has been completed, the success or otherwise of the estimation approach should be reviewed. Which techniques were the most successful and why? Which techniques were the most inaccurate and why? Conclusions reached should be fed back into any future estimation approach. Any appropriate specific data should be stored in the historical databank for future reference and where necessary standard times updated. This kind of review philosophy is a vital step in building up experience and data on task estimation and is clearly good software engineering practice.

A major problem is keeping the estimation knowledge base up with the new techniques. There is a lead-time between a new technique being used by practitioners and their ability to provide estimates for that technique. The reason for this is that it takes time to gain experience with a technique so that significant factors as far as estimation is concerned can be identified and used as predictors. This state of affairs applies to providing software support tools for new techniques too and it is doubtful whether estimation techniques or software support tools will ever catch up with state-of-the-art practice.

The real onus, however, is on the practising computer community to be diligent in creating, storing and reviewing raw data estimates and allowing these to be published, so that the knowledge can be pooled and used by others. The computer industry must not sit back and wait for someone to announce estimation standards. That day is unlikely to ever dawn, if only because the business of computing is too dynamic in terms of changing hardware, software and methods.

14.5 PROJECT ORGANISATION

Project organisation is concerned with how computer staff are grouped to work on a project and in particluar what lines of authority exist. This section will review some popular approaches to project organisation. A fuller discussion is available in Fairley[4].

14.5.1 Functional organisation

The classic organisation structure is functional, which means that the work is done on the basis of functional specialisation, thereby enabling a high degree of skill to be achieved through experience. Typically, within a department there are different functional groups such as an analysis team, design team and so on. See figure 14.12. The functional organisation requires considerable communication between teams and more attention to documentation because it is the major means of communication. Depending on the size of the organisation, each functional area may have a supervisor.

14.5.2 Matrix organisation

The DP manager delegates responsibilities for a project to a particular project leader, i.e. a project organisation is superimposed on the functional organisation. In such an organisation, the DP manager looks to the

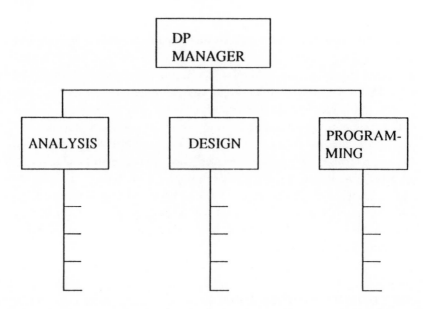

Fig. 14.12. A functional organisation.

functional supervisors to maintain the professional quality of the work being done and to the project leaders to pursue individual project goals. See figure 14.13. Staff therefore have two bosses and this can lead to a conflict of interests. In spite of the problems created by matrix organisations, they are becoming increasingly popular because they are seen as being more flexible than functional organisations.

14.5.3 The degree of structure in a project group

There is a range or continuum on which a project group can sit with respect to how much freedom, or lack of it, exists in the execution of its work. Take the programming group, for example. We will consider three types of team:

- democratic teams
- chief programmer teams
- hierarchical, democratic teams

(1) Democratic teams
In a democratic team, everybody is equal, i.e. there is no supervisor as such and no distinction made in terms of seniority, ability or experience. Democratic teams are, however, difficult to operate because organisations

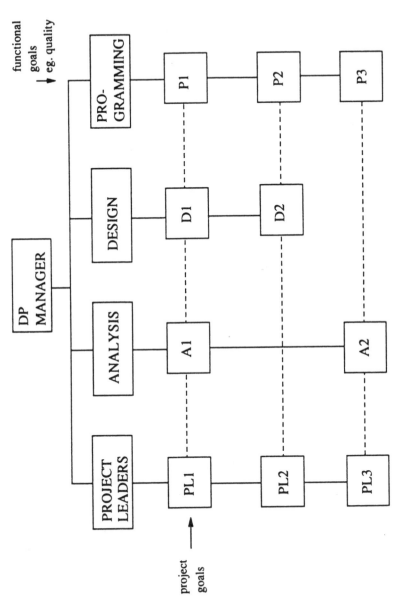

Fig. 14.13. A matrix organisation.

expect people (i.e. not groups) to take on responsibility and therefore accountability for tasks performed, and also there is a necessarily high communication overhead in democratic teams in order for decisions to be taken. However, because of the participative element, it tends to be a source of motivation for individual team members.

(2) Chief programmer teams

In contrast to democratic teams, chief programmer teams are highly structured. Members perform distinctly different tasks. The approach is motivated from the following observations:

- Projects tend to be staffed by relatively inexperienced people.
- Much programming work is clerical in nature involving the storage and maintenance of a large amount of information.
- Unnecessary communication is time-consuming and hence reduces programmer productivity.
- The need for a career path.

Team members' responsibilities are as follows:

Chief programmer.   The chief programmer is the appointed leader of the team and is responsible for critical design and programming activities and also delegating the less-critical to others. The chief programmer must oversee the quality of products produced by the team. Considerable technical knowledge and proven managerial ability are prerequisites for this role.

Back-up to chief programmer.   The back-up to the chief programmer must be able to take over at any time (i.e. be briefed on the current status of the project) and this is the main role. It may be necessary to act as direct assistant to the chief programmer providing advice and assistance when necessary and it will often mean working jointly with the chief programmer on a difficult program.

Project librarian.   The project librarian is responsible for all documentation produced and therefore must keep documentation up-to-date and permit access from authorised personnel. Documentation includes all source programs, job control language, test-data and manuals. Sometimes all project-related clerical and administrative tasks also fall within the responsibility, e.g. collection and submission of weekly timesheets.

Programmers. Programmers perform essentially their expected role, i.e. writing programs. The advantage of the chief programmer team to the programmer is that work is allocated according to ability and because of the existence of the librarian's job the programmer avoids what is sometimes considered 'boring administration'.

Specialist support. The chief programmer team may also receive external support from hardware and system software specialists.

(3) Hierarchical, democratic teams
In an attempt to overcome the disadvantages of both of the above, it is possible to adopt a programming team approach which offers some of the benefits of democratic teams yet still allows for accountability, supervision and a career path. In a hierarchical, democratic team, a senior programmer (who may well report to a programming manager) is responsible for a pool of programmers. Depending on their skill, interests and, of course, the work that has to be done, agreement is reached concerning who does what within the team. This means that individuals can, to some extent, have a say in what they do. This tends to improve the motivation of team members and team identification takes place. This kind of team structure can work well if a team is given part of a system to work on. Even at the level of a structure chart, individual modules can be allocated to team members with integration testing becoming a 'team' responsibility.

14.5.4 Review of project organisation structures

In the author's view, there is no such thing as an organisation structure which is best for all situations. Each individual structure has advantages and disadvantages associated with it and clearly these should be considered in deciding which structure should be adopted in any particular computer department. In chapter 17, a strong plea will be made for the need to involve the user community as much as possible in the decision-making concerning their own information systems. Such involvement requires a commitment from the computer department to 'share the authority' with the users. In deciding which organisation structure should be adopted in a computer department there is no reason why programmers, designers, analysts and so on cannot have a say in deciding which type of organisation is preferred. After all, having participated in decision-making usually means people are more committed to the proposal and will want to make it work.

14.6 QUALITY ASSURANCE

An introduction to quality assurance is included here since the achievement
of quality is fundamental to the success of a project and therefore is very much
the business of project management.

Quality is a difficult characteristic to quantify absolutely. Unlike other
engineering disciplines, there are no materials in software, so the concept of
purity or use of high-quality materials does not apply. One answer might lie
in assessing whether or not the product does what it is supposed to do, i.e. in
the specification of the software product, which should contain the criteria for
its acceptability. So a high-quality software product is considered to be one
which meets its technical specification. This is known as verification, which is
sometimes expressed colloquially as 'are we building the product right?' There
are two ways of verifying tasks in a system. These are the structured
walkthrough and inspection. Although broadly similar in format, inspections
tend to be more specific and detailed in nature. As a general guideline,
inspections are more geared towards verifying code while walkthroughs are
more appropriate for analysis and design.

The complement of verification is validation, paraphrased as 'are we
building the right product?' Here, the concern is external, i.e. that the
specification may not be exactly what the user is after anyway.

Unfortunately, the nature of validation and verification is such that one is
never certain in an absolute sense that they have been performed
satisfactorily, so the notion of quality assurance, rather than quality control,
is used to remind us that all we have is a degree of confidence in the quality
of the product rather than some sort of guarantee or proof of its absolute
workability.

14.6.1 User review

The mechanism for validation is the user review. Along with communication,
validation is one of the main purposes of reviews. As was seen in earlier
chapters, reviews take place at different stages within the project and
therefore the kinds of deliverable which can be shown to the user varies. For
example, DFDs can be shown to confirm system requirements, screen designs
for the user interface and working programs to confirm implementation.
Since reviews may have other objectives, such as to gain agreement to proceed
with the project, it is sensible to have specific validation reviews which are
separate from other kinds of review.

14.6.2 Structured walkthrough

The goal of a walkthrough is to discover and make note of problem areas. This is done by an individual presenting or 'walking through' work products to other members of the project group including the person who specified the task, possibly users, a representative from the quality assurance group and perhaps other technical personnel, e.g. from the operations department. Walkthroughs should not be used for employee evaluation (as this may deflect the purpose of a walkthrough).

Fairley[4] suggests the following guidelines for walkthroughs:

1 Everyone's work should be reviewed – including the project leader's. It facilitates communication amongst team members and lessens the threat to individual reviewees.

2 The emphasis should be on detecting errors. A walkthrough should not be used to discuss how to correct errors. One member of the walkthrough team should become minute secretary so that all errors identified are recorded for subsequent correction.

3 Major issues should be addressed, e.g. basic questions such as 'is the product meeting its specified function' should be the main focus rather than pedantic points of detail. One reviewer should be designated as moderator to maintain a positive atmosphere and keep the walkthrough on track.

4 Limit the session to no more than two hours. This helps to limit the scope of material covered. Time should be allocated in the project schedule for walkthroughs and they should be regarded as an integral part of an individual's load. Time spent on walkthroughs is handsomely rewarded through earlier detection and correction of errors when they are least expensive to fix. Walkthroughs should be conducted in an open, friendly, non-threatening atmosphere. High-level management should not attend walkthroughs since this may affect an individual's willingness to be open.

14.6.3 Inspection

Like walkthroughs, inspections can be used at any stage in the life cycle to assess and improve the quality of deliverables. Inspection teams work from checklists of items to be inspected. Inspections are conducted in a similar manner to walkthroughs, but more formally and each participant has a definite role to play. Inspections may have specific items to assess. For example, items to be inspected in an inspection might include:

- module interfaces
- module verification
- test case generation

An inspection team might consist of moderator, designer, implementor and tester. It may be felt that some roles are aggressive in that they try to prove the code faulty, while other roles are defensive in that they try to refute such claims. Inspections are ideal review mechanisms in, for example, using mathematics to demonstrate the correctness of code with respect to its specification.

14.6.4 The role of quality assurance

In large computer installations it is common to find a quality assurance group. In smaller installations, it may be that there is no separate group. However, the role or function that it performs can be done by staff who are also development staff. The quality assurance 'function' is responsible for assisting the achievement of quality products. It is wrong for the project team to abrogate their responsibilities for quality and leave it to the quality assurance function to pick up the pieces. Indeed, most of the work in quality assurance is prevention rather than cure. The services performed by the quality assurance function can be classified as follows:

(1) Project review
This is the traditional role of quality assurance and it is an important one in many ways. Firstly, the obvious advantage is the opportunity to review progress on the project. This would happen at the end of each major stage in the project and at other points too, e.g. when computer hardware and software is identified and when a detailed testing plan has been generated. These are critical stages in the project. Mistakes at any stage can be costly. This is where the preventative ethos comes in. Take, for example, selecting hardware and software. The quality assurance group will check that the procedures for selecting and evaluating these items have been followed. Have enough alternative suppliers been contacted? Have proper costings been done in the prescribed manner? Although it is a form of policing, it does provide an independent confirmation that project tasks are being tackled properly. But the second benefit is that it affords the opportunity to open up a dialogue on quality with project staff. This is important if a quality ethos is to be established and maintained.

Observe that the different stages of the project will require different kinds and levels of quality assurance. At the latter stages, coding inspections and documentation checks will be typical items for review, whereas in the earlier stages, less tangible deliverables such as project plans, manning levels and cost/benefit justifications will be the rule.

(2) A source of expertise

Quality assurance people can be used as a source of expertise and this can be in two ways. Firstly, in preventative mode, when development staff are confronted with technical problems, they should feel that quality assurance personnel are able to help solve their problem, since sound technical knowledge would be a prerequisite for work in quality assurance. The nature of technical problems can be wide-ranging. There could be problems in using a language, working within standards and so on. The second way is when some abnormality presents itself with an implemented system. Since weaknesses in the quality assurance system will eventually present themselves as errors or problems in the implemented system, it is important that the quality assurance function receives feedback on the success or otherwise of live systems. By analysing errors, it may be possible to identify the specific cause of problems. By analysing error rates and types of errors it may even be possible to pinpoint weaknesses in current procedures.

(3) The creation of installation standards

It is the quality assurance function's job to construct and maintain a set of installation standards including:

- project management standards
- systems analysis and design standards
- programming and testing standards
- documentation standards

(4) The creation of an installation-wide quality ethos

Clearly a quality ethos requires that the previous tasks are being supported. But most important is the need to create the right attitude towards quality. The attitude needs to be an open, learning, egoless attitude, otherwise it just will not work. It should be clear that the role performed by the quality assurance function has a lot to do with the provision of sound project management. One danger though, is that the function itself is seen as an arm of management whose role is to spy or check up on staff. If this can be avoided, the quality assurance function can make a useful contribution to the success of projects.

14.6.5 Internal quality assurance

An alternative to separate quality assurance groups is to perform quality assurance from within the project team itself. In other words, quality assurance reviews are performed by peers in the project team. Working in such a way is a formative experience, because one quickly learns about the difficulties others have faced in trying to resolve certain problems. Now the computer industry is notorious for its shortage of experienced staff. The reality in many project teams is that individual members have often a lot less experience than one would ideally like. Internal quality assurance can be a way of developing a more mature outlook in staff, since it forces them to take a wider view of their environment.

14.7 SUMMARY

Space has limited this review of project management to a brief discussion and to a survey of some of the important issues therein. More is the pity, because clearly project management is a vital component of good software engineering practice and should not be considered something separate or somehow less immediately relevant to software engineers.

The main discussion on project management centred firstly on applying some principles to the project team environment. It was proposed that the style of management adopted is important as well as the kinds of indicators, yardsticks and tactics used to plan and control. These ideas reflect the view that project management is a management activity which demands communication and interpersonal skills and considerable distilled experience to accomplish effectively. But a project manager also needs to be a technical manager in two ways. Firstly, a good understanding of the tasks undertaken within a project is required so that problems can be appreciated. Secondly, a number of project management techniques have to be employed in order to plan and control to a professional standard. A set of such techniques was discussed in some detail. It can therefore be seen that project management is both a management and technical discipline.

The computer industry has not yet succeeded in providing satisfactory techniques for estimating the cost and length of projects. Indeed the basic problem is a complex and dynamic one. Only now are techniques being adopted and used on a widely accepted basis. However, as new methods for development are used and new software such as fourth generation languages pervade the market-place, it will be difficult if not impossible to keep the 'theory' of estimation up-to-date with the practice.

How to organise a project team is an important issue too. Different organisation structures affect the job satisfaction and motivation of team members which inevitably influence the quality of software product generated. The last section considered quality assurance and looked at the role of quality assurance, specific mechanisms for ensuring quality (i.e. reviews, walkthroughs and inspections) and different organisational structures to support a quality ethos.

14.8 FURTHER READING

1   Brook, F. (1975) *The Mythical Man-Month: Essays on Software Engineering*, Addison-Wesley, Reading, Massachusetts, is an interesting and enjoyable account of experiences on a large computer project.
2   Boehm, B. (1981) *Software Engineering Economics*, Prentice-Hall, Englewood Cliffs, New Jersey, gives a much fuller and highly quantitative treatment of COCOMO.
3   Albrecht, A. (1979) Measuring application development productivity. In *Joint SHARE/GUIDE Symposium*, is the original work on function points.
4   Fairley, R. (1985) *Software Engineering Concepts*, McGraw-Hill, New York, provides a discussion of project organisation and structured walkthroughs.

Chapter 15
CASE Tools, Workstations and IPSEs

15.1 INTRODUCTION

In this chapter we will explore how the computer can be used to assist the software engineer in his job. For years, the traditional role of the computer department has been to 'get out there and automate user departments'. It is only in relatively recent times that serious consideration has been given to automating the computer department! This rather ironic situation probably stems from a number of factors, some of which are economic and some to do with the maturity of the industry itself. But one additional factor worthy of discussion here is the trend towards more detailed analysis in methods. The argument here, which is supported by a growing catalogue of evidence, is that by 'front-loading' methods in this way, it is more likely that the specification will be correct and therefore less likely that costly errors will appear further downstream in the development cycle. The cost, for example, of repairing a specification error at programming is much higher than spotting the problem at an analysis walkthrough. This is why most methods, including the one introduced in this book, place so much emphasis on sound analysis – it is cost-effective to do so.

Having committed oneself to a comprehensive and thorough approach to development, the question now becomes 'how can the job be done as productively as possible?' And it is here that we look to the computer to improve productivity.

Now productivity is connected with the factors of time, cost and quality as discussed in the previous chapter. Without the aid of computerised tools on a project, some tasks would take very much longer, so much so that it is perhaps doubtful if some tasks are practical without computer support. What often happens is that quality is sacrificed to meet deadlines. Further, since computers are better than humans at certain things, for example checking, they can be used to improve the quality of some of the tasks in a project. So, two kinds of improvement can be associated with a productivity tool. These are improvements in efficiency and improvements in quality.

Efficiency. The idea of efficiency is that computers can be used to speed up the process. But final product quality is roughly the same, e.g. word processing, graphics editors. The benefits are derived through reduced development time and include:

- Systems are available sooner therefore the company benefits sooner.
- In the long term systems cost less, therefore they become more attractive.
- More can be achieved with fewer people.

Effectiveness. Here, the software has the effect of improving the quality of the final product, e.g. expert systems can be used to, for instance, improve the quality of a decision concerning what hardware to acquire. Without productivity tools, quality often suffers due to lack of available time. Such tools offer the prospect of raising the quality to required levels within acceptable timescales.

The benefits of improved quality include:

- Better systems provide better quality of information to users.
- Savings through fewer mistakes and fewer delays.
- Fewer bugs therefore less maintenance, so more time available for other work.

15.1.1 CASE

CASE stands for Computer-Aided Software Engineering. It can be construed to be any piece of software that supports the software engineering activity – even comparatively large pieces of software that will be defined shortly. Unfortunately, the software industry has not yet matured to a state where all such definitions are agreed and adhered to. To avoid overlap, we will define a CASE tool as a piece of software that supports a single software engineering task. For example, a programmer might use an automatic test-data generator to help him create test data, or an analyst might use a diagram editor to assist drawing DFDs. A CASE tool may improve efficiency, effectiveness or both.

15.1.2 Workstation

A workstation is a set of integrated software with associated hardware which assists software engineers in the execution of their work. Normally, a workstation is associated with a particular type of software engineer, hence the notion of a programmer workstation or analyst workstation. The important distinction here is that unlike CASE tools which assist at the task level, workstations ideally should support all the activities of a particular software engineer. This creates an additional requirement that CASE tools used within a workstation need to be able to communicate with one another, so that, for example, output data from one tool can be passed on as input data to another tool. This is often achieved by the provision of a database at the core of the workstation. Ideally, a workstation should present a standard interface to the software engineer. Workstations are sometimes called workbenches or support environments, e.g. the Ada Programmer Support Environment.

15.1.3 IPSE

IPSE stands for Integrated Project Support Environment. An IPSE attempts to support all activities within a project, i.e. to support all members of the project team in developing the computer system. Just as the workstation incorporates individual CASE tools within it, so the IPSE can be viewed as incorporating the various workstations within its domain. The attraction of the IPSE is that it permits the work of different project team members to be integrated and viewed as a single project. For example, a computerised Project Status Reporting System such as the one discussed in the previous chapter might be part of an IPSE and could use data collected by CASE tools residing in individual workstations. So the IPSE represents a view at project level rather than at the level of individual team members. Figure 15.1 shows

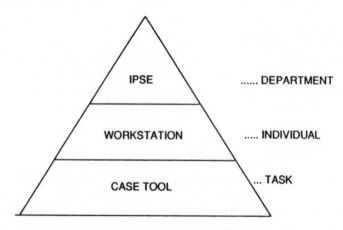

Fig. 15.1. Relative hierarchy of productivity tool.

the hierarchy of IPSE, workstation and CASE tool.

There are currently different generations of IPSE available and being developed (see Mair[1]):

(1) First Generation
This is simply a set of tools brought together under a common computer environment. Typically file-based, the tools are compatible in the sense that files produced from one tool may be input to another tool. However, there is not normally a common user interface.

(2) Second Generation
The main distinction is that they are database IPSEs which means, in effect, that the IPSE is designed from scratch as a product in its own right rather than 'cobbled' from existing tools. There are two distinct types available:

Second Generation – Toolkit.   The IPSE is viewed as a set of tools in a toolkit. The engineer can select tools as appropriate. This seems to typify requirements in the real-time area. However few tools are supplied as standard.

Second Generation – method specific.   The IPSE is viewed as a set of coherent tools related to a particular method and is therefore able to take advantage of the predefined sequence of tasks within that method. Some computer departments believe that their requirements are such that only one method is needed. Method specific IPSEs are designed for that kind of environment.

Recently a hybrid of these two types has emerged:

Populated Second Generation.   This has many tools available together with comprehensive facilities for defining relationships between tools, plus a mechanism for adding new tools. These IPSEs are now becoming available.

(3) Third Generation
These are currently research IPSEs which are knowledge-based and are likely to incorporate the fruits of research into formal methods, specification languages, reusability, distributed computing and user interfaces.

15.2 EXAMPLES OF CASE TOOLS

A programmer in the course of work might use a whole range of CASE tools. Even the humble compiler or interpreter is a CASE tool since the alternative of an assembler or even machine code would normally be a much less efficient use of a programmer's time. In addition, there are a number of options available on some compilers such as link editors, loaders and overlaying facilities. There are also optimising compilers to speed up program execution.

Alternative development options provide another category of CASE tool. This would include the use of 4GLs, report and application generators and packages. Programmers also use utilities, editors, program skeletons and copy macros in the development of their programs.

In testing and debugging there are many CASE tools available and becoming available. These include:

- Test-case generators to automatically create test data.
- Retrieval languages to create test files from existing operational files.
- Diagnostic aids such as cross-reference lists, traces and program flow analysers.
- Dumps and snapshot facilities.
- File comparators and results checkers.
- Automated test harnesses to expedite, for example, the testing of modules in a structure chart.
- Expert system advice on a range of programming related issues, e.g. identifying the likely cause of compiler or run-time errors

Programmers need support in other areas too. For example, in estimating run-times or identifying problems with execution times a programmer might use simulation or modelling languages, time analysers and even test drivers to run tests under differing conditions. Programmers have to document their work products so they need word processors and graphics tools. They need access to maintenance utilities such as space reorganisation programs.

A program could also be written to check for deviations against installation standards.

So it can be seen that there is a wealth of CASE tools, most of which are available today and can improve the productivity of programmers.

The same applies to the analyst activity. Clearly the analyst has a greater involvement with users and therefore electronic mail, word processing and so forth will greatly improve efficiency. More significantly there are also tools which can aid effectivness too. The following is a list of CASE tools which analysts can make good use of:

(1) Programmer workstation software
With the widespread use of 4GLs, there may be 'application development without programmers', i.e. the analyst does the coding. So, an analyst needs to be able to run whatever 4GLs and so on are required plus have access to testing facilities, e.g. test data generators, utilities, program libraries, etc.

(2) Prototyping software
Also desirable is access to prototyping faciliites. A good input/output prototyping facility is required which allows the user and analyst to jointly and incrementally develop the user interface, i.e. to see the screens and reports and make adjustments.

(3) Word processing
This is required for a number of reasons, most of which are documentation-related. Examples include memos, minutes of meetings, feasibility reports, sign-offs and process specifications.

Many documents would be in a standard format (such as system documentation) and uniquely identified. So the ability to retrieve 'blank' documents which are prenumbered would be advantageous.

(4) Electronic filing cabinet
The ability to retrieve, view, modify and store documents and diagrams and also maintain a directory of documents is essential for productivity. A project amasses a lot of documentation, which in turn needs to be stored and retrieved efficiently.

(5) Graphics
A graphics editor is needed for DFDs, data models, structure charts, etc. There is also a requirement for presentation graphs, e.g. histograms, pie-charts.

(6) 'Cut and paste' facility
The ability to merge different types of document together, especially text and graphics for reports, is a major efficiency booster.

(7) Electronic mail
This is used for sending memos and reports to users and elsewhere in the DP department. It is also possible to confirm that a message has been received and request a response from the recipient.

(8) Spreadsheet
This can be used for budgeting and detailed manpower scheduling. During a project an analyst will have to prepare budgets for hardware, software and so on. In particular the ability of spreadsheets to be used to answer 'what-if' questions is of advantage.

(9) PERT/CPA software
This is used for scheduling activities/tasks within a project.

(10) Diary

This can assist the analyst in planning his own workload. It can act as meeting reminder or even enable a boss or colleague, for example, to check where a project member is.

(11) Verification software

Verification software can help to improve the quality of product, so it is concerned with improvements in effectiveness. For example, the quality of dataflow diagrams can be improved by:

- Enforcing installation standards, e.g. ensuring softboxes instead of circles and ensuring that every dataflow name uses a standard convention.
- Automatic consistency checking, e.g. checking that every dataflow is defined in the data dictionary.
- Balance checking, i.e. sum of input dataflows = sum of output dataflows.
- Levelling checking, i.e. checking for consistency across the different levels of the DFD hierarchy.

Verification software can also be used to improve the quality of data in the data dictionary. This would include:

- Checking all dataflows have elementary data dictionary entries.
- Checking all 'nouns' (e.g. dataflows and files) in a process specification are defined in the data dictionary.

(12) Computer based training (CBT)

This is an authoring facility for creating instructional materials to be used as tutorials for users.

(13) Text management

This is different from word processing because it has additional facilities not always associated with word processing and includes special page formatting, indenting facilities, automatic table of contents, automatic index, automatic references and so on.

This is useful for producing user manuals and other documentation. Note that some or all of these are becoming standard in some word processing packages. Indeed 'desk-top publishing' (DTP) is now widely available and has facilities for text management, presentation graphics and 'cutting and pasting', all within a single environment.

(14) Links to data centre/data administration

The analyst may require access to certain information from these areas, e.g.

run-time logs, statistics of machine performance/down time, network plans, and corporate data models.

(15) Expert systems

There is a growing use of expert systems in the software engineering process. For instance, it can be used to help the analyst to identify the best model of VDU in a particular circumstance or identify the most efficient file organisation for a specific application.

15.3 WORKSTATIONS

The major distinction between CASE tools and workstations, as stated earlier, is the provision of an environment which assists a team member in that job. Such an environment must cater for as much of the job as possible, since failure to do so detracts from the ethos of a workstation. This has implications for both hardware and software.

On the hardware side, a workstation clearly must have sufficient power, storage space and so on to provide a comfortable working environment. Although the specification might be less, the list could include colour micro with PF keys, at least a megabyte of memory, hard disk, local laser printer for A4 and continuous stationery and also slides, a colour plotting facility for charts and training materials and, of course, a telephone. Electronic mail would require a linked network.

On the software side, a comfortable working environment would imply that the tools are integrated. There are few things more frustrating than having data in one kind of file and being unable to input it into another tool because of file incompatibility. It is situations like these which inhibit people from doing a task properly, so they end up doing less than they should or doing it poorly. But integration in its fullest sense is much more than mere file compatibility; it must seek to make it easy for the software engineer to do his job in the same way as a car design should make it easy for the driver to drive for long distances comfortably.

Perhaps the best way of illustrating what is possible with workstation software is to examine commercial products available in the marketplace. One such product is Automate+[2] which is marketed by LBMS. By our definition, Automate+ is a workstation in that it attempts to cover as much of the analysis and design activity as possible. Like most good commercial products it is constantly being refined and enhanced, so what is described here is what is available at the time of writing. Nevertheless, it affords a picture of the kind of software on the market that software engineers are actually using. Further, the method it supports is called LSDM, which is similar enough to the method used in this book for the reader to have little difficulty in appreciating the thought that has gone into its design.

Automate+ has a diagram editor which allows a hierarchy of current physical DFDs to be entered and stored within its system. Once the analyst is satisfied with the set of DFDs, they can then be presented to the Automate+ database for internal completeness, correctness and consistency checking.

The Automate+ diagram editor is easy to use. Many types of diagram, including DFDs, data models and Entity Life Histories, are created using the diagram editor which means that the analyst is provided with a consistent user interface for all the diagrams he develops.

15.3.1 Drawing DFDs

The DFD diagram editor is easily invoked through a series of option menus. The editor is mouse-driven, although keys can be used if no mouse is available. Icons (or diagrammatic symbols) appear at the bottom of the screen and these are used in combination with a line of associated commands which are positioned just above the icons. See figure 15.2. So to add a process

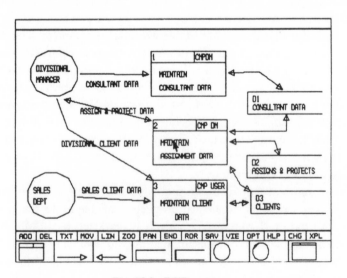

Fig. 15.2. DFD screen.

simply select the 'add' command using the mouse and then the 'process' icon is selected. The analyst then chooses the location on the screen where the process is to be sited. The analyst is then invited to add any appropriate text to accompany that particular symbol. In this manner a picture, in this case a DFD, is progressively built up.

In addition, the diagram editor is able to spot elementary mistakes as the diagram is being created and provides simple on-line messages when it can detect obvious errors or omissions.

For those readers not familiar with graphics products, two commands may be found of interest. These are ZOOM and PAN. ZOOM allows you to enlarge or make smaller the size of the icons and therefore the size of the diagram being viewed. This is particularly useful if the screen is full. By reducing the size of the diagram on the screen, it is possible to continue to add more icons to that diagram. Alternatively, it may be preferred to keep the diagram at the same size and simply move the window to the left, right, upwards or downwards, so that additional icons can then be added. This is what the PAN command facilitates.

The diagram editor treats DFDs as a set, i.e. a hierarchy of DFDs, and it is possible to navigate from one level to the next lower by using the explode (XPL) command. Where lower level DFDs are being created for the first time, the XPL command is used to establish the link between the two levels. For example, if you explode process 3 on a level 1 DFD, a skeleton level 2

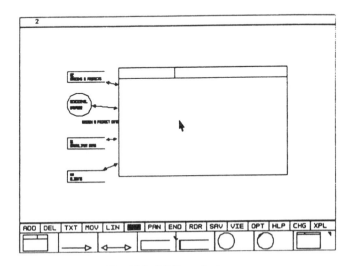

Fig. 15.3. DFD explosion.

DFD is generated. All processes, datastores and external entities connected to process 3 at level 1 appear on this diagram also, but are connected just to the rectangle representing the boundary for process 3. As processes are added to this DFD, the analyst is expected to link these level 2 processes with the appropriate processes, datastores and external entities. In this way, the analyst is reminded of outstanding connections and integrity between levels is preserved. See figure 15.3.

15.3.2 DFD completeness, correctness and consistency checking

The DFD set is presented to the Automate+ database as a set of DFDs. Because there are rules for the drawing of DFDs, these can be used to validate the DFD set, and therefore provide some degree of automatic checking by producing an error report. Essentially there are three levels of checking that are performed – completeness, correctness and consistency. Table 15.1 contains a complete list. The first level checks as far as possible that each diagram is complete. So omissions in naming icons are identified, as are objects (e.g. datastores) which do not have associated dataflows. Correctness checking is the second level of checking. Here, the details in the DFDs are validated against the basic rules for naming and drawing DFDs. So, where icon names do not conform to naming conventions (e.g. a name must start with an alphabetic character) or where icons are related in an illogical way (e.g. a dataflow connecting two datastores), appropriate error messages are generated. The third level, consistency checking, is in fact a form of correctness checking where the software detects inconsistencies in the use of the icons or names with respect to elsewhere in the DFD set. For example if, at level 2, a particular dataflow goes from a process to an external entity, then at level 3 it cannot go from one process to another. Notice that correctness checking addresses quality within the current diagram, whereas consistency checking addresses quality across the DFD set.

This kind of automated support is a valuable contribution in the endeavour to remove errors in analysis as early as possible. However, this is only one class of error detection and is limited to the internal checking that can take place within a DFD set on its own. It is important to recognise that this kind of checking is limited to the rules for drawing DFDs. In other words, there is no guarantee that what is presented to the Automate+ database is correct in terms of providing an accurate picture of, in this case, the current physical system. There may be omitted processes, dataflows or whatever. All that is known is that the DFD set provided conforms to the rules for drawing DFDs.

completeness checks

- missing names or reference number
  simply means that a process box has no name

- no dataflows to or from this object
  a process, datastore or external entity is not connected to anything else

- data flow starts/ends at expansion box
  this a useful check which detects where an analyst has forgotten to connect up external icons to sub-processes while performing an explosion.

correctness checks

- invalid x where x may be datastore name
  external entity name
  data flow name
  datastore reference number
  process reference number

  here the basic rules for defining one of these objects have not been applied

- dataflow joins two datastores
  a process must take data out of one datastore before it can be added to another

- duplicate data flow name
  a data flow name occurs more than once on the same diagram

- duplicate process reference number
  the current diagram has two occurrences of the same process reference number.

consistency checks

- inconsistent usage of data flow
  dataflow must be used in the same way in different DFD pictures e.g. if a dataflow goes from a process to an external entity at level 2 then it cannot go from a process to a datastore at level 3

- cycled DFD, invalid process for this diagram
  in other words, process reference numbers should not refer to processes which exist higher up in the hierarchy of DFDs e.g. finding process 2 in an explosion of process 2.3

- inconsistent process name
  a process reference number must always refer to one and only one process name, whereas the same process name can be used in different processes and hence have different process reference numbers
  where a process reference number appears more than once in a DFD set it must have the same process name
  note that in all likelihood, the analyst has numbered the process wrongly rather than having used the name inconsistently.

- inconsistent datastore name and reference
  either the name or reference number of the datastores occurs elsewhere in the DFD set.

- incorrect process at start or end of flow
  each level of DFD is compared with the next level down where a dataflow exists at the higher level it must exist at the lower. If it doesn't or if one exists at the lower which should appear in the higher, then this error message appears.

Table 15.1. Completeness, correctness and consistency checks.

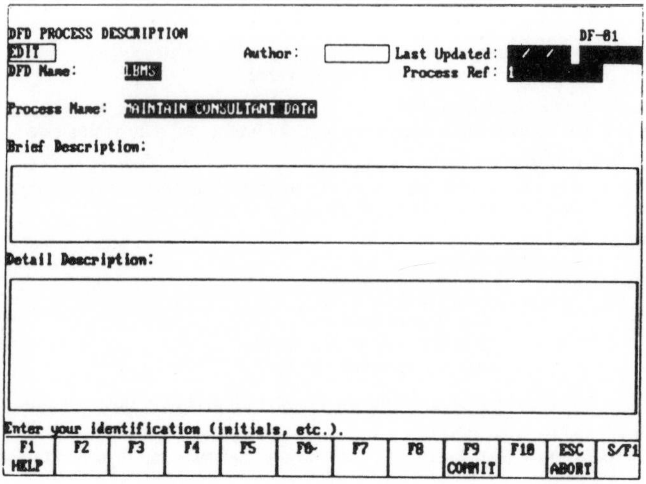

Fig. **15.4.** DFD Process description screen.

Having said that, it is nevertheless a step towards improving the quality of the system model and should therefore be recognised as such.

15.3.3 Specifying processes

Once the DFDs are drawn and entered into the Automate+ database, the details of each process specification can be entered and stored. The option menu is used to find the 'MAINTAIN PROCESS DESCRIPTION' menu. Attributes about the process such as the process number, the author's name and so on are entered. There is also a section for the specification itself, which can be written in structured English form. See figure 15.4.

15.3.4 Drawing the data model

A data model is referred to as a Logical Data Structure (LDS) in LSDM and in Automate+ is created in similar fashion to the DFD. The commands at the bottom of the screen are identical except there is no XPL command, although clearly the icons used are quite different. See figure 15.5.

Included in the icon list are icons which permit optional and exclusive relationships to be shown. An optional relationship (signified by an 'o' on the relationship line) allows for the possibility that a detail occurrence may not have a master. An exclusive relationship, shown by an arc, is where an entity

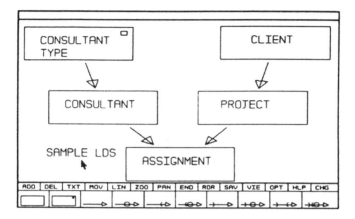

Fig. 15.5. LDS screen.

has a relationship with two or more others, but where any one relationship occurrence excludes the possibility of a relationship occurrence with any of the others. The other symbols are the entity icon itself and the operational master symbol.

Automate+ does not permit many-to-many or indeed one-to-one relationships to be drawn, so it is therefore not possible to store data models which are in the process of being refined.

15.3.5 LDS completeness and correctness checking

Because the data model does not have the hierarchical complexity of the DFD set, there is no need for consistency checking. In fact, only an elementary level of automatic checking can be achieved and is as follows:

- entity not named
- invalid entity name
- invalid relationship name
- duplicate entity name
- duplicate relationship name

Since the data model is used in later stages of the method, it is important that a basic level of quality is established at this stage. Again, however, beware that there is no in-built guarantee that the data model accurately reflects the real world.

318

Chapter 15

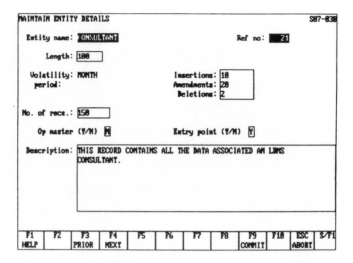

Fig. 15.6. Entity details screen.

15.3.6 Adding entity and relationship descriptions

The LDS chart is a useful overview of the entities and relationships required in a system. But, like DFDs, LDS charts only show, and deliberately so for the same information-hiding reasons, part of the information available. When the LDS chart is presented to the Automate+ database, the details about the entities and relationships are transferred from the chart and stored as initial entries in the database data dictionary. This is called populating the data dictionary and has three advantages. Firstly, it saves the analyst typing in text which has already been added to the LDS picture. Secondly, it removes the possibility of inconsistency through mistyping names. Thirdly, the automatic transfer ensures that the analyst does not forget to add definitions for these entities or relationships.

Entity definitions are created by selecting the MAINTAIN ENTITY DETAILS screen in Automate+. See figure 15.6. The entity name and the reference number assigned to it by Automate+ appear at the top of the screen. This is followed by a number of other fields as indicated in table 15.2. The nature of project investigation is such that probably not all of this information will be known at the time of creating the first-cut data model, although in some projects, for example, where the system is already computerised, much or all of the information if still accurate is available immediately. Where unknown fields exist, they provide a checklist of questions which the analyst

length -	the total data length of the entity occurrence (in bytes)
volatility	
period -	the time period over which frequency transactions are measured (e.g. day, week, month)
insertions -	the average number of entity occurrences added per volatility period
amendments -	the average number of entity occurrences amended per volatility period
deletions -	the average number of entity occurrences deleted per volatility period
no of recs -	the number of entity occurrences
OP master -	enter "Y" if entity contains only key data
entry point -	enter "Y" if entity requires direct access
description -	free text definition of entity

Table 15.2. Operational attributes required by the MAINTAIN ENTITY DETAILS.

will require answered either by recourse to the user or by analysis on the volumes of transactions that are processed.

However, at this stage, the inclusion of all the information is not mandatory, though it should be recognised that the volumetric data is necessary in making decisions concerning the physical database.

The creation of relationship definitions follows a similar dialogue to the entity definitions and is initiated by selecting the MAINTAIN RELATION-SHIP DETAILS screen. See figure 15.7.

Again, what information can be gleaned from the LDS chart is automatically displayed at the top of the screen. Although it is possible to omit naming a relationship, it is good software engineering practice to explicitly name each

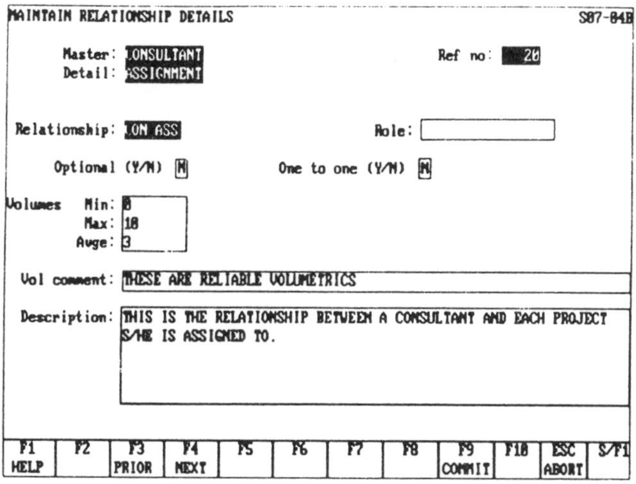

Fig. 15.7. Relationship details screen.

role -	important as a clarification where there is more than one relationship between two entities
optional -	denotes whether or not a detail can exist without a master
one to one -	denotes the degree of relationship
min volume -	the minimum number of relationship occurrences per master
max volume -	the maximum number of relationship occurrences per master
ave volume -	the average number of relationship occurrences per master
volumetric comment -	free text about for example how the volumes were measured
description -	free text definition of relationship

Table 15.3. Operational attributes of the MAINTAIN RELATIONSHIP DETAILS screen.

relationship, since each relationship adds important information to a data model.

The fields on the MAINTAIN RELATIONSHIP DETAILS screen are discussed briefly in table 15.3. As with the entity definitions, volumetric information is vital in physical database design although the inclusion of all fields at this stage is not necessary.

15.3.7 Entity attribute definition

Entity attributes are called data items within Automate+ and are held separately from entities. So it is necessary to set up cross-references within the database.

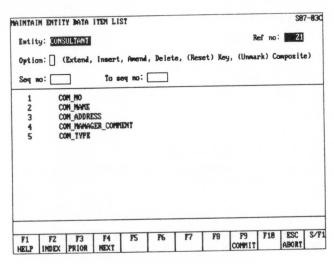

Fig. 15.8. Entity data item screen.

ENTITY -	name of entity
REF NO -	reference no of entity
OPTION -	first letter of option:
	"E" for extend which adds data items to the end of the list
	"I" to insert data item at a particular position in the list
	"A" to amend a particular data item
	"D" to delete a data item from the list
	"K" to set key against a data item or items
	"R" to reset key
	"C" to mark a data item as part of a composite data structure
	"U" to unmark a composite data item
SEQ-NO -	used in combination with OPTION
and TO-SEQ-NO -	to assist with specifying the details of the option

Table 15.4. Operational attributes of the MAINTAIN ENTITY DATA ITEM LIST screen.

The MAINTAIN ENTITY DATA ITEM LIST option allows the cross-reference to be established. This is how Automate+ deals with the decomposition of composite data structures as described in chapter 2. By specifying the LDS chart and entity, the screen in figure 15.8 is obtained. Table 15.4 describes the meaning of the fields on the MAINTAIN ENTITY DATA ITEM LIST. However, the definitions of the data items themselves are held in what is known as the data inventory. If data items already exist on the data

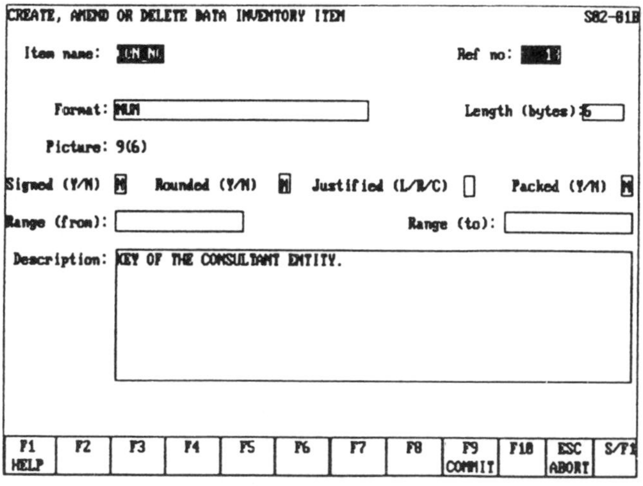

Fig. 15.9. Data inventory item screen.

FORMAT -	either ALPHA or NUMERIC
LENGTH -	length of data item in bytes
PICTURE -	picture clause e.g. 999.99
SIGNED -	whether field is signed
ROUNDED -	whether field is rounded
JUSTIFIED -	field may be right or left justified or centred
PACKED -	field may be packed to reduce storage space
RANGE FROM -	minimum and maximum value of field
RANGE TO	
DESCRIPTIONS -	free text description of field

Table 15.5. Operational attributes for data items.

inventory, then the analyst can call up a list of all data items in the inventory. This is useful where the analyst knows the field exists but has forgotten the exact name.

Data inventory item definitions can be made directly by selecting the CREATE, AMEND OR DELETE DATA INVENTORY ITEM option, or alternatively there is a facility to do so while establishing the cross-references. The screen displayed is shown in figure 15.9 and table 15.5 describes the detailed meaning of each field. This permits the detailed specification of elementary data items as discussed in chapter 2.

Another facility that is available with respect to attributes of entities is the ability to declare synonyms or aliases. The MAINTAIN DATA ITEM SYNONYM screen is used. Having been defined, the synonym can be used to access the definition of the data item and also it will appear on data inventory reports.

By utilising the screen options described above, entity, relationship and data item definitions can be supplied to the database data dictionary. Data item definitions can be easily deleted from the data dictionary; however, in order to delete entity or relationship references, a modified LDS must be reloaded from the LDS picture. This mechanism serves to ensure that the LDS picture and the Automate+ database are always consistent with one another.

15.3.8 Entity/datastore cross-referencing

These cross-references are defined to Automate+ through the MAINTAIN ENTITY/DATA STORE CROSS-REFERENCE screen. Since the datastore through its data items may be related to more than one entity, multiple definitions are often necessary.

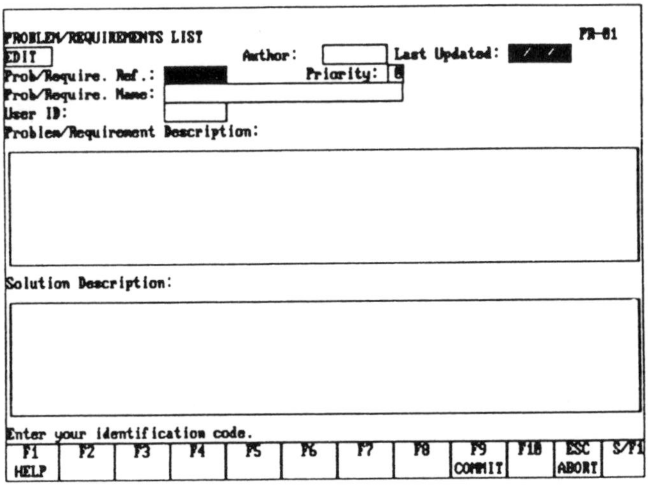

Fig. 15.10. Problem/requirement screen.

15.3.9 Automate+ reports

Three reports are available which provide comprehensive coverage of the contents of the database:

- LDS entity report
- LDS relationship report
- Data inventory report

15.3.10 Maintaining the problem/requirements list

The PROBLEM/REQUIREMENTS LIST screen enables these statements to be formally recorded in Automate+ and also provides for the solution to be recorded when it is identified. See figure 15.10. Table 15.6 describes the meaning of the entries.

AUTHOR -	initials of analyst recording the data
PROB/RQMTS REF -	different codes are possible e.g. P for problem, R for requirement. Also, may include a department code to indicate source
PRIORITY -	from 1 to 9 indicating seriousness of issue
PRB/RQMTS NAME -	name of item (this is mandatory as it is used when all problems are displayed in index)
USER ID -	initial of user involved
PROB/RQMTS DESCR -	description of issue
SOLUTION DESCR -	description of solution

Table 15.6. Operational attribute for the P/R list screen.

15.3.11 A glimpse of workstations in the future

The computing business is both dynamic and competitive. So it is natural as time passes that the current state-of-the-art will be improved upon. In due course, it can be expected that products like Automate+, comprehensive though they are, will be superseded by new generations of workstation. This section will look briefly at the directions a future generation might take.

(1) A multi-analyst environment

In some respects, the boundary between an analyst workstation and an IPSE becomes less clear in the context of a multi-analyst environment. The reality of project life is that, in larger projects, there may be several analysts working on the same system at the same time – the partitioning of the DFD hierarchy, for example, enables this to be done quite easily. The problem comes when it is required to integrate the work of several analysts. Ideally, analysts should be able to work at their own workstations and when required update a master version with the work that has been completed, so that a consolidated picture is obtained. Clearly, this will require a more sophisticated design of workstation as well as, for example, networked communications facilities.

(2) A more flexible working environment

The ideal workstation is one which allows software engineers to work the way they think. The problem is that people think differently and they choose different means to get to the same end. To an extent, the current generation of (method specific) workstations has perhaps tended to be a little bit prescriptive in following the sequences of tasks within a method. In one sense, this has been useful, because it has allowed a generation of software engineers to acclimatise themselves to working with a workstation and the method behind it, yet still have a well-defined path to follow. Many such software engineers have now reached a level of maturity and familiarity with their work environment that it is no longer appropriate to limit or restrict the way things are done. What is required is a workstation environment which allows software engineers the flexibility they need, yet still retaining a safety-net in terms of ensuring that the underlying essential tasks and sequences within the development process are not compromised. Again this has significant implications for the design of the workstation. The workstation database has to be more flexible to allow the recording of data in perhaps alternative sequences, e.g. low level DFDs before higher level DFDs. But at some point and presumably when appropriate, there needs to be the ability to check that the integrity of the data is still intact. In the above example, the software engineer will still want to check the consistency between different levels of DFD.

The use of 'windowing' technology is another development which makes for a more flexible working environment. In such an environment you can display two documents side by side on the screen for comparison purposes or overlay one document on top of another. The facilities offered are more akin to working at a desk and again allow software engineers flexibility in the way things are done.

(3) Help support

It is possible to provide sophisticated forms of help support. For example, the most immediate form of help is context-sensitive help, where the workstation can provide guidance based on the particular point in the dialogue. A second category of help can be provided concerning the method itself. Software engineers might use such a facility to remind themselves what is to be done next and how it should be done. The system could even prompt the software engineer about tasks which are becoming vital or overdue. Lastly, a form of help support could be obtained in the guise of an expert system designed to help the software engineer in resolving error messages or warnings arising from integrity problems in the database.

(4) Automatic code generation

Given that so much information has already been captured within the analyst workstation, it seems such a relatively small step to convert this into executable code. Certainly, it is already possible to create record or database definitions for most target languages. The next step is to take the logic in the process specifications, validation rules in the data dictionary and so on and try to construct the source code from these. In fact, this is by no means trivial, but the more that can be done automatically, the less that needs to be done in an error-prone manual fashion. This brings us closer to being able to effectively prototype from a system specification. Prototyping is discussed in chapter 17.

15.4 IPSEs

Discussion in this section, in fact, covers two perspectives. These are project leader's view, where the interest is on a single project, and the view of the system development manager who is concerned about all the projects in the department. However, for brevity, these are discussed as one.

Computer departments like most other departments have a need for what may be termed a 'departmental database' which can support all its activities and therefore improve its productivity. It must meet the needs of the programmer and systems analyst, as previously discussed, but further it needs to assist the project leader in the planning and control of a single project and then also the systems development manager who is interested in all the work being done in the department. Certain other groups have not been mentioned such as librarians and, if the department has one, the data analysis group, who are the custodians of the organisation's corporate data model.

The following are typical of the kinds of facility which could form part of an IPSE.

15.4.1 An integrated project status reporting system

This would be linked with analyst and programmer workstations and be based on completed deliverables, e.g.:

- a program entered into a program library
- a DFD entered into a directory
- a report sent by electronic mail

Each task has a time allocated to it. So as a task is completed, it is registered as complete and the actual time to complete is entered against it. This information is consolidated at project level to produce an up-to-date picture of the status on the project. This would allow for percentage complete and, more importantly, estimate-to-complete information to be provided.

15.4.2 Current status reporting

In addition to the normal reporting cycle discussed above, it would be advantageous to be able to obtain an up-to-the-minute status of a project or indeed projects. This is feasible because all the information is already in the database; it only needs to be retrieved and displayed.

15.4.3 Long-term manpower planning

This would be done by the systems development manager to address long-term requirements, i.e. not to make decisions about who does what and when within a project but to decide who is available for the next project and roughly when. Again the raw information to do this would be available from the departmental database.

15.4.4 Project histories

When a project is completed, it is usually quickly forgotten. However, there is a lot that can be learnt (and perhaps reused) from previous projects, provided that the information, which may be both qualitative and quantitative, is stored in such a way that it can be conveniently retrieved.

15.4.5 Databank of time estimates

Each DP installation needs to build its own set of estimates for tasks (not just for programming tasks but for documentation, design tasks, analysis tasks, handovers, data analysis, training, etc). As the nature of the work changes, so do the estimates. A databank of this information needs to be set up and maintained.

15.4.6 Sub-networks

There are patterns of activities which are repeated in many projects. For example, tasks within a method usually follow a strict sequence. When planning a new project, these 'sub-networks' can be lifted from a standard library and inserted into the new project. This also helps to ensure that standards are adhered to, since, for example, standard reviews would be built in. Time estimates may or may not be applicable.

15.4.7 Change control system

A change control system is a natural candidate for computerisation under an IPSE, since all basic information would already exist. The benefits of computerisation would include automated change impact assessment, change tracking and the sending of reminders to team members of deadlines.

15.4.8 Problem management system

Like the change control system, a problem management system lends itself to computerisation under an IPSE. Historical information would be readily available to recover the details of who developed the product that is causing the problem, as would information about the impact and likely effect of the problem (e.g. which programs use an offending module) and who is available with the requisite skills to solve the problem (since the IPSE would know what had been done, when deadlines were due, etc).

15.4.9 An interrogation facility

With all this potentially useful information available, it is possible to retrieve and display it in a variety of ways. The power and usefulness of such a facility is demonstrated in the following example:

1 Standard reports reveal that a programmer has been 50 per cent over target in three programs within the current project.

2 Displaying the work breakdown structure, it is observed that the same analyst specified all three programs. Furthermore, the analyst has specified a number of other programs, but none of these has been written yet. So:
   • Is the programmer poor?
   • Is the analyst too tight on his estimates?
   • Is it a combination of both?
   • Is there some other cause (e.g. m/c failure, bottleneck)?

3 (a) Extract data on all previous (recent) programs written by the programmer and calculate the ratio of total actual time to total planned time. (b) Extract similar data for the analyst. Note that it may be necessary to select out only certain categories of work, e.g. only on-line, database programs.

4 Inevitably, this leads to further questions being raised, which may require further retrievals or perhaps to utilise different tools, e.g. suppose you conclude that the analyst has been underestimating by 30%. What will be the effect on the project? The programs specified by the analyst can have their estimates revised and the effect on the critical path established.

5 Assuming this affects the critical path, it becomes necessary to add an additional member of staff to the project team. The manpower plan is reviewed and various alternatives to identify who will be added to the team and when will be considered. So through successive interrogations of the database, conclusions can be reached. Other software tools may then be used in combination with the retrieval facility to analyse the impact of the situation.

15.4.10 The central role of the database in an IPSE

The design of an IPSE is clearly a complex task. It has to be able to store data and retrieve the data required by different staff who may need to view the data at different levels. Because of the requirement for multi-user access (here the 'users' are programmers, analysts and so on) and to avoid the consequences of duplication and inconsistency of data, it is virtually mandatory that the heart of an IPSE would be a database which permitted copying up and down to individual workstations only under strict rules. This is essential for preserving the integrity of the data within the IPSE.

One can imagine the kind of entities the development database would have to contain. For example, entity PROJECT would contain many TASKs in which the actual time and planned time would be held as attributes. For each TASK occurrence there would be an associated set of deliverables such as compiled program, tested module or whatever. It is clear that the data contained in an IPSE would be substantial. Another part of the database would be devoted to what we have called the data dictionary. Ideally, a single set of definitions of composite and elementary data needs to be maintained for the organisation. Again, the use of a database is justified. Composite data items will contain many elementary data items, elementary data items will be used in different modules and so on.

Though it is absolutely crucial that the designers of IPSEs get the design of the database right, they have an additional problem in making it as flexible as possible in terms of meeting the needs of everyone in the development department. Now this is a typical dilemma that developers of information systems face – how do you anticipate the kinds of questions that people are going to ask? In the author's view, the answer lies in the following:

- The provision of a basic database which can be modified or extended to meet specific requirements.
- A powerful query facility which can interact on entities in the database, thereby allowing questions to be explored fully.
- The ability to incorporate new tools within the IPSE.
- The capability to change the flexibility obtainable from an IPSE. For example, experienced staff should be permitted to take alternative routes to solving problems if appropriate, whereas perhaps it is better for inexperienced staff to work through the basic sequences inherent in a method.

15.5 SUMMARY

It was felt important to spend some time illustrating in detail how automated productivity tools can support the work of the software engineer. Inevitably, the use of such tools changes the way in which things are done – it forces the analyst to document fully using certain notations and standards, it forces use of a microcomputer and so on. The industry as a whole has now caught on to the idea that productivity tools are vital if costs are to be kept down and quality up and it is to be expected that the next decade will see a growth in the use and sophistication of CASE tools generally.

But it is in the realm of workstations and IPSEs that the real improvements will be made. Workstations like Automate+ provide a great deal of support in assisting the analyst. Emphasis is on producing major deliverables such as the data model with perhaps less support in how the intermediate deliverables are generated. For example, a relationship matrix would be drawn on paper. Nevertheless, Automate+ does provide comprehensive support in all the major deliverables required. Specifically, these are the creation and mainten-ance of diagrams including the LDS, DFD and ELH pictures, a data dictionary facility which permits definition of a number of objects used in later stages, and lastly a comprehensive report facility which enables useful documentation to be generated with minimum effort. Given the iterative nature of software engineering, the ability to easily modify a diagram several times if necessary and then regenerate the documentation automatically is clearly advantageous.

Projects within an installation can vary substantially, and even more so across installations. So it is important that a method, and therefore any supporting workstation, not only tolerates but is supportive of the variety of development situations. This can be achieved by emphasis on deliverables and permitting therefore alternative routes to that goal. This enables circumstances such as the existence of a corporate data model or an existing computerised (but insufficient) system to be subsumed within the method. Automate+ is flexible to the extent that not all properties of attributes, for example, need to defined to the database. This accommodates situations where more or less is known at a particular point in time during the analysis. Also, given the iterative nature of analysis and design, it is imperative that facilities exist to go back, modify and regenerate deliverables with relative ease. A good example of this in Automate+ is the reload command, which resubmits a DFD set or LDS chart to the database after modification of the appropriate picture. When the DFD set and the LDS chart are loaded into the data dictionary database, the software checks for errors in terms of completeness, correctness and consistency. Although it does not ensure that the diagrams are any more correct with respect to the real world objects they represent, it does trap 'syntactical' errors at an early stage. Early correction of such errors saves time and effort in later stages and is therefore a worthwhile activity.

To a degree, it may be that the boundary between workstations and IPSEs could become blurred, as facilities are extended and, for example, the potential for automatic code generation becomes more real. Having said that, an IPSE by our definition must explicitly cater for the needs of project management (i.e. the project and departmental dimensions) as well as individual and task needs. Because of its charter, an IPSE is a complicated and comprehensive piece of software. It may be some time before the suppliers of IPSEs get their their products completely right and probably some time after that until widespread use of IPSEs will be seen. But make no mistake, the challenge of creating a fully functional IPSE is here to stay. Computer staff are notoriously expensive and scarce. It makes sense to use such resources productively. Like workstations, it is imperative that IPSEs reflect current practice and, for example, are able to incorporate new software tools which reflect new techniques, otherwise they will become obsolete and fall into disuse. Given a flexible IPSE, the advantage to project management is immense and provides the opportunity for a level of project supervision not possible today. The next decade will see considerable development in IPSEs and no doubt much still has to be learnt in how to use such facilities to best effect.

15.6 FURTHER READING

1   Mair, P. (1986) *Integrated Project Support Environments: State of the Art Report*, NCC, Manchester. This technical report discusses IPSE generations in some depth. It also surveys a number of IPSEs currently available in the marketplace.
2   *Auto-Mate Plus Users Guide* (Vols 1, 2 and 3) (1987) obtainable from LBMS (Learmonth and Burchett Management Systems), London, gives details of the operation of Automate+.

Chapter 16
The Need for Quantification

16.1 INTRODUCTION

The reason for this chapter is quite simple. Many software engineers do not attempt to make quantitative estimates in areas of work where it is possible to do so. Part of the problem lies in that there has not been a tradition for gathering quantitative data upon which to make estimates. In order for the profession to advance past the 'practice of ignorance' it is vital that a positive attitude towards quantification is inculcated in every software engineer. The purpose of this chapter is to demonstrate some areas in which quantification is practical. These areas cover the spectrum of activity in software engineering from 'hard' areas such as quantifying hardware resources through to 'soft' areas such as trying to quantify intangible benefits.

Some of the issues dealt with below impinge on the territory of queuing theory and statistical theory generally. Such discussion is unfortunately beyond the scope and introductory nature of this textbook. The discussion below should therefore be considered an absolute minimum and sometimes insufficient treatment of the subject matter. However, it is hoped that it presents some of the important issues in quantification as well as providing a starting point for some degree of decision-making.

16.2 QUANTIFYING RESOURCES

Consider the design problem in the SBM case study. For the sake of discussion in this section, assume that two alternative design solutions are proposed, i.e. one based on customers continuing to send their orders by post with the staff inputting these on-line to the system (option 1), and the other based on customers telephoning orders directly to staff who update the system at a terminal while the customer is on the phone (option 2). It is required to establish how many terminals are needed.

16.2.1 Option 1

This situation is known as pseudo-batch, because orders are received through the post and processed by computer serially.

The number of terminals is calculated as follows:

(1) Calculate the average time to process one order

The processing of an order is broken down into tasks. Each task is given an estimated average time. The estimates are obtained using a combination of stop watch and experience.

1 The clerk checks for any omission on the order which will make computer processing infeasible. This takes 15 seconds.

2 Input order header. By analysing each field in the order header the following is concluded:

Order-no. This is automatically generated by the system when the screen is displayed. No effort.

Customer-no. Say 25% of customers include their customer-no, while 75% do not. If included, the copying across takes 4 seconds. If the index has to be searched, this takes 20 seconds including copying across. Average time to insert customer-no is therefore 16 seconds.

Date. Date is automatically generated.

So, average time to insert order header is 16 seconds plus 2 seconds response time, making 18 in all.

3 Input one order-line

Product-code. 20 seconds for clerk to search product-code index and key product-code

Product-description. Generated by product-code

Unit of measure. 4 seconds

Quantity. 4 seconds

This makes 28 seconds plus 2 seconds response time, making 30 seconds in all.

4 Time for all order-lines. Assume the average order contains 5 lines. This makes 150 seconds.

5 Completion of order. When all order-lines have been entered, the program will check stock and credit limit. Stock not available implies order-lines are moved onto an outstanding order list. Insufficient credit also removes order-lines from the order. Assume this is done by machine and takes, say, 3 seconds.

6 Average time for a valid, accepted order is therefore 186 seconds.

7 Assume there is a 10% mistake allowance which adds 10% to the time taken so that mistakes in entering data can be corrected. Total time for an accepted order is 186 + 19 is 205 seconds.

8 Suppose omissions occur in 5% of all orders received. This means that in those cases processing proceeds no further. So average time for an order is 15 × 0.05 + 205 × 0.95 = 195.5 seconds.

9 An allowance for productivity is now added, since no one works flat out all day without interruptions, etc. Say, productivity is 85%. Adjusted time for one order is 230 seconds.

(2) Identify the demand
To identify the demand, an analysis of the number of orders received per day can be performed. This would then be modified to incorporate any likely trends as a consequence of the new system. It is acceptable to group these into bands to facilitate further analysis. Table 16.1(a) contains an analysis of the transactions received each day over a year (assume 200 working days per

No of transaction/day	*Mean*	*No of days*
40-79	60	25
80-119	100	65
120-159	140	90
160-199	180	20

		200

Table 16.1(a). Analysis of transactions received.

$$Number\ of\ terminals = \frac{No\ of\ orders\ \times time\ for\ one\ order}{working\ day\ time}$$

$$= \frac{197 \times 230}{6 \times 60 \times 60} \text{ (assume 6 available hours in a day)}$$

= 2.1 (which needs to be rounded up to 3)

Table 16.1(b). Calculation to cope with worst day of year.

year). From the table we can see that, for example, on 25 days of the year the number of transactions received was in the range 40 to 79.

(3) Decide on the number of terminals
This decision is not as mechanical as it might appear, because it depends on how complete the coverage needs to be. If it is desired, for example, to cope with the worst day of the year, say 197 orders, then the calculation is as in table 16.1 (b).

So, 3 terminals are required to cope with the heaviest period. However, it is also clear that for most of the time, 2 terminals would be sufficient. On the other hand, if there was a substantial increase in orders placed because the computer system offered a better quality of service to customers, then 3 terminals might be needed after all. Another aspect is seasonal variation. Some companies, e.g. manufacturers of ice cream, experience vast differences in demand depending on the time of year. It could be, in our example, that there is a peak time of, say, a fortnight or three weeks where demand is exceptional. It may be acceptable to offset this by overtime working. Only a deeper analysis of the data and background factors will reveal the answer.

16.2.2 Option 2

This option represents the situation when the arrival of orders is random or approximately random. Since in the SBM system, the majority of orders are sent by post, there is no hard data to use, although often there will be for this kind of option. However, with the clerks' help and possibly by contacting customers, a picture of likely dialogues and arrival rates can be built up.

(1) Calculate the time to process one order
This case is different from the previous one because the order is made by telephone.

1 Allow 20 seconds for initial introductions and pleasantries.

2 Input order-header. The time taken will be similar to the previous case for keying and response but add 1 second per keyed field as overhead, since customer has to read out his requirements. Allow 19 seconds (i.e. 18 + 1).

3 Input one order-line. Again the time for keying and response is similar but 3 seconds overhead (1 second per keyed field) are added, making 33 seconds per line.

4 Time for all order-lines. Assume 5 lines on average, making 165 seconds.

5 Adjusted time for order-lines. Because of the on-line nature of the dialogue, problems which occur during processing can often be rectified on the spot. For example, alternative items or sizes may be ordered if the product available is not in stock. Assume this leads to a 10% overhead while inputting order-lines. This gives 181.5 seconds.

6 An allowance of 10% is again provided to correct keying mistakes. This is applied over all keying i.e. order-header plus order-lines, which is (19 + 181.5) + 10% = 220 seconds.

7 Assume another 20 seconds for confirmation of order.

8 Total time to deal with order is 20 + 220 + 20 = 260 seconds.

9 Lastly, there is likely to be an interruption factor of say, 5%, making 273 seconds in all.

(2) Identify the demand
In this case the arrivals are collected into half-hour periods throughout the

time	no of arrivals
9.00 - 9.30	1
9.30 - 10	3
10.00	12
10.30	14
11.00	16
11.30	12
12.00	1
12.30	4
1.00	5
1.30	5
2.00	6
2.30	8
3.00	15
3.30	10
4.00	5
4.30	4

Table 16.2. Analysis of arrival rates during the day.

day. Table 16.2 shows that there are two peaks during the day, one between 11.00 and 11.30 am, the other between 3.00 and 3.30 pm.

(3) Decide on the number of terminals

Again, the decision will be based on what is acceptable. The worst period in the day is in the morning, when it is estimated there are 16 arrivals. Now these orders will arrive randomly during the half-hour period, i.e. it is still likely that there will be gaps in that period between one order being completed and the next phone call. This means that unlike the pseudo-batch option, where one order can be processed after another, there will be times when the terminal is not in use. Another complicating factor is that a customer may find the phone engaged because the clerk is dealing with another customer. But ignore this for the current calculation. Assume the utilisation rate for the terminal is 90% i.e. it is used 90% of the time.

Let M be the number of minutes processing time that must take place in the half-hour slot. Then:

M = peak no of orders $\times$ time to process one order
  = 16×273 seconds = 72.8 minutes

Applying the utilisation factor this gives approximately 81 minutes processing required in a 30 minute period. So three terminals are required. Incidentally, three telephones are required too.

Now, the average arrival rate for the day is much less – around 7.5 in any half-hour period. At this arrival rate, about 38 minutes of processing time is required, so 2 terminals would be required to cope with an average daily load.

Observe that option 2 is likely to be the preferred option in terms of customer goodwill and business generated. Customers and staff are likely to build up working relationships, problems can be resolved interactively on the telephone instead of rejection notes being sent through the post. The amount of business done will increase. The cost of this may be a requirement for more hardware to provide the level of service needed to maintain customer goodwill. Again peak days and seasonal variations will have an impact on requirements as they did in option 1. So costs and perceived benefits determine the basis of the final decision.

16.3 QUANTIFYING COMPUTER TIME

Another area which has been largely ignored is in estimating the time a program takes to execute. In the past, as long as programs worked within reasonable limits, there was no great concern shown by management. It was only later at, say, periods of peak demand when things started to go badly wrong, that questions were asked. By then of course it was too late.

Today, especially with on-line transaction processing systems, it is important that the response time for transactions which involve human interaction is reasonable and is geared to holding the concentration of the human participant.

Usually, response times should be within 2 seconds to facilitate this. After 4 seconds, concentration tends to slip. So there is a need to quantify program execution times and other related times. At the same time, it is becoming more difficult to do this in today's sophisticated computer environments. The response time may well include factors for delays in transmission through a communications network, execution of various language features (e.g. multiple module calls), time to navigate through entities in a database and operating system overhead. There are three ways in which one can begin to quantify such factors.

16.3.1 Supplier's modelling tools

A notable trend is occurring with some suppliers of software. They are supplying tools which allow computer personnel to model the effects of running their software on certain machines. Typically the tool will require quantitative input concerning the nature of the application, e.g. number of entity occurrences, how many entities navigated, etc. From this the modelling software can provide an insight as to the expected execution time on a certain class of machine. One important benefit of this is that, if the projected time is not acceptable, alternative ways, if available, can be explored to meet the needs of the program. This is all done at the design stage, before the program is actually written.

16.3.2 Machine instruction analysis

This is a kind of 'bottom-up' approach which can sometimes be used to advantage. This involves quantifying the basic machine instructions or operations that take place in a program or module. For example, to establish the access time to read a record on disk, the following formula can be used:

access time = channel transfer time + seek time + rotational delay

Clearly, a sound knowledge of the physical characteristics of how a particular machine and its associated software operates is necessary to perform this kind of analysis adequately. However, this demands a substantial amount of expertise to estimate adequately. Such expertise is not always available. Even when it is, it needs to be continually updated as new computers, machines, and software change the basic formulae. But the real problem is that this area is only one of many in which software engineers are expected to be competent. Is it realistic to expect software engineers to carry around such vast amounts of knowledge over an ever widening domain?

16.3.3 Benchmarking

The idea of benchmarking is to quantify an activity by measuring it in its operational environment. Benchmarking can be performed both prior to and after implementation. If used after implementation it provides the necessary confirmatory data about actual execution times. It can be used before implementation in the following way. Suppose it was required to benchmark the time taken to calculate a person's wage. A typical wage calculation can be relatively complex with overtime and bonus payments, tax and other statutory deductions. A small program can be written which goes through a typical calculation and CPU clock readings taken before and after the calculation. If there are a variety of different calculations then a representative set can be used. In this way, the calculation time component can be established and carried forward to the final total. (Clearly other components such as database access and telecommunications delay could be added in.)

If it is established that a particular transaction is taking excessively long, then the question of what to do about it arises. Experience shows that often the Pareto rule applies, which can be paraphrased as '10% of the modules account for 90% of the execution time'. By investigating the detail of the delinquent module(s), alternatives, if available, can be identified and implemented. Often, however, there may be nothing that can reasonably be done without re-examining user requirements.

16.4 QUANTIFYING AND COMPARING COSTS

When potential projects are being investigated, ways have to be found to enable the perceived value that one project might bring to be compared against the value another project or a variation of the original project might bring. This is a difficult area to address and one fraught with danger, because there are many complicating factors. One problem area is how to quantify the benefits that may arise from an implemented computer system. Some of these may be tangible in the sense that they can be quantified relatively easily, e.g. if a system is currently run manually, the costs incurred in doing so are avoided (and replaced by the computer costs). Others are intangible, e.g. the benefit of increased customer goodwill because a superior service is offered. However, before these issues are considered, there is a more pressing one which is concerned with techniques for assessing the value of projects. In this discussion, it is assumed there is some mechanism for quantifying benefits.

Four techniques are discussed:

- payback period
- return on investment
- net present value
- internal rate of return

16.4.1 Payback period

This is a very simple technique which involves calculating the length of time for the benefits of the project to 'payback' the original investment. See table 16.3.

Unfortunately, there are a number of problems with using the payback period. These include:

- Benefits may continue to accrue long after the payback period is reached. This technique does not take account of this. In practice computer systems typically have a heavy investment while the system is being developed, followed by many years of potential benefit.
- The scale of the investment is not considered. The two projects in the

	Project A	Project B
Investment	(10,000)	(50,000)
year 1	1,000	30,000
year 2	2,000	15,000
year 3	7,000	10,000
payback period	3 years	2.5 years

Table 16.3. Payback period.

example have roughly the same payback period. If this was the only criterion used, one would be tempted to assume that they are equivalent. However, the investment required for project B is five times that of A, so clearly they are not equivalent in that sense.
- The timing of the cash flow is ignored. Looking at the example again, after 2 years, project A has only recovered 30% of its outlay, whereas project B has recovered 90%. Clearly, there is advantage in recovering costs sooner rather than later.

16.4.2 Return on investment (ROI)

This technique addresses one disadvantage of the payback period. It quantifies the total value of benefits over the whole life of the project. ROI is the ratio of net benefit to investment expressed as a percentage over the life of a project. See table 16.4.

However, ROI does not address the other weaknesses of payback period, i.e. the scale of the investment and the timing of cash flow.

More significantly, both ROI and payback period have another important drawback which has not yet been discussed. That is, that they do not consider the time-dependent value of money. Money changes its values over time because of inflation. One pound or dollar this year will buy you more than it will one year hence and far more than ten years hence (assuming that inflation continues). What is required therefore is a technique which takes account of this change in the value of money and compensates for it in its calculation.

$$ROI = \frac{\Sigma B_i - I}{I * n} \times 100$$

where B_i = the benefit in year i
         I = investment
         n = the project life span in years

Example
Consider project B,

$\Sigma B_i = 55,000$
$I = 50,000$

$$ROI = \frac{5000}{50000 \times 3} \times 100 = 3\frac{1}{3}\%$$

Table 16.4. Return on investment.

Consider project A again.

Year	Benefit	Inflation Factor	Present Value (PV)
1	1,000	$\frac{1}{1.1} = 0.909$	909
2	2,000	$\left(\frac{1}{1.1}\right)^2 = 0.826$	1652
3	7,000	$\left(\frac{1}{1.1}\right)^3 = 0.751$	5257

The net present value formula is given by:

$$NPV = \sum_{i=1}^{n} PV_i - I$$

where PV_i is the present value in the ith year
and I is the investment.

$$PV_i = \frac{B_i}{(1+r)^i}$$

where B_i is in benefit in the ith year
r is the inflation factor.

Table 16.5. Net present value.

16.4.3 Net present value

This technique converts the value of benefits which will accrue in the future to the value it is worth today, i.e. its present value. To do this one has to apply a factor for inflation for each year in the future. It is customary, although not necessarily valid, to apply the same inflation factor for each year over the life of the project. Assume that inflation is 10%. This means that after one year, a pound is worth 10% less, i.e. 0.909 pounds. Two years hence, a pound today is worth even less, i.e. 10% less than it will be one year hence i.e. 0.909 * 0.909 = 0.826 pounds and so on. See table 16.5.

So, in the example, NPV = 7818 – 10000 = (2182). Clearly, if as in this case the NPV is negative, then the project is not worthwhile. Only positive NPVs are profitable.

16.4.4 Internal rate of return (IRR)

One difficulty in using the NPV method is that a value for the inflation factor must be provided. But no one really knows what inflation is likely to be. The IRR technique looks at the problem from a different perspective. Instead of find an r such that

$$\sum \frac{B_i}{(1+r)^i} = I$$

Table 16.6. Internal rate of return.

Consider project B. Suppose the inflation factor had been 10%.

Year i	Benefit	Inflation factor (10%)	Present Value
1	30000	0.909	27270
2	15000	0.826	12390
3	10000	0.751	7510
			47170

NPV = 47170 - 50000 = (2830)

In other words, the inflation factor of 10% is too high. So try an inflation factor which should yield a positive NPV, say 5%.

Year I	Benefit	Inflation factor (5%)	Present Value
1	30000	0.952	28560
2	15000	0.907	13605
3	10000	0.864	8640
			50805

NPV = 50805 - 50000 = 805

So   NPV at 10% gives -2830
and NPV at 5% gives   805

Table 16.7. Using IRR.

$$IRR = r_1 - \frac{NPV_1}{(NPV_1 - NPV_2)} * (r_1 - r_2)$$

where r_1 and r_2 are the respective inflation factors
and NPV_1 and NPV_2 are the respective NPVs.

$$= 10 - \frac{2830}{3635} * 5$$
$$= 6.1 \text{ (approx)}$$

So an inflation factor of around 6% is required to exactly recoup the project costs.

Table 16.8. Interpolating the IRR.

assuming an inflation factor, it asks the question, 'what would the inflation factor have to be, so that over the life of the project the costs are recovered?' Table 16.6 shows this question expressed in mathematical form. Now this expression is a polynomial in r. In mathematics there is no easy way to calculate r directly. Fortunately, a close approximation is relatively easily reached. See table 16.7.

Clearly to get costs to exactly equal benefits the inflation factor must be somewhere between 5% and 10%. In fact, a good approximation can be obtained by simply interpolating the results. See table 16.8.

Some organisations use IRR as a way of eliminating projects as not viable. They tend to take the following view. If they were to invest the capital for the project in a bank or in other ways, they could expect to get a return on their investment of n%. If the IRR is less than the threshold n, then it is not worth investing in the project. Also, there is a high risk factor in projects – if it fails the benefits will not accrue, but the costs will have been incurred. To compensate for this, organisations raise the value of the IRR threshold, so that only projects which have the potential to yield high returns are considered viable.

16.5 QUANTIFYING BENEFITS

Returning now to the earlier point about benefits, in order to produce a quantified cost/benefit analysis, it is necessary to be able to quantify, as far as possible, the benefits accruing from a project. One can view benefits on a continuum with totally quantifiable benefits at one end, through to effectively unquantifiable benefits at the other. Examples of quantifiable or tangible benefits include situations where it improves the control the company has over its assets, e.g. in stock control where the value of stock carried can be reduced and in debt control where bad debts can be minimised. But clearly the more difficult area is how to, if not quantify intangible benefits, bring them into an arena where they can at least be compared with other benefits and costs. Examples of comparatively intangible benefits include:

- goodwill
- improved service
- better quality of information in terms of accuracy, timeliness and appropriateness
- improved user satisfaction

- reduced degree of risk associated with project
- congruence to business objectives

One approach is to ask user or senior management to put a monetary value on intangible benefits. For example, customer goodwill may bring in more business and a value could be put on that. However, it is less clear how to allocate a value for the degree of risk associated with a particular computer project.

16.5.1 Weighted ranking by levels method

An alternative to putting monetary values is to use non-financial criteria as a measure of goodness. The technique recommended is called the weighted ranking by levels method. However, a number of other simpler techniques and their weaknesses will be briefly reviewed to demonstrate why the above method is recommended.

(1) Attribute counting

The simplest technique is to just list the desirable criteria. Table 16.9 shows the desired criteria for the purchase for a microcomputer. A selection has to be made between two different micros. If the machine has the characteristic then a 'Y' is entered in the appropriate box; otherwise an 'N' is entered. The machine selected is the one with the most 'Y's.

characteristic	micro A	Micro B
Does it have 512K memory?	Y	Y
expandable to 1 megabyte?	Y	Y
IBM compatible?	Y	Y
colour monitor	N	Y
hard disk	Y	N
standard software	Y	Y
free extras	N	Y
training disks/manuals	Y	Y
good price	Y	Y
reasonable maintenance fee	N	Y
supplier reputation	Y	Y
	8	10

Table 16.9. Attribute counting.

characteristic	micro A	micro B
Does it have 512K memory?	10	10
expandable to 1 megabyte?	10	10
IBM compatible?	10	10
colour monitor	0	10
hard disk	10	0
standard software	7	7
free extras	0	7
training disks/manuals	5	8
good price	10	7
reasonable maintenance fee	2	5
supplier reputation	5	10
	69	84

Table 16.10. Ranking using scores.

(2) Ranking using scores

One disadvantage of the attribute counting method is that it does not take into account the relative advantage one option may have over another. For example, the criterion for 'yes' against cost, may be that the micro costs less than 1000 pounds. But micro B may cost 999 pounds, whereas micro A could have been 700 pounds, which is a big difference. If a score is attached to each criterion (say a mark out of 10), then this will permit relative advantages to be, to some extent, incorporated into the decision. See table 16.10.

characteristic	weighting factor	micro A	weighted mark	Micro B	weighted mark
does it have 512K memory?	15%	10	1.5	10	1.5
expandable to 1 megabyte?	5%	10	0.5	10	0.5
IBM compatible?	15%	10	1.5	10	1.5
colour monitor	5%	0	0	10	0.5
hard disk	20%	10	2	0	0
standard software	5%	7	0.35	7	0.35
free extras	5%	0	0	7	0.35
training disks/manuals	5%	5	0.25	8	0.4
good price	10%	10	1	7	0.7
reasonable maintenance fee	5%	2	0.1	5	0.25
supplier reputation	10%	5	0.5	10	1.0
			7.7		7.05

Table 16.11. Weighting ranking.

(3) Weighted ranking

The next difficulty is that each criterion is assumed to be equally important, i.e. they are all marked out of 10. This may not be so. Some criteria may be several times more important than others. This is overcome by applying a weighting factor to each criterion. It is customary to contrive the weighting factors such that the sum of weighting factors equals 100%. See table 16.11.

Now it is not absolutely necessary for the sum of the weighting factors to be 100%, although it does provide a completeness check that all weighting factors are included. Against this, there is a problem if it is required to increase

characteristics	weighting factor	micro A	weighted mark	micro B	weighted mark
: hardware category (contribution 35%)					
does it have 512K memory	25%	10	2.5	10	2.5
expandable to 1 megabyte?	10%	10	1.0	10	1.0
IBM compatible?	25%	10	2.5	10	2.5
colour monitor?	10%	0	0	10	1.0
hard disk?	30%	10	3.0	0	0
sub total			9.0		7.0
category sub total			3.15		2.45
: software category (contribution 25%)					
standard software?	35%	7	2.45	7	2.45
free extras?	30%	0	0	7	2.1
training disks/manuals?	35%	5	1.75	8	2.80
sub total			4.2		7.35
category sub total			1.05		1.8375
: cost category (contribution 20%)					
good price?	70%	10	7	7	4.9
reasonable maintenance free	30%	2	0.6	5	1.5
sub total			7.6		6.4
category sub total			1.52		1.28
: supplier category (contribution 20%)					
supplier reputation	100%	5	5	10	10
sub total			5		10
category sub total			1		2
grand total			6.72		7.5675

Table 16.12. Weight ranking by levels methods.

or decrease a particular weighting factor. It means that all other weighting factors have to be adjusted to maintain the total at 100%.

(4) Weighted ranking by levels

Another disadvantage with weighted ranking can arise when the number of individual factors becomes high – say over 20. It is not easy to manage! Around this number, it becomes difficult to cope with the relative importance and therefore weighting of one factor against the others, e.g. in absolute terms is expandability to 1 megabyte more important than a supplier's reputation? Most people would be happy with the additional memory, but the supplier reputation is important too – he may not have the necessary skills or resources to perform the expansion to 1 megabyte!

A more realistic approach is to divide and conquer, i.e. identify main classifications and then divide these further in sub-classifications and so on. For the example in table 16.12, the main classifications are cost, hardware, software and supplier rating. Having identified these classifications it is reasonable to apply weighting factors to each. Then each classification is considered in turn and sub-classifications are identified with corresponding weighting factors. This process is repeated until all levels of classification have been identified and weighting factors allocated. So a hierarchy of classifications is developed. The significance of insisting that weighting factors add up to 100% should now be clear. It preserves the consistency of the hierarchy and the relative weighting between classifications.

16.6 COST/BENEFIT ANALYSIS

At the end of the day, decisions have to be taken in environments where some of the factors are not totally quantifiable, as has been discussed above. A cost/ benefit analysis (CBA) attempts to do this. However, a CBA is not simply a table with costs and benefits. It is a much wider discussion in which qualitative factors are also included.

Specifically a CBA should include:

- cost/benefit statement
- ratio analysis
- factor analysis
- qualitative analysis

16.6.1 Cost/benefit statement

This is a simple statement of all costs and those benefits which are able to be quantified. It can be set out as follows:

- expected life of project
- once-off costs
- recurring costs
- once-off benefits
- recurring benefits

These figures are quoted as non-discounted figures, i.e. no adjustment is made of the time-dependent value of money at this stage.

16.6.2 Ratio analysis

This term comes from accountancy, where it is common practice for accounting to use ratios (or percentages) to gauge a company's performance. In selecting a computer project the ratios are those techniques which allow us to quantify the costs and benefits, i.e. ROI, NPV, etc. If IRR is used in a company, then it acts as a filter, i.e. only those projects which pass the IRR threshold are available for selection. Payback period, ROI, NPV and IRR may all appear in a ratio analysis. However, payback period and ROI should use discounted values for the returns identified.

16.6.3 Factor analysis

Factor analysis uses the weighted ranking by levels method to introduce the less quantifiable benefits. The beauty of this technique is that a host of different factors can be included for analysis. Conclusions from the earlier sections of the cost/benefit analysis can be converted to factors, e.g. costs, length of payback period and so on. Also, other issues which were not able to be quantified can be incorporated. This would include the riskiness of a project, the scale of cost of a project and the timing of returns, i.e. whether the major returns come quickly in the first years or not.

It is important that the construction of the factor analysis is done with the involvement of the users. Although the software engineer may have a list of factors, he may have overlooked others. Also, the users will be able to assist in the quantification of weighting factors. Since the ultimate decision to proceed with the project lies with the users, it is folly not to use this opportunity to discuss the relative merits of a project using factor analysis as a vehicle.

16.6.4 Qualitative analysis

This is a straightforward narrative which discusses individual aspects of a project in some depth. The only criterion for inclusion here is that the discussion has some bearing on the selection of the project.

16.7 SUMMARY

This chapter examined quantification in software engineering in three main areas.

16.7.1 Quantification of resources such as computer terminals

It was shown by extracting simple statistics that information about the amount of resource required is easily generated. What is required is that the software engineer takes the time to research the data and perform the calculations. Although the example used referred to computer terminals the same approach to quantification can be applied to other resources such as printers, network loadings, etc.

It should be recognised that much deeper analysis is possible if the reader has an understanding of statistics and operational research (OR) techniques. Resources with complex interrelationships often need complex techniques to model them, otherwise bottlenecks are not identified. Ideally people with an OR background should assist in making such decisions. The sad fact is that all too often nobody makes any attempt to quantify the problem at all.

16.7.2 Quantifying computer time

Approaches to this kind of problem can be classified as:

- *Macro-level*, in which a relationship between the whole entity and its time estimates is asserted, e.g. the use of suppliers' modelling tools.
- *Direct*, in which a straighforward estimate of an item is produced. Benchmarking (before the actual program is written) is a direct method for quantifying computer time.

- *Bottom-up*, in which basic relationships between components of the item and the item itself are used to create the time estimate. Machine instruction analysis can be used to predict computer execution time.

16.7.3 Quantifying costs and benefits

In examining costs and benefits, the time-dependent value of money was recognised and a method for discounting for this was introduced. Also a quantification continuum was discussed, which asserted that some benefits are more quantifiable than others. The weighted ranking by levels method was introduced as a technique for considering all types of factor within a single framework.

The main challenge to software engineering is to create a culture which is positively motivated towards quantification. Attitudes are notoriously difficult to change and it has to be recognised that the situation, although improving, is still not good enough within the professional computing community. But the onus is not just on practising professionals, it is also on researchers to find better models and on manufacturers and software suppliers to provide more and better modelling tools and even expert systems. Some degree of responsibility is even on software engineering students to acquire the basic skills and be prepared to share these with more experienced practitioners. Only then will the necessary environment be realised which will enable the community to move forwards. The act of quantification should become a natural every day way of life to all software engineers. Individual companies must be prepared to make public their experiences in using different techniques so that industry-wide statistics can be compiled. Achieving this will bring software engineering closer to the level achieved in other engineering disciplines where standard times and other formulae have been used for years.

As an example of how important this culture is, let's return to the example used at the beginning of this chapter when the number of terminals for option 2 was being quantified. The example had a utilisation factor of 90%. Most authorities would agree that a 90% utilisation is far too high – 70% is much more reasonable. It is only by working with and using such figures in real environments, that such statistics will become meaningful and be recognised amongst practising engineers.

Chapter 17
The Need for a Contingency-based Approach to Developing Systems

So far we have discussed software engineering in the context of a fairly well-defined environment in which decisions about many things have already been taken. For example, it has been assumed that someone has given the go-ahead to begin a computer project and that users have a clear idea about what they want. Unfortunately, the real world is somewhat different. There are lots of factors in the software engineering environment which are unclear or undecided and some of these are so fundamental that one is forced to consider whether it is desirable to have a single approach to developing information systems such as the one described in Part B. These are, if you like, pressures on the software engineering group to decide how they will respond. After all, they are employees of an organisation which has put the planning of the use of computers in their hands. Because the pressures are many and pervasive, the response often has to be sophisticated. What this means is that there have to be many tools in the tool-box to meet the variety of problems encountered. Of course, any one project is not likely to require all the tools in the tool-box, so the software engineer has to make decisions about what tools to use in what circumstances.

This chapter is split into three sections. The first section will review some of the major pressures facing the software engineering group. The nature of some pressures is that they can have solutions for which it is appropriate to respond in the form of a technique. The second section will discuss briefly those techniques. However, other pressures have responses which are not techniques as such but more reflected in how the software engineering group deals with specific issues. The 'software engineering strategy' is the name given to a statement of how the software engineering group intends to execute its function, and therefore one can expect to find details of how specific issues are being addressed in such a statement. The third section discusses a software engineering strategy. As the discussion unfolds in this chapter, it should become clear why it is less practical to hold the view that any one method can meet the wide range of situations that computer departments are confronted with.

17.1 PRESSURES FACING THE SOFTWARE ENGINEERING GROUP

This section identifies pressures which might cause the software engineer to question whether a single development method is sufficient to cope with all situations. The pressures are reviewed under the following headings:

- technological
- the need for participation
- corporate

17.1.1 Technological pressures

The main source of technological pressure as far as this topic is concerned, comes from the availability of 'fourth generation languages'. The idea behind fourth generation languages is that the software product can be produced much quicker than with other languages. First generation was machine code, second generation was assembler and third generation was so-called 'high' level languages such as COBOL, Fortran, Pascal and Ada. Third generation languages have been around since the late fifties.

As each generation of language came along, significant gains in productivity ensued. An important reason for that was that the programmer became further removed from the machine and its instruction set. However, and certainly topically so with respect to fourth generation languages, the price paid for this is often in terms of its functionality, i.e. the breadth of problem it can address.

Let's look briefly at software which it is argued is fourth generation.

(1) Report program generators (RPGs)
Report program generators can produce reports very quickly. Typically, the data required on the report and positional information is simply declared to the RPG, which then generates the code which produces the report. Simple calculations such as totalling, subtotalling, counting and averaging are usually available; however, pure report program generators are limited to producing reports. Screen output or input is not available. Neither is validation nor update.

(2) Application generators
As the name suggests, application generators are able to generate whole applications. This implies that facilities must be available to input data, manipulate it, update files or databases and provide reports. Again the style

is typically one of making declarations rather than instructions. Languages which have a declarative style are referred to as non-procedural in contrast to, for example, third generation languages where calculations are performed through the constructs of sequence, selection and iteration (as well as GOTOs). Such languages are known as procedural.

(3) Database management systems (DBMS)

Some people argue that DBMSs are fourth generation in that the provision of facilities in a DBMS allows an application to be developed more quickly. Such facilities include built-in security, back-up and deadlock avoidance as well as the basic database mechanisms for database navigation. Many DBMSs have built-in data dictionaries which can speed up development significantly.

A true 4GL would perhaps be better named a fourth generation development system since many of its components would be declarative rather than language-based. To obtain function across the full spectrum of development activities, components would include:

- a report generator
- screen-handling software
- end-user query language
- built-in link to DBMS
- basic 4GL facilities to permit validation and updating
- data dictionary

Examples of potentially true 4GL systems include Cincom's MANTIS and ICL's QuickBuild. Today's marketplace is full of products which are promoted as fourth generation. Some claim productivity factors as much as ten times that of 3GLs. One complicating factor is that software develops over time. Consider COBOL. Over the years it has been extended to include facilities to permit screen-handling and to access a number of different kinds of databases.

At the end of the day, the software engineer has to choose from a bewildering list of alternatives. 4GLs are probably not as efficient and there will be an initial investment and learning curve. Against this is the carrot of increased productivity and reduced development time.

If fourth generation technology is to be used in developing a system then clearly it affects the method. For example, many fourth generation systems work at the program level, so there is no scope for using modules, i.e. no structure charts, module reuse and so on. The danger is that the 'baby might be thrown out with the bath water'. For example, how easy is it to test a fourth generation program? If it is as complex as a 3GL program then it will be equally difficult to test. Remember that in the method in Part B, we were able to effectively ignore the difficulties of testing a program by concentrating on testing modules! However, the attractions of fourth generation technology are such that ways will be sought to minimise its disadvantages and methods will have to adapt to accommodate the use of such technology.

Fourth generation technology also provides scope for prototyping because the potential speed of development is so quick. Prototyping is used in other branches of engineering. Its original purpose was to produce quickly a rough mock-up of the final version in order to obtain certain clarifications. In other words, the original purpose of prototyping was to assist in the definition of the system.

Although 'paper' prototypes have been used in the past, current interest and debate in prototyping centres on the ease and speed with which ostensibly, highly realistic models can be constructed using fourth generation technology. Users involved in a prototype often cannot understand why the prototype is not made immediately available to them as a working system perhaps with a few relatively minor modifications to address those 'highly-technical' problems the analyst seems to be over-concerned about.

Probably the most common reason for prototyping is to assist the user in visualising the system, i.e. to specify the human-computer interface. Users, even today, often have little or no experience of computers. Even if they do, they may not be aware of the range of alternative interfaces available to them. Clearly, a good way of providing that understanding is to show their inputs and outputs actually working on a computer. Note that the computer, operating system and software used for the prototype may not be the same as required for this final system.

From the analyst's point of view, a prototype can also be used to help him to understand the requirements better. Although many users are excellent communicators, some are not. The prototype is an excellent medium for establishing or confirming requirements, since by incremental means the user can eventually point to the screen and say 'Yes, that's exactly what I want!' Sometimes, the analyst may have difficulty in eliciting the details of an algorithm from users, particularly where informal rules of thumb are employed. By formalising impressions in a program, the analyst can then run through relevant scenarios and obtain the user's confirmation.

Prototyping has become increasingly popular and rightly so. As far as the ethos in this book is concerned, as long as prototyping is performed as a technique within a method and not seen as a complete method in itself, it is a highly valuable addition to the tool-box.

Prototyping has a clear impact on a method, because it changes the traditional sequence of tasks in parts of the method. Given that the advantages outweigh the disadvantages, then it is the method that will have to adapt to accommodate prototyping.

17.1.2 The need for participation

Participation is concerned with getting users involved in the development of their own information system. The participation of the user community (management and workers) is a critical success factor if information systems are to be used by an organisation successfully. However, there are different ways and levels in which users can become involved with systems development. In the last section prototyping was discussed and this clearly involves participation at the level of defining the user interface. But there are other forms of participation which involve decision-making at higher levels. Systems analysts have traditionally made decisions about the shape that the new system should take. In doing so, they have very much decided how and in what way users will do their jobs. This is certainly not morally or ethically right. Ways have to be found to involve users in making decisions about how they do their work. The fact that a user's work is done on a computer does not change that need. But there is a higher level of potential involvement of users yet. This is in the area of deciding what kind of computer system is appropriate. Take the marketing department for instance. What kinds of computer system could be identified to assist that department in its work? Does it need a straightforward sales information system? Does it need access to an outside database of potential customers or better production schedule information or both? In other words, who decides what the priorities and problem areas are? Clearly, the users themselves must have a major involvement in this.

17.1.3 Corporate pressures

The question here is how the work of the computer department interfaces with the business plan specifically and supports the needs of the business generally. Computer departments do not exist in a vacuum; the reason for their existence is that they should support the effective operation of the organisation's business. So it is necessary for the software engineering group to synchronise computer plans with the wider elements of the business and to be able to demonstrate and justify the linkages.

In considering business needs, it is immediately obvious that organisations need access to corporate data, i.e. data that transcends that held or used by any one department or area. This is why the goal of constructing a corporate data model has been so important. Unfortunately in practice, the achievement of a corporate data model which actually provides the level of information desired by users and management is, so far, perhaps the exception rather than the rule. Martin and Finkelstein[1] identify four classes of databases which distinguish how effective their use is in terms of meeting business need:

(1) Class I

A class I environment is one that uses files. As discussed in chapter 3, eventually for the majority of cases, files bring more problems than they solve. Certainly file-based systems are easy to generate but they introduce redundancy and inconsistency, which create a massive maintenance headache. When this is coupled with the trend towards more on-line query systems, the problem becomes untenable. Where the query requires data from different files, the workload for the programmer increases dramatically, often to the point where the information cannot realistically be provided to the user in the timescale required. In other words, a file-based environment is not likely to be suitable for meeting a high query load from users.

(2) Class II

Class II environments involve the use of application databases. An application database is one in which a single database system is developed for each application. This means that some advantage is gained over Class I environments but only to some extent. For instance, where a query requires data, all of which is held within the application database, then there is no problem. However, more frequently, and often where the information is highly valuable to the organisation and needed very quickly, the data required resides in different application databases. Observe too, that it is likely there will still be a significant degree of inconsistency and redundancy, because certain data such as customer or stock data will be replicated from one application to another.

(3) Class III

A class III environment uses subject databases. Subject databases divide the corporate data model into distinct areas, each one of which is as low-coupled as possible from the rest.

If it were manageable only to have one corporate database, then this would be a class III environment. However, in practice, especially with large corporations, subject databases are the best compromise. Clearly, because of the low-coupling, redundancy and inconsistency are kept as low as possible. So typically customer data, stock data and so on, will only reside in one subject database with all the advantages that brings.

(4) Class IV

The class IV environment is sometimes called the information systems environment. This is because of the need for efficient information retrieval. It can be viewed as a development or extension to the class III environment, since it needs an integrated database approach in order to supply it with the raw data for retrieval. However, in computing terms, it often demands a different approach, because if a database is tuned for high-volume updating then it is less likely to be efficient at retrieving information, for example. Either an alternative tuning strategy is adopted or the database at appropriate intervals may be copied into a different environment whose software and access methods are more geared to efficient query handling. The software here is often more user-friendly which allows the users to make their own queries; a relational database approach makes the data more manipulatable.

17.2 TECHNIQUES FOR MITIGATING PRESSURES

In the last section, pressures facing the software engineering group were discussed. Some of these pressures can be resolved or at least mitigated by introducing additional techniques into the overall development process. We will look at three techniques:

- The Soft Systems Methodology which it is proposed can help users identify those areas of their work which would most benefit by computerisation.
- The ETHICS method which it is suggested is useful in involving users and getting them to make decisions about the shape of information system.
- Business System Planning which is a technique for linking computer plans with business needs.

Discussion in this section will focus on what the techniques are, and in the next section, we will look at how they can fit in to a software engineering strategy.

17.2.1 The Soft Systems Methodology (SSM)

The Soft Systems Methodology[2] is an example of the 'Human Activity System' approach. Human Activity Systems emphasise the importance of the human participants and the way in which they relate to each other through the work that they perform. Hence the use of the adjective 'soft' to describe the human and sometimes fickle dimension in which, because so many people are involved who have different viewpoints, a consensus or pluralistic approach is often taken. By contrast, 'hard' methods assume that there is much less scope for difference of opinion, that is, there is basically only one best way of solving a problem.

SSM is relatively easy to follow. Some of the steps are described as real-world activities, which by definition involve people in the problem situation. Other steps are 'systems thinking' activities which can be considered equivalent to the abstract activities carried out by systems analysts and designers without users being present. The main stages are summarised below:

Stage 1 (real-world)
The problem situation is the area of interest for the method. It is identified in an unstructured way in this stage because it is important firstly to allow all perspectives and opinions to be taken into account. Typically, however, the boundary of the problem is pre-set.

Stage 2 (real-world)
Once this is done, an attempt is made to come to some level of agreement amongst the participants concerning the problem situation. Through the achieving of consensus the problem is described (structured) in real-world terms. This is sometimes called a rich picture, because it is supposed to reflect the width of view felt across all participants. There are no rules as such for the format that a rich picture must conform to. What is important is that the users get the opportunity to describe the problem as they see it. Figure 17.1 shows an example of a rich picture drawn by a student. Much insight can be gained by analysing a rich picture. For example, in figure 17.1 the people who buy boats do not seem to be the same group who receive the newsletter. This may point to a problem in marketing.

Stage 3 (systems thinking)
Obtain root definitions of identified systems. A root definition is a concise statement of the activities carried out by a system. Included normally in a root definition are the following components:

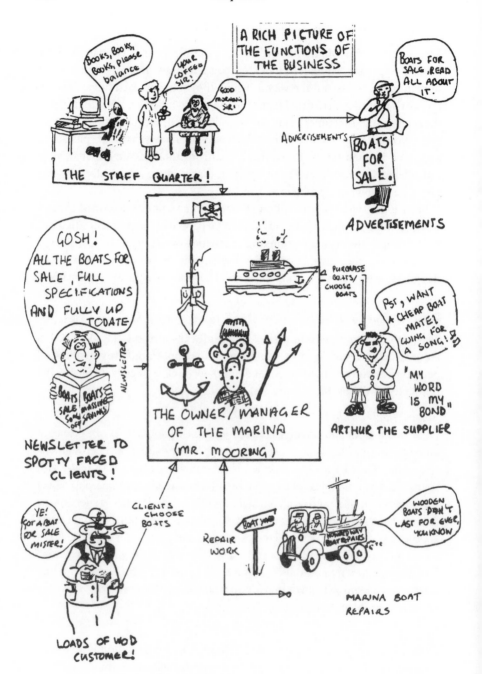

Fig. 17.1. Example of a rich picture.

customers	These are the people who are affected by the system and its activities.
actors	These are the people within the system who actually carry out its activities.
transformation	This is the means by which inputs are converted into outputs.
Weltanschauung	This is a German word which approximates to an outlook or perspective that underpins the root definition.
owner	The owner or owners of the system is the group responsible for the system and therefore has ultimate power over the system.
environment	The environment includes any external conditions which are of direct significance to the system.

Stage 4 (systems thinking)

In this stage conceptual models based on the root definitions are built. The conceptual model can be in any appropriate format. They may be, for example, bubble diagrams showing the sequence of and relationship between activities. Activities may be relatively 'hard' such as performing a clerical task; equally they may be quite 'soft' or unstructured, for example, choosing the best design for a dress.

Stage 5 (real-world)

The conceptual model should then be compared against the perceptions of the people whose opinions generated the root definitions. The proposed model should reflect what each said; however, it is a global model and therefore each person's view is only a part of the whole.

Inevitably, this generates discussion and debate about the model and its validity, which is the desired purpose. Ultimately an agreed conceptual model is obtained.

Stage 6 (real-world)

Changes are identified which are feasible to implement and agreed generally as desirable. A high degree of creativity is required here to maximise the potential for improvement. Changes need not require computerisation but if they do, the likely costs and benefits need to be examined.

Stage 7 (real-world)

The changes identified in stage 6 are implemented and hopefully these improve the problem situation. This will create a new problem situation, thus permitting the whole approach to be reiterated in due course.

So, if you take the example of a marketing department again, the boundary would be the work done in the marketing department. After discussion and possibly debate amongst the staff in the marketing department, a rich picture of what people do in the marketing department is drawn. The rich picture is a useful vehicle because it is non-verbal, i.e. much can be gleaned from the imagery used. Root definitions are then created and from these a conceptual model drawn. The important benefit of the technique is that in an organised way, discussion takes place amongst users about their problems and priorities. Although the technique has definite stages, it is not a 'structured' technique in the sense that it does not force people to use certain rules for drawing diagrams or whatever. Indeed, the opposite is true. The technique tries to give as much opportunity for people to work in a free-format unrestricted way, yet still have a forum for discussion. The end result of such an analysis on the marketing department would be the starting point for developing a system, because what we have, in effect, is a terms of reference statement.

17.2.2 The ETHICS method

The ETHICS method[3] is an acronym for the Effective Technical and Human Implementation of Computer Systems. It is an example of the socio-technical approach, the aim of which is to integrate the technical objectives of the system with what may be termed people objectives, i.e. the quality of work experienced by people. The ETHICS method assumes that job satisfaction is critical in achieving success in using computer systems; if users do not enjoy using the computer system, its use will not be maximised. For the purpose of the ETHICS method, job satisfaction is defined as 'the attainment of a good 'fit' between what the employee is seeking from his work – his job needs, expectations and aspirations – and what he is required to do in his job – the organisational job requirements which mould his experience'. In other words, does the job actually match what the employee wants out of the job?

The approach including post-implementation has nine steps:

(1) Diagnosis
In this step the needs of the social system are identified through the use of questionnaires and follow-up interviews. It provides the data for identifying the job-satisfaction needs which are used in the design process.

The replies to the questions should be analysed against the following categories:

Knowledge fit. This is the degree to which employees feel that knowledge and skills are being utilised by the organisation. Perhaps they would like to be stretched more; perhaps not.

Psychological fit. This is an assessment of how close needs such as recognition, responsibility and status are being met in an employee's work.

Efficiency fit. This is the extent to which employees perceive salary as equitable and controls on work such as the need to be supervised as reasonable.

Task-structure fit. Work often offers the opportunity for the employee to exercise control over the variety of tasks performed, target-setting, quality-setting, decision-making and so on. The task-structure fit is the degree to which one's job meets these kinds of expectations.

Ethical fit. This is to do with the organisational environment. Does the employer's ethics and philosophy match the employee's in, for example, the degree to which an employee is consulted before a change which affects the employee is implemented?

In terms of the discretion allowed for change in the context of implementing computer systems, the task-structure fit and the knowledge fit are the two areas where change is most likely to be effected. The others are more likely to require changes in company policies, promotions or demotions, etc.

(2) Socio-technical systems design
(Please note that the word 'design' is used here in its broadest sense.) The purpose of this step is to identify and list human objectives. Such objectives are, at this stage, only set out in broad terms. They are, if you like, the broad conclusions which emerge from the analysis in the diagnosis step. However, these need to be reviewed against the technical system since it may not be possible, because of the nature of the computer system, to meet any or all of these. Also, particular resources or constraints in the technical system may mitigate against their creation. Typical human objectives at this stage include increased job satisfaction, more job security, etc.

(3) Identify alternative solutions
The output from this step contains two lists. One is a list of social solutions; the other is a list of technical solutions. It is important in this step that the

design group are encouraged to think creatively so as not to overlook potentially good solutions. Each solution is then assessed in terms of its ability to meet both social and technical objectives. Obviously technical solutions will tend to meet technical objectives and similarly for social solutions, but this is a necessary step in recognising a solution's potential for mixing with other kinds of solution.

(4) Identify possible socio-technical solutions
In this step the social solutions are matched with the technical solutions. It may be that some socio-technical combinations are incompatible. These are discarded, leaving a set of compatible socio-technical pairs.

(5) Rank the socio-technical solutions
A cost/benefit analysis is performed here to identify the best socio-technical design. This, however, is not an easy task, since one must try to quantify human benefits such as job satisfaction, recognition and so on, so that they can be compared against the costs.

(6) Prepare a detailed socio-technical design
So far, the socio-technical designs have only been specified at an overview level. It is now necessary to address the detailed design of the tasks. In doing so, the following job design principles apply:

Task variety.   The secret is to try to achieve optimum variety. Just enough to obviate boredom and fatigue, but not enough to lead to inefficiency or frustration.

Skill variety.   If employees are asked to use a variety of skills, e.g. problem-solving, manual and so on, then it is likely this will lead to greater job satisfaction.

Feedback.   Feedback is important as a means of reinforcement. It leads to confidence if targets are being met and should spur on effort if not. This is particularly true if employees are involved in setting their own targets.

Task identity.   It is important that each group or individual has a set of tasks which are distinguishable from others in a logical and meaningful way. This visibility enables a sense of identity to develop, which is important if people are to take a pride in their work.

Task autonomy.   Where possible, the exact manner of how a task is executed, or how tasks generally are worked through, should be left to the discretion of the individual.

(7) Implement the socio-technical solution
For computer systems this implies carrying on with the rest of the technical analysis process. Remember also that there may be other issues which have arisen out of the socio-technical analysis. These could involve the changing of job descriptions or departmental policies or procedures.

(8) Monitor the system
When the computer system is eventually implemented it needs to be monitored to ensure that the human design aims are being realised. Any major deviation must be identified and steps taken to correct it.

(9) Evaluate the socio-technical system
The acid test is to use the diagnostic questionnaire once again to see if the new system has provided a closer fit in terms of job satisfaction. This should be done once the system has generally settled down and the workers have had an opportunity to gain experience with it.

In terms of its relationship to the systems development method, ETHICS as proposed here would be part of the requirements analysis activity. The act of incorporating one technique into an existing method or indeed using one method as a pre-cursor to another (as with SSM) is sometimes called 'blending'. Basically, as well as the other activities in requirements analysis, the analyst uses the ETHICS method to establish user preferences (requirements) in more detail. In other words, it is both a vehicle and an opportunity for the analyst to do the job better.

17.2.3 Business systems planning

Business System Planning (BSP)[4] is a technique for incorporating the goals and aspirations of the company as perceived by top management into an information systems plan. Top executives are interviewed to identify their perception of the organisation's needs. These needs may be seen as business priorities, issues from the environment that must be addressed, basic performance problems and so on. These needs are then converted to a list of broad information system solutions to these problem areas. In doing so the link between business priorities and information system planning is established. The list of information systems is examined and sorted to take account of the most efficient implementation path in terms of data availability, i.e. data in the corporate data model which already exists or will exist. So the technique analyses business needs and tempers this with implementation feasibility to produce a prioritised information system plan.

Business Systems Planning is a way of establishing a long-term plan for the work of the software engineering group. It therefore ought to be done in advance of individual computer projects so that the computer department's work is integrated with the rest of the organisation.

17.3 A SOFTWARE ENGINEERING STRATEGY

17.3.1 The organisation of resources

A major issue for software engineering management is the organisation of development resouces. Martin[5] suggests a three-point strategy which covers maintaining the investment in existing computer systems, developing new systems on a solid foundation and meeting other high-value needs.

1 A maintenance team needs to be set up to look after non-strategic systems, i.e. systems which are not part of the long-term plan. Examples include file-based or application database systems which eventually would be converted to a class III environment. Also included would be any prototyped systems. Over time it is hoped that the number of systems being maintained by this group would drop off.

2 The development group would be involved in producing the basic transaction processing systems for the company. These would be subject databases and if possible use fourth generation technology. However, for efficiency reasons third generation languages are often needed, because of the high volumes involved. These transaction processing systems support the basic operations of the company. They are the foundations on which all computing is built. Therefore it is important that they are constructed soundly, hence the need for solid software engineering.

3 The third component is the information centre. The information centre is a mechanism for achieving more effective use of the organisation's computer resources by enabling users to gain better and easier access to the computer in order to assist in solving business rather than computer problems. In other words it puts the users in the driving seat. Users come along to the information centre when they have a problem which can be addressed by some use of the computer. Often such problems have a high importance as far as the organisation is concerned and the future success or even existence of the company may depend on the right decision being reached quickly. Clearly the traditional software engineering approach is not appropriate for this kind of problem.

Sometimes the user will want to form a solution based on data that is on the organisation's computer. If the environment is class IV, then this is easily achieved. Often, in such decisions, recent trends are more important than the need for the data to have up-to-the-minute currency. Alternatively, users may only need to use a micro to aid the decision process. The range of powerful software products available on micros today is awesome. Examples include spreadsheets, network analysis tools, relational databases, modelling languages, expert systems and so on. Power and flexibility are enhanced by the provision of mainframe-micro copy facilities. Information centre staff provide a range of support and training services.

A majority of the work undertaken in the information centre, because of its time-critical nature, is work which is not inappropriate for solution by the main development group. In other words, the information centre can address a whole class of business computing problems which have no real alternative solution. If the information centre can be dovetailed with the other groups, then this makes for a coherent and extremely effective software engineering strategy. Observe that the information centre is a realisation of the class IV environment discussed earlier. As such it feeds off the class III environment created by the development group.

Another use for the information centre is to off-load certain kinds of work from the development group. Given user-friendly software, the users themselves can get involved in writing their own reports and display screens. Clearly, this may need some technical support. Also, the correctness of the software produced should be verified since users are just as likely to make mistakes. However, it can significantly reduce the workload of the development group, it promotes participation and commitment in users and it also means that any maintenance associated with user-generated software can be handled by the users themselves. This leaves the development group to get on with creating a stable class III database environment.

17.3.2 A blended approach

A critical mistake made by some who consider so-called rival methods is to assume they are mutually exclusive, i.e. you can use one or the other, but not both! In fact, most of what is discussed earlier can be considered complementary, i.e. can blend together in the sense that methods can be used alongside each other to enhance the development process.

Blending is an important concept for the software engineer. It has significant implications for the level at which the software engineer must work. This is because blending is motivated from a contingency-based view of software engineering, i.e. that basically each project situation is different and therefore may require different approaches or techniques to effect a good solution. This means that:

1 The software engineer has to be able to recognise different project situations.

2 The software engineer must have available and be able to select the appropriate tools for the job rather than blindly following a specific method.

3 In order to be able to select the appropriate tools for the job the software engineer has to know the tools well enough (and the method well enough) to be able to evaluate them and synthesise them. A fuller discussion of this important issue appears in Avison and Fitzgerald[6].

Let's now review the techniques discussed in the previous section to see how they could be blended together.

The Soft Systems approach is a useful vehicle for:

- Analysing part of an organisation.
- Stimulating debate amongst workers.
- Achieving a better understanding of what one does and how it affects the organisation.
- Getting involvement and commitment, i.e. achieving participation.
- Implementing change in an organisation.

SSM is often described as a 'general problem-solving' approach because of its general applicability to many types of problem situation. It has, for example, been used to perform information systems planning, i.e. an alternative to BSP. But the important use from our point of view is to identify potential systems for computerisation. Because the conceptual model identifies human activity systems it is an important source for identifying critical or high-value systems, some of which may be totally computerised or, if not, some degree of computer support offered. So, here the Soft Systems approach is used to promote user participation and identify systems which are appropriate for computerisation based on human activity considerations.

Socio-technical paradigms like the ETHICS method are also relatively general problem-solving approaches. Their strength lies in their ability to marry both social and technical considerations and therefore one important, though again not the only, use of this approach is in the analysis phase once the broad area for computerisation has been identified. Here, the technique encourages participation and the full analysis of options in order that job satisfaction can be improved. Once the option has been chosen the technical side of the method takes over.

Business System Planning is a useful tool for identifying a company's long-term computer needs. Such needs are based on what senior management view as the important business areas for the company to succeed in. A Business System Plan can provide a five or ten year plan for computerisation in a company, albeit at a non-detail level. It also prioritises systems and identifies an idealised sequence of implementation. Clearly top management are likely to be very keen to promote the business system plan, yet they must ensure commitment all down the line and also need their staff to provide more detailed input. This is because the output from the business plan is necessarily high-level, leaving a lot of scope for deciding exactly how an area or function might be computerised. The Soft System approach can assist here, although a problem in practice lies in that the BSP looks to the future and may identify areas in which the company is not currently operating, e.g. a company may be considering exporting its products. Although the root definition can be used to specify future scenarios it is arguably better at describing what the company currently does. However, by inputting future aspirations into the discussions of the conceptual model (stage 5) and then reiterating through the method, the shrewd analyst can use the Soft Systems approach to further the goals of Business System Planning.

The existence and success of fourth generation technology brings a number of challenges to software engineering and it is good that it should. The tradition of software engineering is steeped in analytical approach which is time-consuming but its advantage is in its thoroughness. The legacy of hastily developed systems is all around us. Nevertheless, fourth generation technology is not a bad thing in itself; it is how it is used that is open to question. For instance, consider prototyping. There is great pressure on computer departments to implement systems by prototyping only. The advantage of course is speedy development, albeit that if fourth generation technology is used, the system may be somewhat inefficient. The trouble with this is that it is a short-term expedient. The resulting data class will be either class I or class II. In other words prototyping on its own, will not achieve the benefits of class III and IV environments. However, prototyping does have an important role to play in the software engineering of information systems. Firstly, it can be incorporated into a structured method in the same way as methods such as ETHICS can be bolted on. Prototyping serves as an ideal way of confirming the human computer interface. Secondly, there are occasions when for

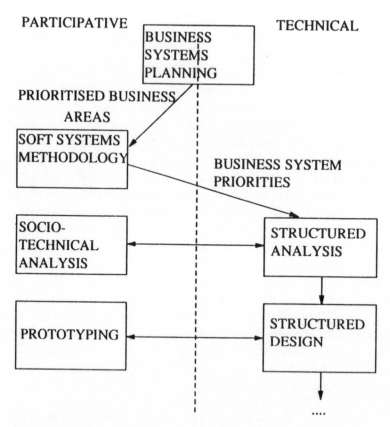

Fig. 17.2. Contingency-based approach to developing information systems.

business or political reasons in a company, systems have to be developed expeditiously. As long as user management fully appreciate the implication of such a decision, then this is acceptable. Because of business pressure, the danger is that all users will want a prototyped system in order to get a quick implementation. It takes strong software engineering management who are credible with the user community to convince them of the folly of such an approach.

Figure 17.2 shows an approach to blending which summarises the above discussion. It is by no means the only way in which the above techniques could be used together, but it illustrates the general philosophy of blending. For a more in-depth discussion of this area see Wood-Harper, Antill and Avison[7].

17.3.3 The implications of a contingency-based philosophy

The introductory chapter explored why a method is important and one of the reasons given was that it provided a pathway for the software engineer to follow and that would tend to reduce the risk of failure in a project. The discussion above has demonstrated that the variety of pressures in the software engineering environment and the kind of solution responses that are appropriate make a 'single development philosophy' unhelpful in terms of being an aid to thinking about the development process. A more sophisticated model is needed (i.e. a contingency-based model) which requires that for any one project the software engineer, along with perhaps the project manager, decides what set of techniques is appropriate. Now this is not to say that we are abandoning all the good that is in a well-tried method, since the techniques themselves can still be followed to the letter, but to acknowledge that the variety of needs is such that selection of techniques from a 'tool-box' is unavoidable. Of course, this imposes a responsibility on the software engineer to be able to make sound selections. Though this would be reasonable and desirable for experienced staff, it is probably better for inexperienced people to learn the ropes, as it were, through following well-tried routes. As more experience is gained, then more discretion would be permitted as more skill and understanding are acquired.

But there still needs to be something in the environment that is tangible, something which allows us to measure progress in the development project and it is suggested that emphasis should be on the deliverable rather than the technique, i.e. the end itself rather than the means to an end. This is not to say that techniques are unimportant. Of course they are important and quality assurance procedures still need to applied to techniques to confirm they are being done properly. But the control of the project is best achieved against the deliverables themselves rather than trying to 'control' the technique. This allows software engineers to be in a position to make the necessary choice of techniques as the circumstances require, yet still ensure that the project is being progressed in a logical way.

This discussion is really about the maturity of the software industry with respect to its use of methods. Nolan[8] describes the stages of DP growth that a DP department goes through until it reaches a mature state. This growth manifests itself in a number of ways including the roles that staff perform, the degree of control exercised and so on. This path to maturity also applies to the use of methods. The software industry has for some time now attempted to use a wide variety of methods and techniques, each competing with the other for supremacy. More and more there is a recognition that there is no one best approach. What is more disturbing perhaps, is that people have spent a lot of precious time debating which one is best. This has meant that they have been deflected from the real debate which is recognising what is good and necessary in a method.

17.4 CONCLUSION

Having examined and explored the issues in this book, we can make a number of deductions about what is desirable in a method for the software engineering of information systems. These characteristics are described in non-specific terms:

- A method should facilitate user communication via physical models and analysis through logical models.
- The analysis phase should create a process model (e.g. a DFD), a data model and a time-dependent model (e.g. an SDD).
- Techniques should be available to address social issues as well as technical ones.
- The number of models in a method should be kept to a minimum as conversion from one to another is time-consuming and error-prone. This is why it is preferable to refine a physical DFD into a logical DFD rather than create a totally different model.
- A method should contain techniques which permit the cross-referencing of one model against the other as a means of improving integrity.
- Quality assurance techniques should be able to be blended into a method where required.
- Methods and techniques should be simple enough to be taught to apprentice software engineers.
- A method should be amenable to automation.
- A method should be flexible enough to permit, where appropriate, the swapping of alternative techniques (e.g. the use of decision tables instead of structured English).
- A method should cover all stages of the life cycle (from information systems planning to maintenance) and be so structured that it lends itself to contingency-based development.

17.5 FURTHER READING

1 Martin, J. and Finkelstein, C. (1981) *Information Engineering* (vols I and II), Prentice-Hall, Englewood Cliffs, New Jersey, provides a fuller discussion of database classes. In addition, the approach contains some interesting techniques (such as the event diagram) which may be seen as alternatives to some of the techniques introduced here.

2 Checkland, P. (1981) *System Thinking, System Practice*, John Wiley, Chichester, contains a complete discussion of SSM. A shorter discussion appears in Avison and Fitzgerald[6].

3 Mumford, E. and Weir, M. (1979) *Computer Systems in Work Design – the ETHICS method* Associated Business Press, provides details of the ETHICS method.

4 Martin, J. (1980) *Strategic Data Planning Methodologies* Savant Institute, Carnforth, Lancashire, discusses Business Systems Planning.

5 Martin, J. (1984) *Information System's Manifesto* Prentice-Hall, Englewood Cliffs, New Jersey, describes a three-point strategy for organising development resources.

6 Avison, D. E. and Fitzgerald, G. (1988) *Information Systems Development: Methodologies, Techniques and Tools* Blackwell Scientific Publications, Oxford, is an up-to-date reference text covering many important issues in system development.

7 Wood-Harper, A. T., Antill, L. and Avison, D. E. (1985) *Information Systems Definition: The Multiview Approach*, Blackwell Scientific Publications, Oxford, provides more insight into the business of blending in respect of human, business and participative considerations as well as technical ones.

8 Nolan, R. (1982) *Managing the Data Resource Function* West, St Paul, Minnesota, contains a detailed discussion of growth stages in DP departments.

Appendix
Case Study

PART 1

Superior Builders Merchants (SBM) is a small private limited company selling building materials mostly to the construction industry. It is a merchandising company, i.e. it manufacturers no products, simply relying on purchasing its goods from a variety of specialist suppliers and reselling them to its customers in convenient quantities. SBM's ability to deliver goods to the customer's premises coupled with the wide selection of materials it holds has meant that in the last five years the business has grown substantially, to the extent that the administration of the business is barely keeping up with the current volume of trade.

In particular, the SBM Sales Administration System (SAS) which is currently operated manually, is under considerable pressure and customer goodwill is low. Management have requested it be computerised and after interview with the appropriate departments the following information has emerged.

Sales order processing
SBM has about 500 credit customers, the majority of whom send orders on their own company's order form. Alternatively, they telephone their order to SBM. SBM's own standard order form is created either by transcribing from the customer order form or interactively while the customer is on the telephone. If there are omissions on the customer's order form, e.g. no quantity for an item, then that line is deleted from the order and the details of any deleted lines sent back to the customer by post. Any difficulties with telephone orders are handled interactively.

The standard order forms are then sent to the credit control section to check that the customer's credit is greater than the value of the order. To do this the order has to be priced by reference to a price catalogue. The price for each line on the order is calculated and then totalled to obtain the value of the order. Where the value of a customer's order is greater than his current credit, the whole order is rejected and notification of this is sent back to the customer.

Orders which have passed the credit check are then sent to the stock control department, where the quantities for each item on the order are checked against the stock levels in the stock file. If there is insufficient stock for an item then that complete order line becomes part of an outstanding order.

Invoicing

The remainder of the order, however, is accepted and passed to invoicing. Standard invoice forms are used and the details from the standard order form are transcribed onto the invoice as well as price data from the price catalogue. The standard invoice form is in fact a multiple set. The top copy is sent back to the customer; the second to accounts to maintain the sales ledger and the third and fourth copies to the warehouse who use them to pick the items from stock (i.e. as a picking list).

Sales ledger maintenance

The purpose of the sales ledger in SBM is to keep account of each customer's record of payment in respect of credit sales. So, as customers obtain goods from SBM, summary details of the transaction are recorded in the sales ledger awaiting payment, in due course, by the customer.

The details on the sales transaction are inserted into the sales ledger by taking some details from the invoice copy sent to the Accounts department. At the end of each month a 'statement of account' is sent to each customer containing the details of all events concerning the account during the month. These events include payments made by the customer and invoices and credit notes sent to the customer. Credit notes are issued when the value of the original invoice was greater than what it should have been. This may have been because the goods delivered were faulty in some way or perhaps because insufficient quantities were delivered. Naturally, the customer is not going to pay for faulty goods or goods not received, so the value on the credit note reflects this difference in value. A credit note is one kind of adjustment made to a sales ledger and is necessary for keeping the sales ledger accurate.

The statement of account contains a tear-off slip called a remittance advice note (RAN) which is sent with the customer's payment. The customer is able to indicate which particular invoices he wishes to pay by simply ticking against a list of all outstanding invoices. The details from the RAN are inserted into the sales ledger.

If a customer does not pay an invoice within 30 days of the date on the statement of account, then that invoice becomes overdue. A reminder letter is sent to customers with overdue accounts around the middle of each month.

Lastly, sales management are interested in information about the overall sales performance in each month. Only two reports are currently produced. The first is a sales report which indicates the sales this month of each stem stocked. The second report is an 'aged debit analysis', which provides information about how much debt there is and how old (i.e. overdue) it is.

PART 2

Upon attempting to draw the DFD set, it was discovered that there was insufficient information to complete it. This was particularly so in respect of how outstanding orders are dealt with. A further interview with the Sales Order Processing department revealed the following information.

The standard order form is created in the following manner. The order-no is obtained from a master-index held in the department. The master-index is simply a series of numbers on paper. When a clerk uses up a number, it is crossed out from the sheet. Sometimes the customer order form contains the SBM customer-no. Where this is so, the customer-no is simply copied onto the standard order form. Otherwise a customer-name index is used, which contains, in customer-name order, a list of all customers with their corresponding customers-nos.

The date on the standard order form is the current date. Incomplete order details are sent back to customers for a number of reasons. Firstly, as was stated earlier, because one or more of product description, unit of measure or quantity fields are not on the order line and clearly all are necessary for acceptance. Secondly, SBM may not carry that particular item. This can be checked by the clerk by using the product catalogue, which contains product descriptions in alphabetic sequence. Each description has a corresponding product code. If an item is not in the product catalogue then it cannot be accepted. Note that descriptions are formed hierarchically, i.e. the basic material is described first, e.g. paint, then follow the colours of paints. Thirdly, where the quantity ordered is not obtainable in multiples of those units stocked, the line is deleted from the order. In all cases, the reason for rejection appears on the incomplete order form.

The value of the order is established by obtaining the unit price and multiplying by the quantity ordered. The sum over all order lines is then calculated and then 15% Value Added Tax (VAT) applied. The customer's current available credit is held in an index which is in customer-no order. Where an order is rejected a rejection stamp is applied to the standard order form. The stamp contains boxes in which the customer's current credit and the order value are added. This is then sent back to the customer.

Outstanding orders are held in a file in customer-no sequence. For each customer, a list of outstanding items is held. Once each week that list is reviewed to identify items that can now be fulfilled. An accepted outstanding order is created for those customers where one or more items can now be delivered. The accepted outstanding order is identical to the first time accepted order in format. A unique order-no is obtained by contacting the sales order processing section. Either the accepted outstanding order or the first time accepted order are used to generate an acknowledgement which is sent back to the customer. The customer acknowledgement is simply a photocopy of the accepted order with an acknowledgement stamp applied.

SUPERIOR BUILDERS MERCHANTS

STANDARD ORDER FORM			123 Renfrew Road Glasgow Scotland

ORDER NO	CUSTOMER NO	DATE
017321	0324	15/10/88

Item	Product Code	Product Description	Unit of Measure	Quantity
01	PA129	Paint - Royal Blue	5 Ltr	100
02	MH005	Mahogony - Strips	1	15
03	CM002	Cement	cwt	50
04	BR031	Bricks - Standard Red	100	200
05				
06				
07				
08				
09				
10				
11				
12				
13				
14				
15				

Appendix

SUPERIOR BUILDERS MERCHANTS

123 Renfrew Road
Glasgow
Scotland

INVOICE

CUSTOMER NO: 0324

J Smith, Blg Contractors
36 Inchinnan Road
Renfrew
Scotland

INVOICE NO: 018758

ORDER NO: 017321

INVOICE DATE: 24/10/88

ORDER DATE: 15/10/88

DATE DUE: 30/11/88

Item No	Product Code	Product Description	Unit of Measure	Quantity Delivered	Unit Cost	Amount
01	P A 1 2 9	Paint - Royal Blue	5 Ltr	100	7.50	750.00
03	C M 0 0 2	Cement	CWT	50	5.50	275.00
04	B R 0 3 1	Bricks - Standard Red	100	2000	22.00	440.00

TOTAL AMOUNT: 1465.00

TOTAL VAT: 219.75

TOTAL DUE: 1684.75

SUPERIOR BUILDERS MERCHANTS

STATEMENT OF ACCOUNT

CUSTOMER NO
0 3 2 4

STATEMENT NO
003397

STATEMENT DATE
31/10/88

CUSTOMER
J Smith, Big Contrs
36 Inchinnan Road
Renfrew
Scotland

DOCUMENT NO	DOCUMENT DATE	DESCRIPTION	TRANSACTIONS SELECTED	INVOICES DUE
017892	1/9/88	Invoice	510.15	
001477	9/9/88	Credit Note	150.15	
018097	20/9/88	Invoice		1710.00
018641	3/10/88	Invoice		542.50
003097	15/10/88	Payment	360.00	
018758	24/10/88	Invoice		1684.75
			Balance	3937.25

Total Overdue

1710.00

SUPERIOR BUILDERS MERCHANTS

REMITTANCE
ADVICE
NOTE

123 Renfrew Road
Glasgow
Scotland

RAN NO
003397

CUSTOMER NO
0 3 2 4

STATEMENT DATE
31/10/88

INVOICE NO.	INVOICE VALUE	TICK
018097	1710.00	
018641	542.50	
018758	1684.75	

Payment

Index

abnormal life analysis, 92
access, to and from datastores, 25
actual task times (ATT), 288
Albrecht, A., 290
alias, 107
Antill, L., 370
application generators, 353
assumption model, 4
atomic access, 199
attribute, 53, 198, 222
attribute amendment analysis, 92, 226
attribute checking, 139
attribute counting, 345
auditing, 210
Automate+, 311–23, 330
automatic code generation, 325
Avison, D., 368, 370

balanced architecture, 124
batch program, 237
batch runchart, 238
batch transaction, 236
benchmarking, 339
big-bang testing approach, 253
binary chop, 191
black box, 17
blending, 367
Boehm, B., 1, 303
bottom-up testing, 254
boundary, 17
boundary value analysis, 189
Brook, F., 278
Business System Planning (BSP), 365

calculated field, 109
CASE tools, 305, 307
CASE construct, 44, 76, 166
cause analysis, 190
cause-effect graphing, 153
change control, 282, 327
changeover plan, 257

Checkland, P., 373
chief programme teams, 296
COCOMO, 288
Codd, E., 94
codification, 154
cohesion, 117
    coincidental, 120
    communicational, 117
    functional, 117
    logical, 120
    procedural, 117
    sequential, 117
    temporal, 120
composite data, 33
composite key, 97, 218
composite logical data design (CLDD),
        219, 225, 228, 231
compound key, 97, 218
computer-based training (CBT), 259
configuration management, 282
consistency checking, 140
constraint, 225
constraint analysis, 91
constraint avoidance, 122
context diagram, 18
contingency, 270
cost/benefit analysis, 348
coupling, 114
    common, 117
    content, 117
    control, 117
    data, 117
    stamp, 117
critical path analysis (CPA), 274, 309
Cutts, G., 94

data analysis, 52
data dictionary, 37
data model, 52, 60, 68, 198, 217, 231
data retention, 211
data space, 158